Studies in Church History

Subsidia

6

FAITH AND IDENTITY
CHRISTIAN POLITICAL EXPERIENCE

FAITH AND IDENTITY
CHRISTIAN POLITICAL EXPERIENCE

PAPERS READ AT
THE ANGLO-POLISH COLLOQUIUM OF
THE BRITISH SUB-COMMISSION
OF THE COMMISSION INTERNATIONALE
D'HISTOIRE ECCLÉSIASTIQUE COMPARÉE
9–13 SEPTEMBER 1986

EDITED BY

DAVID LOADES AND
KATHERINE WALSH

PUBLISHED FOR
THE ECCLESIASTICAL HISTORY SOCIETY

BY

BASIL BLACKWELL

1990

© Ecclesiastical History Society 1990

First published 1990

Basil Blackwell Ltd
108 Cowley Road, Oxford OX4 1JF, UK

Basil Blackwell Inc.
3 Cambridge Center
Cambridge, Massachusetts 02142, USA

British Library Cataloguing in Publication Data
A CIP record for this book is available from the British Library

Library of Congress Cataloging-in-Publication Data
Anglo-Polish Church History Colloquium (1986 : Gonville and Caius
    College)
    Faith and identity: Christian political experience: from an
Anglo-Polish Church History Colloquium held at Gonville and
Caius College, Cambridge, 9–13 September 1986/edited by David
Loades and Katherine Walsh.
        p.   cm.—(Studies in church history. Subsidia: 6)
    ISBN 0–631–17163–0
    1. Christianity and politics—History—Congresses.
2. Nationalism—Religious aspects—Christianity—History—
Congresses. 3. Poland—Church history—Congresses. 4. Great
Britain—Church history—Congresses. I. Loades, D. M.
II. Walsh, Katherine. III. Title. IV. Series.
BR115.P7A53   1986
261.7´09–dc20
                                                        89–14977
                                                            CIP

Typeset by Joshua Associates Ltd, Oxford
Printed in Great Britain by
Billing and Sons Ltd., Worcester

CONTENTS

v

CONTENTS

PREFACE

Historical scholarship, like History itself, has been frequently shaped, and occasionally perverted, by nationalist enthusiasm. The modern historian is very conscious of this, but conscious also of the continuing human need for a sense of identity in a world which becomes smaller and more uniform with every passing decade. Consequently, scholars endeavour to follow the practices and principles of international collaboration, while taking as their subject matter the social and cultural traditions which make their respective communities distinctive. This volume is an example of that process. The Commission Internationale d'Histoire Ecclésiastique Comparée (CIHEC) has long devoted itself to the study of Church History as a vehicle for the promotion of international understanding. Not only has the Christian Faith (and even the institutional Church) always in theory transcended the feuds and conflicts of secular society, it has even occasionally done so in practice. At the same time, its own internecine strife has cut across political frontiers more often that it has coincided with them, so that those who follow its history have an excellent opportunity to develop a sense of perspective and proportion. Ironically, CIHEC has developed largely through the work of its national Sub-Commissions, but these have, for the most part, acted in the spirit of the Commission, by promoting bilateral meetings and conferences. In September 1986 the British Sub-Commission entertained its Polish equivalent at a colloquium held in Gonville and Caius College, Cambridge, on the appropriate theme 'Religion and national identity'. The papers published in this volume are a selection from those offered to the colloquium.

Like every successful enterprise, that meeting was the result of long and careful preparation, going back to informal contacts between Professors Christopher Brooke and Jerzy Kłoczowski in 1968. In 1971 Christopher and Rosalind Brooke visited Poland as guests of the Polish Academy, and gave lectures at the Catholic University of Lublin. During their stay, which lasted ten days, Sister Urszula Borkowska acted as their guide and interpreter. This visit was followed up by further personal contacts, which included exchange visits by Francis Brooke and Paweł Kłoczowski, the sons of the professors. In 1974 the British Sub-Commission acted as hosts to a general colloquium of CIHEC, held at St Catherine's College, Oxford, and a number of Polish delegates attended, sponsored by the Friends of Lublin and by the British Sub-Commission itself. Professor and Dr Brooke, in association with Dr Roger Highfield of Merton College, entertained the Polish delegation to lunch at Merton during the conference. By that time it was known that CIHEC would be holding a major conference in Warsaw in 1978, and it was hoped to be able to use that meeting to broaden and develop the contacts which already existed between the British and Polish Sub-Commissions. That process was significantly advanced in 1977, when Urszula Borkowska was able to spend some time in both Oxford and London, and to meet the officers of the British Sub-Commission, Dr Derek Baker and Miss Brenda Bolton. During the very successful conference at Warsaw in the following year, the participants visited the University of Lublin, and it was there that the specific proposal for a bilateral Anglo-Polish meeting was raised and discussed. Further discussions then took place in 1979 and 1980 between Brenda Bolton and Urszula Borkowska, both at the John of Salisbury conference and at a private meeting in Bruges. In 1981 the British Sub-Commission organized a further general CIHEC colloquium at the University of Durham, which was attended by a small Polish delegation, and the firm decision to hold an Anglo-Polish conference in Britain was taken, although at that stage neither the date nor the place could be determined. In 1983 Urszula Borkowska spent a further period in Oxford as a visiting Fellow at University College, and later in the same year both British and Polish delegations attended the CIHEC colloquium in Strasbourg. It was then decided that the much-discussed bilateral meeting should take place in Cambridge, in September 1986. Christopher Brooke had been appointed to the Dixie Chair of Ecclesiastical History at Cambridge in 1977, and had returned to a Fellowship at Gonville and Caius College. It was therefore natural that his college should be the venue, and that Professor Brooke himself should preside over the occasion, along with Professor James Cameron of St Andrews (the Chairman of the British Sub-Commission) and Professor Jerzy Kłoczowski.

The final programme, including the dates and theme, were decided in 1984, during a visit by Brenda Bolton to the University of Lublin. Papers were then invited, and a list of potential participants compiled. Much detailed labour followed, particularly on the part of Brenda Bolton as conference secretary; but almost a decade of planning finally came to fruition on 9–13 September 1986, when thirteen Polish and twenty British scholars assembled in Cambridge for an extremely fruitful exchange of ideas, both formal and informal. Because of the nature of the occasion, many of the most interesting contributions were not in a form suitable for subsequent publication, but at the final session it was decided to publish a selection of the proceedings as a *Subsidia* volume to the series *Studies in Church History*. The editorial work was entrusted to David Loades and Katherine Walsh, who, from her base in Austria, was in a good position to keep in touch with the Polish contributors. In July 1987, Urszula Borkowska was able to attend the annual conference of the Ecclesiastical History Society (the parent body of *Studies in Church History*) at Maynooth, in Ireland, a meeting also attended by the editors and several of the British contributors. At that time the final selection of papers was made, and the specific editorial work commenced.

The result has intellectual coherence, but is not, and could not be, a systematic exposition of the theme. Although the majority of the papers describe English or Polish experience, the related cases of Ireland and Bohemia at critical times in the emergence of their collective consciousness are also examined. John of Salisbury was acutely aware of national identity, but, writing in the mid-twelfth century, did not associate it with political states in the later sense. Anselm, some sixty years earlier, was concerned about a very different type of identity, the citizenship of the City of God, but he was equally sensitive to the fact that the Christian Faith was not simply a question of the convictions of isolated individuals. Believers and non-believers alike belonged to a society which fostered and reinforced their positions, and the former community needed to be constantly guarded and protected against the insidious assaults of the latter. By the time that Anselm wrote, Christendom had long been a physical as well as a metaphysical concept, a development which was not logically inherent in its origins. This had come about through the adoption of the Faith, and consequent patronage of the institutional Church, by the Emperor Constantine and the majority of his successors. So it is appropriate that a volume concerned with the social and political identity of Christians should commence with Constantine, and proceed via Anselm and John of Salisbury, before reaching the more obvious aspects of nationalism. No two Christian nations have enjoyed (or suffered) the same experience, but Britain and Poland are alike in having been profoundly influenced by their contrasting religious backgrounds. In Britain (or, more strictly, in England), the distinctiveness of the national Church was an essential element in the formation of a national State during the sixteenth century. Thereafter, with their statehood and their autonomy increasingly assured, the English became progressively more indifferent to institutional religion until, in the late twentieth century, only a tiny minority are effective members of the Established Church. By contrast, Poland, with a bitter history of invasion, partition, and conflict with powerful alien cultures, has adopted the Catholic Church as the symbol and cement of its identity. Never has this been more obvious than during the eighteen years which it took for the Anglo-Polish colloquium to proceed from personal contact to academic fruition.

The editors, however, would like to look forward, rather than back. What we are here presenting is a promising start; the fruit of much friendly collaboration and a common struggle against financial and bureaucratic obstacles. Hopefully, in the years to come, Anglo-Polish co-operation will be able to capitalize on this start and proceed, as Anglo-Dutch co-operation has already done, to produce a regular series of profitable encounters and publications.

David Loades
Katherine Walsh

LIST OF ILLUSTRATIONS
(pages 171–92)

The photographs are reproduced by kind permission of the Polish Academy of Sciences, Warsaw

CONTRIBUTORS

ANNA S. ABULAFIA
Fellow, Clare Hall, Cambridge

URSZULA BORKOWSKA
Professor of History, Catholic University of Lublin

MIECZYSŁAW BRZOZOWSKI
Lecturer in History, Catholic University of Lublin

STANISŁAW BYLINA
Professor of History, University of Warsaw

TADEUSZ CHRZANOWSKI
Professor of Art History, Catholic University of Lublin and
University of Cracow

CLAIRE CROSS
Professor of History, University of York

STUART G. HALL
Professor of Ecclesiastical History, King's College, University of
London

STEFAN KIENIEWICZ
Professor of History, University of Warsaw

JERZY KŁOCZOWSKI
Professor of Humanities, Catholic University of Lublin

DAVID LOADES
Professor of History, University College of North Wales, Bangor

JOHN McLOUGHLIN
Assistant Registrar, London School of Economics

JANUSZ TAZBIR
Professor, Historical Institute, Warsaw, Member of the Polish
Academy of Sciences

KATHERINE WALSH
Professor of Medieval History, University of Salzburg

CONSTANTINE AND THE CHURCH

by STUART G. HALL

CONSTANTINE was already on his way to sainthood when Eusebius of Caesarea delivered panegyrics in his honour in 335–6. His *Laudes* are in the tradition of pagan panegyric, in which the virtues of the emperors were praised, especially their piety to the gods and the divine favour to them. Such had earlier been given to Constantine himself, relating him to his persecuting predecessors. But now it is his services to the one God the Creator, who inspired him with justice and wisdom to rule the Empire, to root out idolatrous error, and to set up the symbol of the Cross for mankind's salvation. In the *Life of Constantine*, which must be largely or wholly from Eusebius, the whole career is surveyed in a form which combines panegyric, biography, history, and proclamation. The Emperor was, it was claimed, deeply, skilfully, and consistently Christian. He had fulfilled apocalyptic prophecy by destroying the persecuting dragon that corrupted the world, represented chiefly by Licinius. Constantine had filled the Empire with churches and Christian governors; he had pacified barbarians and brought them to the knowledge of God and the rule of law. In death he lay between monuments of Apostles, sharing the prayers of the Church to whose bosom he had finally been received in baptism. Coins depicted his ascent to heaven on a quadriga (a pagan tradition which Eusebius saw with Christian eyes), and the sons of his body continued to exercise his single, quasi-divine government of the world.

It is no surprise that the Empire, increasingly centred on the new Rome, which everyone called 'Constantine's town', Constantinople, upheld his memory. Early, though not in Eusebius's day, his statue stood on a high porphyry column in the centre of the city, sunrays shining from his head, which had been converted from one of Apollo. By the time Justinian built Hagia Sophia, he was depicted in mosaic wearing a halo. Hagiography enlarged the miracles of Eusebius's *Life*, on which it was usually based. With his mother, Helena, he is among the saints of Greece to this day; their feast is 21 May. He has a large, modern church in Athens. Every great emperor was hailed as a 'new Constantine'. The West could not accept so straightforwardly a hero whose relics and city were in the East. Constantinople's pretensions were suspect. The story went in the sixth century that Pope Sylvester had healed Constantine, converted and

I

baptized him (and not Eusebius of Nicomedia, as was in fact the case). The Emperor consequently turned from persecution to support the Church. He then went East to found his new city and seek out the true Cross. But if the coincidence of the cross of light of Constantine's vision and the discovery of the true Cross by Helena on his behalf made a delightful theme for story-tellers, papal lawyers could do better. By the eighth century, Constantine had appointed Sylvester head of the Church, and entrusted to him the imperial regalia. The documentation of Constantine's 'Donation' in the *Constitutum Constantini* reinforced the setting up of the Western Empire in 800. The document retained its authority until its authenticity was refuted by the researches of such humanists as Laurentius Valla in the fifteenth century. When medievals such as Dante criticized the *Constitutum*, it was not on the grounds of authenticity, but of impropriety; Constantine had no right to concede the Empire's prerogatives to the Church, and the Church had no right to accept them.

Constantine's stock did not, however, drop at the Reformation. Dethroning the pope made the godly monarch a necessary ally. In England, for instance, the claim was consciously made that the realm was 'an empire', implying royal jurisdiction even over spiritual officers and councils. The model was clearly Constantinian and Byzantine. Wherever the principle of *cuius regio eius religio* prevailed, so did Constantine. A few Anabaptists might associate him with the slaughterous Antichrist who had seized the Church, but for reformers generally the secular arm was not the cause of the Babylonish captivity of the Church, but its cure. Kings must rise like the biblical Josiah to vindicate the Word of God against the false priests.

Yet some criticism there had always been, both Christian and anti-Christian. Eustathius of Antioch cast aspersions on Helena and her mission, and was deposed. Athanasius regarded the Emperor's schemes for Church unity as less important than the prerogatives of the popes of Alexandria in their own domain, and named his episcopal critics an Arian conspiracy. Constantine with his wider perspective pressed Athanasius to readmit the wayward presbyter Arius; Athanasius was finally exiled, and blamed the Emperor bitterly for meddling with the decrees of the bishops at Nicea. Similar rebukes, more bitter still, were to fall on the head of Constantius II, when he sought to set the Church free from dogmatic division; to the generally irenic Hilary of Poitiers, Constantine's son was Antichrist. But the memory of Constantine as heretic was to fade rapidly, as the Eusebian vision prevailed, supplemented by the city of Constantinople and by the true Cross, with its world-famous memorial in the cult at the Church of Anastasis in Jerusalem.

Paganism launched its own counterattack. Julian the Apostate, a generation later, put about slanderous reinterpretations of Constantine's history. So did the orator Libanius and pagan historians such as Eunapius and Zosimus. His fiscal and military programmes were criticized, probably ineptly. It was alleged also that he became a Christian only after the appalling crime of murdering his son Crispus and his wife Fausta in 326. The guilt of this parricide no religion could expunge, until Christian priests offered the pardon which others, loving justice, refused. This is a sort of pagan afterthought, reinterpreting facts already in the public domain, as the legend of Sylvester is a Christian afterthought. If it has any kind of historical basis, it might be that Helena's mission to Palestine, immediately following the dismal slaughter, was some kind of atonement for Crispus; but that is uncertain. This pagan critique was to surface again in the Enlightenment. Constantine had weakened the Empire by undoing its unity, according to Montesquieu and Gibbon. The intellectual freedom of the classical world was subjected by him to ecclesiastical dogmatic control, said the Encyclopaedists. Voltaire fulminated against the bloodthirsty, superstitious tyrant who brought his Empire under the black shadow of the clergy. The prejudiced accounts of the pagan historians were too readily believed, and the extravagant panegyrics of Eusebius too readily dismissed as worthless. From that methodological error we took a long time to emerge.

Jakob Burckhardt was the first writer whose work still compels attention for critical thoroughness.[1] He shows Constantine not unsympathetically, but as an unprincipled, diabolically clever politician, outmanœuvring all opponents, and deploying the new religion to make unbeatable support. To achieve this interpretation, the numerous letters and decrees preserved in Christian literary sources had to be dismissed as frauds perpetrated on the Emperor's behalf by Christian supporters. Otto Seeck allowed him some religious ideals, but still dismissed the letters. So did Eduard Schwartz, for whom Constantine was quite irreligious, driven only by a will to power. English-speaking historians brought up on a famous lecture by Norman Baynes will recognize the point the argument has now reached.[2] But although a series of passive authorities has agreed with Baynes in accepting the personal authorship of all or most of the documents attributed to Constantine, the sceptical view has an important afterlife.

[1] Burckhardt, *Die Zeit Constantins des Grössen* (Basel, 1853, 1880; Darmstadt, 1970).
[2] N. H. Baynes, *Constantine the Great and the Christian Church* (London, 1929, 1975).

3

First, it has seemed to some that the Christian sincerity of Constantine could be impugned by showing that the stories of his 'conversion' are false. The two basic versions, very different from each other, by Lactantius and Eusebius, can perhaps be shown to be Christian improvements upon a different experience of Apollo as the Unconquered Sun. The triumphal arch, the coinage, the official Latin panegyric of the period, show that, while Constantine attributed his victory over Maxentius to his god, that god was Sol Invictus. The vision, real or imagined, took place at Grand, in Gaul, at the earlier time when Maximian was defeated. It gave impulse to Constantine's Gallic troops as they fought their way to Rome. Not surprisingly, such views have French-speaking advocates like André Piganiol and Jean-Jacques Hatt. There is truth in them: the same crucial panegyric[3] which described Constantine's vision of the sun god was also the one which set out his claim to authentication independent of the Tetrarchy. Constantine's father had been a Tetrarch, and from that position, sealed by marriage to the daughter of Maximian, Constantine had begun. Now his descent from Claudius II Gothicus was revealed, descent from a worshipper of Sol Invictus and hero of third-century history, in order to make a claim for primacy among or over the other Tetrarchs. But these views fail to explain the Christianity of Constantine's letters about Donatism, which begin immediately after he took Rome. Further, to dispose of the 'conversion' does not dispose of Constantine's Christianity. It is probably wrong to regard Lactantius and Eusebius as recounting a 'conversion' at all. A vision or dream of a god before a battle is a standard historical *topos*. And even in the late Eusebian account, in which Constantine sees the cross of light superimposed upon the sun, it is only after he prays to his father's god to identify himself that Christ appears to him in a dream. Constantine does not claim a conversion, but an answer to prayer for divine aid, which takes the form of the sign of the cross: 'Conquer by this'. He later indicates that he was not always aware of the truth: but he had somehow to account for his years at the courts of the persecutors. In any event, showing the stories of the vision to be fictitious does not show that Constantine was not genuinely and officially a worshipper of Christ.

Secondly, residual doubts about his Christianity have combined with Athanasian resistance to imperial meddling in one recent synthesis. Alistair Kee's book is hardly a work of scholarship in the vein of

[3] *Pan. Lat.*, 6 (7). J. J. Hatt, 'La Vision de Constantin au sanctuaire de Grand et l'origine celtique du labarum', *Latomus*, 9 (1950), pp. 427–36.

4

Burckhardt or Baynes.[4] Its author is an advocate of revolutionary third-world theology; for him Constantine represents a deliberate perversion of the pacifist Christ into the military one, the cross of triumphant suffering into the *labarum* of authoritarian power, the gospel of liberation into a theology of political subjugation. The trouble with this is that it merely states that Constantine was not the kind of Christian Kee wants him to be. It wants historical context: most Christians of Constantine's day would not understand Kee's criticisms, and would fall outside his definition of Christian. In particular, their religion was more God-centred and less Jesus-centred than he seems to think proper. A more persuasive criticism comes from J. H. Yoder.[5] Standing in the Mennonite tradition, he offers to contemporary interfaith dialogue an alternative to 'Constantinian', hierarchic, European Christianity. The non-Christian world could more easily engage in dialogue with a more serious, spiritual, Jesus-centred faith, free from state control and sacral hierarchy made absolute in papacy, episcopate, or anything else. Significant though that may be in contemplating the fall-out of Constantine, it is a critique of developments of which he is the emblem, rather than a report of anything he did. Constantine invented neither the Christian hierarchy, with its presumptuous claims, nor the sacral state; he did perhaps combine them.

Serious scholarship has moved considerably since Baynes. In some ways the most significant work was that of Hermann Dörries, *Das Selbstzeugnis Kaiser Konstantins*, in which all the documentation is described, and the thought of the Emperor fully expounded, on his mission, religion, the Church, and theology.[6] Like Baynes, Dörries regards the authenticity of the letters as vindicated. It is partly because they show remarkable internal consistency, coming from a variety of sources: Optatus's Donatist dossier, Eusebius's writings, Athanasius's polemical collection. The consistency is partly of style and tone—a forceful angularity which makes forgery unlikely and personal drafting probable. But it is also of content: the same fear of the Divinity, the same expectations from him, the same abusive permission to practise pagan cults, extend not only to the letters, but to laws preserved in the *Codex Theodosianus* and even the contemporary inscriptions preserved at Hispellum and Orcistus. Add to this that Eusebius can be convicted in at least one place of misinterpreting what Constantine wrote, so that we know the historian was not himself the

[4] A. Kee, *Constantine versus Christ* (London, 1982).
[5] J. H. Yoder, 'The disavowal of Constantine. An alternative perspective on interfaith dialogue' in *Aspects of Interfaith Dialogue*, ed. W. Wegner and H. Harrelson (Tantur, 1976).
[6] H. Dörries, *Das Selbstzeugnis Kaiser Konstantins*, AAWG. PH, ser. 3, 34 (Göttingen, 1954).

forger; and that A. H. M. Jones identified a papyrus copy of one of the most important and improbable of Eusebius's documents, having been in official use in Egypt before Eusebius wrote, and the case seems overwhelming.[7]
Leading writers now adopt a moderate and constructive view. In England, Jones was persuaded of Constantine's seriousness about the God of the Christians, and even defended the authenticity of the heavenly vision. In his massive researches on the organization of the Empire he saw Constantine's fiscal and military policies in a favourable light.[8] In Germany, Joseph Vogt and, in France, J.-R. Palanque both perceived a development in Constantine's religious beliefs and policies going hand in hand, but did not doubt his Christian seriousness. Ramsay MacMullen in America has pursued a similar line, but takes a severe view of the moral character and consequences of Christianity and its application in Constantine. Some writers have exaggerated. Alfoeldi was too excited by the occasional use of the 'XP' emblem on coins, and tried to shut out the general truth that the coins of Constantine did not reflect much anti-pagan sentiment, and had no explicit Christianity, by misinterpreting a few issues.[9] Timothy Barnes has done excellent work on the timing and character of Constantine's career and campaigns, and has tried his hand at the Christian documents. But he is mistaken in asserting, for instance, that in 312 the Roman army 'became officially Christian'.[10] That was not the way the military could operate. In such an area familiar documents deserve closer scrutiny. The military prayer of *Vita Constantini*, 4, 19–20, is not specifically Christian, and is confined to the Constantinople garrison. Eusebius himself emphasizes that Constantine could not get his message across to his military colleagues, and that his baptism separated him from them. Raban von Haeling has demonstrated that the higher officers of the Empire remained non-Christian until the reign of Theodosius I.[11] The group of officers who carried out the *putsch* after Constantine died did not put his sons in power for the sake of Christianity; they were the sort of men who could successively sustain in power the Arian Constantius II, the neo-pagan Julian, the orthodox

---

[7] A. H. M. Jones and T. C. Skeat, 'Notes on the genuineness of the Constantinian documents in Eusebius's *Life of Constantine*', *JEH*, 5 (1954), pp. 196–200.

[8] A. H. M. Jones, *Constantine and the Conversion of Europe* (London, 1948; Harmondsworth, 1962).

[9] P. M. Bruun, 'The Christian signs on the coins of Constantine', *Arctos*, ns, 3 (1962), pp. 5–35.

[10] T. D. Barnes, *Constantine and Eusebius* (Cambridge, Mass. and London, 1981).

[11] R. von Haehling, *Zur Religionszugehörigkeit der hohen Amsträger des Römischen Reiches von Constantin I. bis zum Ende der theodosianischen Dynastie* (Bonn, 1978).

Jovian, and Valentinian I, who had little time for religion on the ground that he was a soldier: there were probably many like him.

This comment on a detail of Barnes's work shows how far one can be from understanding the conditions and compromises of the reign of a Christian in the Roman world. Hence my suspicions about the work of Paul Keresztes, who uses the apparatus of scholarship, and no small learning, to revive the hagiographic view of Constantine.[12] He works out parallels with St Paul, and sweeps aside doubts about his character and orthodoxy in undue reliance on his self-testimony and the panegyric of Eusebius. Fortunately the latter is now getting some of the attention he deserves. We have a useful English text and commentary on the *Laudes* from H. A. Drake, and a new edition of the *Vita* from F. Winkelmann. It is to be hoped that an English version with up-to-date analysis will soon be forthcoming.

Where does all this lead us on the question of Constantine's effect on the Empire and Church of his day? First the Empire. There is little doubt that both Diocletian and Constantine promoted the cult of the Emperor. Eusebius gives the game away when he describes the lying-in-state of the deceased monarch, with the staff and military

> entering the chamber at the appointed times, and saluting their coffined Emperor on bended knee, as though he were still alive. After them the senators appeared, and all who had been distinguished by an honourable office, and offered the same homage. These were followed by multitudes of every rank.[13]

The deification of the Emperor by the Roman Senate went on after his death, though he was downgraded by Christians to being a servant of God: he is accepted into the company of the immortals on the quadriga as his predecessors had been, and still rules his Empire from Heaven.

In his lifetime Constantine retained the title *Pontifex Maximus*, high priest of the gods, in which capacity he could limit and control pagan religion at his discretion. More to the point, he behaved as *Pontifex Maximus* to the Christians. His activity, though expressly reluctant, within the Church included not only the reconciliation of divergent forces, as at Nicea, but the removal of obstacles to unity like Arius, Eusebius of Nicomedia, Eustathius of Antioch, and Athanasius of Alexandria, and their restoration when appropriate. It included making theological proposals,

[12] P. Keresztes, *Constantine; a Great Christian Monarch and Apostle* (Amsterdam, 1981).
[13] *Vita Const.*, 4, p. 67.

7

like the formula *homoousios*/consubstantial at Nicea, and the preaching of moral and theological sermons at court—and apparently once in church, since the *Oratio ad sanctorum coetum* is now recognized as probably an authentic address for Easter Eve. So the royal supremacy merges into the headship of the world-wide Church, in which no universal papacy or patriarchate has yet emerged to challenge him: Caesaropapism.

One thing alleged of Constantine appears to be false. He certainly perceived his mission as God-given, but in none of his own statements does he suggest that rule by *one* emperor is essential or divinely ordained, much less than (as Eusebius maintains) that his sole monarchy is a model of Christ's Kingdom. Constantine accepted for a time the alliance of the Tetrarchy, and even when he claimed superiority through his Claudian ancestry he co-operated with Licinius, formed a marriage bond with him, and appointed Caesars. He never ruled without at least one designated colleague, though they were always related by blood or marriage. On his death he had distributed the realm between five, though the military soon disposed of the nephews and left only the three sons. As in many things, he continued the decentralizing policy of Diocletian, a trend never effectively reversed.

As to the Church, the well-known ideas remain true. Its buildings were enlarged, adorned, or built new, in part with spoils of the temples, whose doors were unlocked and treasures diverted. Its clergy were endowed with lands, subsidized by grants, or exempted from taxes. The priesthood became a respectable calling for educated gentlemen. Churches were filled with stately rituals, partly modelled on those of the court, with processions, incense, robes, and acolytes. They were also thronged with indifferent Christians, gossiping at service, apt to attend also vulgar entertainments, and unorthodox religious groups, a nightmare to serious-minded clergy like Cyril of Jerusalem. Small wonder that flight to the desert monastery, or deviation into puritan schism, attracted some abler people; there was still a suffering Christ to be imitated and loved: 'Quid ecclesia imperatori?' as the Donatists said. And this very tendency would serve as a tool by which ambitious churchmen might unseat their rivals. How better to defeat your opponent than to prove him a false prophet, disobedient to the Church's creed, and thus to the Empire which enforced the decisions of Church councils? Eusebius thought that Constantine had brought the Church to its God-appointed goal: the Church was to take the Gospel to all the world, and then the end would come. In the fusion of Church and Empire that was achieved: no other earthly end was envisaged. But it did not work.

We still live with the fall-out of what Constantine was called to do. I cannot accept the view that he should not have done it. Those entrusted with governing their fellow men cannot escape responsibility for their spiritual welfare; Constantine in a famous remark called himself 'bishop of those outside'. Rulers must see that the best buildings and the best minds in their domain are given to God, not only because God is God and deserves it, but because it is better for people to give these things to him. Where we must undo the Eusebian and Constantinian view is at a point unthinkable to them. For them the whole habitable world, the *oikumene*, consisted of the Roman Empire, plus a few satellite barbarians, who were defined in terms of their relation to Rome, and whose interest lay in recognizing Roman hegemony. Eusebius claims that even the Persians and Indians did so in Constantine's day, when all things were well. The ages of medieval Christendom, European empires, and the missionary move-ments all extended the same general assumption: there was Christian civilization, and there were the heathen outside. Now we know differently. While Rome rose and fell, great empires continued in the East. Before Europeans arrived in Africa and America, they had their empires too. No doubt each of these empires saw itself as the centre of the world, just as we have done and do. That presumption in us is as unreasonable as it was in them. It is not so much Constantine we must disavow as the imperial presumption which we share with him and his predecessors. It is wrong to regard our empires and our cultures as giving us special privileged status before God as against the rest of mankind, just as it is Antichrist so to regard our man-made sects and religions. The living God is above all these things, large and small. Constantine certainly saw better than the Donatists, and better than his imperial predecessors, that God was the one God of all the world. What he lacked was what could be available to us, a wider vision of what the world is. The next stages of Church History must take account of that wider vision.[14]

King's College
University of London

---

[14] Other relevant works: A. Alfoeldi, *The Conversion of Constantine and Pagan Rome* (Oxford, 1948) Eusebius, *Über das Leben des Kaiser Konstantin*, ed. F. Winkelmann; *GCS, Eusebius*, I, 1 (Berlin, 1975). H. A. Drake, *In Praise of Constantine* (Berkeley, Los Angeles, and London, 1976). J. W. Eadie, ed., *The Conversion of Constantine*, European Problems Series (Huntington, 1971; New York, 1977).

ST ANSELM AND THOSE OUTSIDE THE CHURCH

by ANNA S. ABULAFIA

I

WE know from Eadmer's *Vita Anselmi* that Anselm would eat little when he sat down to meals with his monks. Instead of having one of his monks read from an appropriate book at mealtimes, Anselm would instruct the community himself. Indeed, Anselm talked so much that, according to his biographer, it would take a separate book to record all that he said.[1] In fact, Anselm's sayings were collected, and it is to one of these that I wish to pay particular attention.

In the original version of the collection of Anselm's sayings, the *De moribus*, Anselm is recorded as having compared God's kingdom to the world in the following way. In the world there is a city ruled by a king. In the city there is a castle, and within the castle is the keep. Outside the city is where the king's enemy holds sway. Often the enemy prince invades the city. When this occurs, only those in the keep are completely safe: they cannot be reached by the enemy, and they would never venture forth from their haven. The inhabitants of the castle are safe too, but only as long as they stay put and distance themselves both physically and mentally from what is happening in the city. If they heed the wails of terror of their families who are being ravished by the enemy, or even if they so much as peep through the gaps of the castle walls, they will be lost. In the city there are some inviolable buildings which can withstand the enemy onslaught. But most structures are flimsy; they are stormed easily enough, and their occupants are taken away.

The world stands for God's kingdom, the city for Christendom, with God as its king, the castle for the institution of monasticism; the keep is the abode of angels; the town houses are individual Christians; and the enemy prince is the Devil. The whole area outside the city (and I imagine this to be the countryside beyond the city walls) is within the Devil's control; it is where the *Iudei* and the *pagani* live. In other words, Anselm is quoted as having told his monks to imagine Christendom as God's city.

[1] Eadmer, *Vita Anselmi*, ed. R. W. Southern, NMT (1962); repr. OMT (1972) [hereafter *VA*], ii, 11, p. 78: R. W. Southern, *Saint Anselm and his Biographer. A Study of Monastic Life and Thought, 1059–c.1130* (Cambridge, 1963) [hereafter *AB*], p. 219.

Within Christendom there is the society of angels and the institution of monasticism. The walls of Christendom are constantly being breached by the Devil. Only the society of angels is perfectly impervious to these raids; monks are safe as long as they adhere to their renunciation of the world in thought, word, and deed. Most other Christians are not safe and will be carried away by Satan. Outside the walls of Christendom are the Jews and the pagans, who are incapable of putting up any resistance to the Devil, and who will end up in hell.[2]

Without wishing to press the details of Anselm's simile too far, I propose to investigate to what extent Anselm's treatises and letters conform to the views put forward in it. Moreover, the reference to the two groups outside Christendom has pricked our curiosity. Who are these Jews? Are they contemporary Jews or simply the Jews of the Bible? And even more interestingly, who are the *pagani*? Finally, it is hoped that, in its turn, the simile will be able to help us understand better the many and varied allusions in Anselm's writings to 'unbelievers', that is to say, to those outside the Church.

II

There can be no doubt that Anselm was convinced that it was more feasible to attain salvation within the confines of a monastery than without. As he wrote to a certain Helinandus, who was wavering in his decision to become a monk:

> . . . it is very much more difficult to preserve a life of sanctity out of free choice than to do so within the enclosure of a monastery under the discipline of a rule of life. . . . No one refrains from the intention of becoming a monk in order to live a better life; . . . every type of person comes to monastic life in order to come closer to God.[3]

Anselm's letters also attest to the fact that he felt very strongly that once a monk had renounced the world he should be impervious to what happened in it. For instance, Anselm was adamant that monks had no business leaving their monasteries to go on crusade. As he put it to Osmund, Bishop of Salisbury, in 1095: 'Send out orders to all the monasteries in your diocese that no monk is to presume to undertake the

[2] *De humanis moribus per similitudines*, ed. R. W. Southern and F. S. Schmitt, *Memorials of St Anselm*, ABMA, 1 (1969), 75–6, pp. 66–7.

[3] *Ep.* 101, *S. Anselmi . . . opera omnia*, ed. F. S. Schmitt, 6 vols (Edinburgh, 1946–61) [hereafter *S*], 3, pp. 233–4.

journey to Jerusalem, and prohibit this under pain of excommunication'.[4] But Anselm's letters concern situations which come much closer to the scenario of the simile, which demands of monks that they be deaf to the calls for help from their families when the Devil invades God's city. Henry, who was later to become Prior of Christ Church, Canterbury,[5] wanted desperately to leave his monastery to go to the aid of his sister, who had run into trouble in Italy. Anselm implores him not to go.[6] Even more telling is the letter in which Anselm begs a young man called William not to help out his brother in Jerusalem but to seek Christ instead. In other words, even a lay person is advised to become a monk rather than to give succour to a member of his family. Anselm says to William:

> You say to me . . . 'I love not these [evils of the world] but my brother enwrapped in them; and therefore I hasten to be enveloped in them with him in order that I may help and defend him . . .'. Why O man do you not rather say 'I love not these things but Christ, my God; and therefore I flee from them and hasten to him that I may be helped and safeguarded by him'? Now that the noise of the world crashing down on your brother has been heard, are you going to ignore Christ's call and are you really going to run to the ruin itself so that you manikin can help and defend a manikin, so that you a worm can help and protect a worm from such a confused weight and from such weighty confusion? . . . Who will help and protect you while you are helping and safeguarding him? God, whom you are less eager to follow than your brother? Will you ignore Christ who is calling you to follow him in peace and in your homeland and among your neighbours and friends so that you may . . . possess the kingdom of Heaven; will you run to your brother through so many and such great difficult hardships of travelling, through the turbulences of the seas and stormy tempests into the confusion of war . . . so that you will see him defending the kingdom of Byzantium; and do you think that God will help and protect him more through you than without you, or you yourself because of him rather than because of himself? God will do so even less. For he will be angry if he sees anyone loved more by anyone than himself.[7]

[4] *Ep.* 195; *S*, 4, p. 85.
[5] I am relying on Schmitt's notes in dating Anselm's letters and in identifying the people in them.
[6] *Ep.* 17; *S*, 3, pp. 122–4.
[7] *Ep.* 117; *S*, 3, p. 251.

According to Schmitt, the letter was composed during Anselm's second sojourn in England, before he became Archbishop of Canterbury. The date of the letter would then be c. 1092–3.[8] William's brother was probably one of the Norman mercenaries employed by the Byzantine emperor to fight against the Turks.

Of all Anselm's letters, only two concern Jews and Judaism. While in exile, Anselm wrote one letter to Prior Ernulf and Archdeacon William of Canterbury and another to Gundolf, Bishop of Rochester, to ask them to see to it that a convert from Judaism, now called Robert, was not suffering penury. The act of conversion is described as 'fleeing from Judaism to Christianity', 'passing from perfidy to the true faith', and 'fleeing from the hands of the Devil'.[9]

The designation of Judaism as *perfidia* (probably in the meaning of unbelief rather than actual treachery[10]) and of Jews as being in the hands of the Devil is common enough; and it is for this reason that Gilbert Dahan described these words as banal, implying that they are meaning-less.[11] But common usage of images and terms does not necessarily render them without significance. Whether or not Anselm gave any particular thought to his precise choice of words—Dahan assumes he wrote the letters very quickly[12]—the fact remains that the words of the letters concur exactly with the description of the position of the Jews in his simile: Jews are inhabitants of the countryside outside of the city walls of Christendom, and they are natural prey for Satan. Moreover, the emphasis of the concept of flight in the process of converting from Judaism to Christianity easily evokes the image of someone escaping from the dangerous area outside a city to the relative safety found within its walls. These letters prove that Anselm was, at least in one instance, directly involved with a Jew. Thus we can assume that the *Iudei* of the simile

---

[8] *S*, 3, p. 252.

[9] *Epp.* 380, 381; *S*, 5, pp. 323–4. Letter 380 contains the words: '. . . quatenus ille cum familiola sua nullam duram patiatur indigentiam, sed gaudeat se de perfidia transisse ad veram fidem, et probet ex ipsa nostra pietate quia fides nostra propinquior est Deo quam Iudaica'. G. Dahan, 'Saint Anselme, les Juifs, le judaïsme' in *Les Mutations socio-culturelles au tournant des XIe–XIIe siècles* (Paris, 1984), p. 521 deduces from the fact that Anselm says here that the Christian Faith is closer to God than the Jewish faith that Anselm concedes that Judaism is a faith and has some proximity to God. I think, however, that because these words are part of a sentence in which Judaism is contrasted to Christianity as being a *perfidia* rather than the *vera fides* that Anselm's use of the comparative *propinquior* does not necessarily imply that he is conceding any closeness to God to contemporary Judaism.

[10] B. Blumenkranz, 'Perfidia', *Juifs et Chrétiens patristique et moyen âge*, 7, Variorum Reprints (London, 1977).

[11] Dahan, p. 521.

[12] *Ibid.*

certainly include contemporary Jews. Another unambiguous piece of information we have about Anselm and the Jews of his day comes from Eadmer. In the *Historia novorum*, Eadmer narrates how travellers from England tell Anselm's party in exile that William Rufus received money from the Jews of Rouen in exchange for permission to Jewish converts to Christianity to return to Judaism.[13] It seems likely that these Jewish converts were Jews who were baptized against their will during the persecutions of the First Crusade. But even without these references one could take for granted an awareness on Anselm's part of the existence of Jews. Bec lies close to Rouen, which was a centre of Jewish activity and learning; and it was from Rouen that Jews came to London after 1066.[14]

However, it is to Anselm's treatises that we must turn to learn what Anselm actually knew about Jews and their faith. Anselm mentions Jews and Judaism explicitly, once in both recensions of the *De incarnatione verbi* and several times in the *Cur Deus Homo* and the *Epistola de sacrificio azimi et fermentati*, a piece defending Latin usage of unleavened bread for the celebration of the Eucharist against the Greeks. Many, if not most, of these references clearly concern the Jews of the Bible, others are general references and could allude to contemporary Jews as well. Thus in the *Cur Deus Homo* the question is asked why the Jews [of the New Testament] persecuted Jesus unto death.[15] In another chapter of the same work, Anselm explains to Boso that the Gentiles would have been called to Christ even if the Jews had not rejected Jesus.[16]

The discussion of Jews and Judaism in the *Epistola de sacrificio* pivots around the question whether or not Latin Christians judaize when they use unleavened bread for the Eucharist. *Judaizare* is defined as imitating Jews for the sake of Judaism.

> They said that we judaize, but that is not true, because we do not celebrate the Eucharist with unleavened bread in order to keep the old law, but in order that the celebration takes place more diligently, and we imitate the Lord who did not do this in order to judaize. For when we do something which the Jews *did* in order to preserve

---

[13] Eadmer, *Historia novorum in Anglia*, ed. M. Rule, *RS*, 81 (London, 1881), 2, pp. 99–100.

[14] Also Anselm's pupil Gilbert Crispin knew a Jew and wrote a disputation reflecting the conversations he had with him. See R. W. Southern, 'St Anselm and Gilbert Crispin, abbot of Westminster', *MRSt*, 3 (1954), pp. 78–99; A. S. Abulafia, 'The *Ars disputandi* of Gilbert Crispin, abbot of Westminster (1085–1117)' in C. M. Cappon *et al.*, ed., *Ad Fontes Opstellen aangeboden aan prof. dr. C. van de Kieft* (Amsterdam, 1984), pp. 139–52.

[15] *Cur Deus Homo* [hereafter *CDH*], i, 9; *S*, 2, p. 61.

[16] *CDH*, i, 18; *S*, 2, p. 78.

Judaism, we do not judaize if we do not do this for the sake of Judaism but on account of another reason.[17]

The fact that Anselm uses the imperfect tense when he speaks about the Jews, and not the present—we do something which the Jews did—implies that he is thinking here especially of the Jews of the Bible. Elsewhere he writes:

If [the Greeks] dare assert that Christ made his body of unleavened bread for the sake of Judaism in order to preserve the law given about unleavened bread, they are erring in the most absurd way in that they think he would have spoiled such a genuine novelty with the leaven of oldness.[18]

In another passage of the same treatise, Anselm says:

We say that we do not judaize when we hold to the symbol of unleavened bread, for we do not signify that the Christ will come without the leaven of sin as the Jews do; but we demonstrate that he has come thus [that is, without sin], as Christians and in this way we admonish ourselves to exhibit ourselves thus—such is our *pascha* which we eat. They [the Greeks] display themselves to be neither Jews nor Christians in this, because they do not signify that God will come by the symbol of their leaven, as Jews, nor, as Christians, that he has come; but rather they seem to favour pagans who judge him to have been corrupted by sin as other men.[19]

Underlying Anselm's argument in the *Epistola de sacrificio azimi et fermentati* is the traditional assumption that the Old Testament is full of figures to which the Jews continue to adhere. Anselm's knowledge of Jewish teaching about the coming of the Messiah is very shaky indeed. In addition to our last example, there are two more instances in Anselm's *oeuvre* where he mentions Jews in conjunction with pagans. We shall examine the example shortly. For the moment, it suffices to say that one of these references shows Anselm to be ignorant of the Jewish rejection of the doctrine of original sin.[20]

There is one final passage in the *Cur Deus Homo* which needs to be discussed here. In book ii, chapter 15, Anselm explains to Boso that the

[17] *EpSac.*, 3; *S*, 2, p. 226.
[18] *EpSac.*, 2; *S*, 2, p. 225.
[19] *EpSac.*, 4; *S*, 2, p. 227.
[20] See below, p. 20.

murderers of Christ did not know Jesus was God and that, therefore, they were ignorant of what they were really doing. No one, says Anselm, would knowingly kill God. Thus the murderers could be forgiven for their sin.[21] These words have led scholars (notably Amos Funkenstein; Dahan basically follows his lead) to argue that Anselm abandoned the concept of collective Jewish guilt for the Crucifixion. Funkenstein sees in the *Cur Deus Homo* a spirit of rational tolerance which would be sadly lacking in the anti-Jewish polemics of most of Anselm's successors.[22] I would argue that this passage has less to do with any conception of tolerance on Anselm's part than with the momentum of Anselm's argument in the *Cur Deus Homo* and his own conflicting feeling about the Passion.

The *Cur Deus Homo* was meant to demonstrate the necessity of the Incarnation for man's salvation. If, however, one of the steps in the scheme of redemption could be shown to cause some men to lose the possibility of being saved, then Anselm's argument would no longer be valid. To repay man's debt to God, Christ needed to die on the Cross; for Christ to be crucified there had to be those who crucified him. To exclude the perpetrators of the Crucifixion from the proposed scheme of salvation would be nothing less than to deny the total efficacy of the Incarnation. Thus Anselm had to reason that these murderers could be saved because they did not kill Christ knowingly. This line of thinking finds a parallel in Anselm's *Meditation on Human Redemption*, where he wonders how he can rejoice in his salvation when it was brought about by the untold suffering of Jesus. How could he grieve because of the cruelties of Jesus' murderers and at the same time rejoice in the benefits which Jesus' suffering brought about? Jesus Christ underwent his death freely.

> Thus, I must condemn their cruelty, imitate your death and sufferings, and share them with you, giving thanks for the goodness of your love. And thus may I safely rejoice in the good that thereby comes to me. Now, little man, leave their cruelties to the justice of God, and think of what you owe your Saviour.[23]

In other words, Anselm did not think it was up to him to revenge Christ's death on anyone. He seems to be far more concerned with the consistency

[21] *S*, 2, p. 115.

[22] A. Funkenstein, 'Basic types of Christian anti-Jewish polemics', *Viator*, 2 (1971), p. 378; Dahan., p. 522.

[23] *Med.*, 3; *S*, 3, p. 89: trans. B. Ward, *The Prayers and Meditations of St Anselm* (Harmondsworth, 1973), p. 235.

of his own feelings. Finally, it cannot be wholly insignificant that Anselm does not mention the Jews specifically in either of these passages or in any of the other places in his work where he dwells on the same subject, for instance his *Prayer to the Holy Cross*.[24] Technically speaking, the context of his words does not even exclude the possibility that he had the Roman soldiers in mind who actually crucified Jesus.[25] But it is very likely that for Anselm, Romans and Jews were not mutually exclusive categories in this instance. As Anselm's pupil, Gilbert Crispin, writes when he tries to explain how the same words can have different meanings: 'We say the Jews crucified the Lord and yet it was not Jewish soldiers who crucified the Lord but Gentile soldiers. The Jews crucified the Lord by their judgement, the Gentile soldiers by matching their decisions'.[26] The important point is that what seems to have mattered to Anselm was what the implications were of Christ's death at the hands of men for his argument about God's scheme of redemption, rather than the fate of the descendants of those men, whoever they might be.

Anselm refers to pagans only three times in his treatises and not once in his letters. And each time he mentions pagans he does so in conjunction with Jews. We have already quoted the passage in the *Epistola de sacrificio azimi et fermentati* where Anselm says that the Greeks behave more like pagans than Christians or Jews when they use leavened bread for the Eucharist. In both versions of the *De incarnatione verbi* Anselm has Roscelin say, 'Pagans defend their law; Jews defend their law. Therefore we Christians must defend our faith'.[27] In the final chapter of the *Cur Deus Homo*, Boso is made to say:

> Because you prove that God became man out of necessity in such a way that, even if the few things which you have taken from our books were removed, such as what you said about the Three Persons of God and about Adam, you can satisfy not only the Jews, but also the pagans with reason alone, and because the same God-man himself establishes the New Testament and confirms the Old, thus just as it is necessary to acknowledge that he himself is true, so no one can deny that there is nothing in the Scriptures which is not true.[28]

[24] *Oratio*, 4; S 3, pp. 11–12.
[25] Dahan, 'Saint Anselme', p. 522, says the killers must refer to the Jews of *CDH*, i, 9, but Anselm is referring to the murderers of I Cor. 2.8, whose identity is not specified.
[26] *De altaris sacramento*, sections 15–16, ed. G. R. Evans in *The Works of Gilbert Crispin*, ed. A. S. Abulafia and G. R. Evans, *ABMA*, 8 (London, 1986), pp. 126–7.
[27] *De inc. verbi*(1), 5: S, 1, p. 285; *Ibid.* (2), 2; S, 2, p. 10.
[28] *CDH*, ii, 22; S, 2, p. 133.

The triad, Christians, Jews, and pagans, matches exactly the inhabitants of the world of the simile, but it does not necessarily bring us closer to an understanding of who these *pagani* are. All that we can surmise from our references is that Anselm used the term *pagani* to describe all those people who were neither Christians nor Jews. *Pagani* share no common ground with Christians, and they seem to have to be approached *sola ratione*.[29] Pagans consider Jesus Christ to have been as sinful as any other man. Finally, pagans stand up for their own points of view. So who are they?

For Roques the solution to the problem was plain enough. Anselm's *pagani* were not simply figures of literary fiction, meant to recall the heathen of classical antiquity, they were flesh and blood 'heathen' of his own day, that is, the Muslims. To give credence to his viewpoint, Roques quotes the *Vita Anselmi*, book ii, chapter 33, where Eadmer speaks of the Muslims in the army of Roger, Count of Sicily, whom Anselm encountered at Capua in *c.* 1098. Eadmer says that the Muslims might well have been converted to Christianity by Anselm, but that Roger would not countenance any such thing. Eadmer gives no value judgement of the incident, and does not record what Anselm thought about the affair.[30] As Roques admits, the *Cur Deus Homo* would have been completed by the time this incident took place. Furthermore, Roques points out that in twelfth-century vernacular literature (for example, the *chansons de geste*) Muslims are commonly referred to by the misnomer *paiens*. And Muslim polemics against Christianity are predominantly based on reason. Roques is sure that Anselm would have been conversant with the gist of these polemics.[31] Some scholars have followed Roques, for example, Julia Gauss, who identifies almost every non-Jewish 'unbeliever' in Anselm's work as a Muslim;[32] others have not. Charlesworth can discover no Muslim traits in Anselm's *pagani*. He sees

---

[29] It is not clear whether *sola ratione* in *CDH*, ii, 22 applies only to *pagani* or whether it refers to the Jews too. R. Roques favours the latter view (*Pourqoui Dieu s'est fait homme, Sources Chrétiennes*, 91 [Paris, 1963], p. 461), Schmitt's translation is a bit ambiguous (Darmstadt, 1970, p. 155), but in his article 'Die wissenschaftliche Methode in Anselms 'Cur Deus Homo', *Spicilegium Beccense*, 1 (Le Bec Hellouin and Paris, 1959), p. 355 he implies it applies only to pagans.

[30] *VA*, ii, 33, pp. 110–12.

[31] Roques, *Pourquoi Dieu*, pp. 72–4 and 'Les *Pagani* dans le *Cur Deus Homo* de Saint Anselm' *Miscellanea Mediaevalia*, 2 (1963), pp. 192–206.

[32] J. Gauss, 'Die Auseinandersetzung mit Judentum und Islam bei Anselm', *Analecta Anselmiana* 4, 2 (1975), pp. 101–9 and 'Anselmus von Canterbury zur Begegnung und Auseinandersetzung der Religionen', *Saeculum*, 17 (1966), *passim*.

them as a specific category of non-Christians who will listen only to arguments based on reason, but he gives no further clues to their identity.[33]

It seems excessive to deduce from the fact that Anselm seems to imply that *pagani* must be approached *sola ratione*, and from the fact that the *Cur Deus Homo* is based on the use of rational arguments, that Anselm knew of the rationalistic polemics of the Muslims against Christians. There is not one word in any of Anselm's writings that betrays any knowledge at all of Islamic teachings. On the contrary, if Anselm knew so much about Muslims, and if he had them in mind when he wrote the *Cur Deus Homo*, he could not have based the work on the concept of original sin as he did. In the same way as the Jews, Muslims do not adhere to this doctrine. When, in the quoted passage from the *Cur Deus Homo*, Boso admits that what had been said about Adam would have to be removed to convince Jews and pagans, he is not referring to original sin but to the question whether or not Adam would be saved by Jesus Christ (*Cur Deus Homo*, ii, 16).[34] Nor does Anselm's view in the *Epistola de sacrificio azimi et fermentati* of what would constitute pagan ideas about Jesus Christ conform to Muslim thoughts.[35] If *pagani* meant Muslims to Anselm, he certainly did not know much about their teachings. But did it?

Eadmer does not only use *pagani* in the sense of Muslims. In chapter 30 of the first book of the *Vita Anselmi*, he talks about Anselm's first visit to England and Lanfranc's discussion with him about the veneration of Elphege in Canterbury. Anselm advises Lanfranc not to suppress the cult. Archbishop Elphege of Canterbury was murdered on 19 April 1012, by, as Eadmer puts it, *inimici Dei pagani* or *pagani persecutores*.[36] These *pagani* are without question Danes.[37] Thus it is certainly not true that besides Jews, Muslims were the only non-Christians Anselm was aware of. Here we have concrete evidence that Anselm was confronted with the case of a man who had been killed only sixty years earlier by as yet unchristened Danes. Both Eadmer and Osbern, a monk of Canterbury, embellished the history of Elphege by claiming that the main reason the Danes killed him

[33] M. J. Charlesworth, *St Anselm's 'Proslogion' with a reply on behalf of the Fool by Gaunilo and the Author's to Gaunilo* (Oxford, 1965), pp. 32–3n.

[34] *S*, 2, p. 119, *contra* Gauss, 'Anselmus', p. 349 and Roques, *Pourquoi Dieu*, p. 460, n. 1.

[35] *EpSac.*, 4; *S*, 2, p. 227.

[36] *VA*, i, 30, pp. 51–2.

[37] *ASC, anno* 1012; Thietmar of Merseburg, *Chronicon*, ed. R. Holtzmann, trans. W. Trillmich, *Ausgetwählte Quellen*, 9 (Berlin, 1958), vii, 42, p. 398.

was that he tried to convert them.[38] Anselm's visit to England took place long before he first used the term *pagani* in his writings.

The use of *pagani* for Danes or Vikings is, of course, not peculiar to Eadmer. In the *Gesta Normannorum Ducum* of William of Jumièges (written *c.* 1070–1) *pagani* is used exclusively in this meaning. And when Orderic interpolated the *Gesta* (between 1109 and 1113) he copied this usage, changing only one occurrence of *pagani* to *barbari* for stylistic reasons.[39] In his *Historia ecclesiastica* (written between 1123 and 1137) Orderic uses *pagani* for Danes but for Muslims too.[40]

Both William of Jumièges and his predecessor as a historian of Normandy, Dudo of St Quentin, emphasize the recent heathen background of the Normans. Herluin, the founder of Bec, was a descendant of the Vikings through his father, Ansgot. Herluin's biographer, Gilbert Crispin, goes on to tell us that it was not easy for Herluin to find his way:

> for in Normandy at that time there was little indication of what the right way of life was; priests and prelates were freely married and carried weapons as if they were laymen; everyone still lived according to the customs of the ancient Danes.[41]

At the Council of London of 1075 held by Lanfranc, legislation was passed against vestiges of heathen observance.[42]

There is only one unequivocal reference in Anselm's *oeuvre* to Muslims. In a letter written between 1100 and 1103 Anselm regretfully informs Bishop Diego of Santiago de Compostela that England cannot send out soldiers to help the Bishop fight the Saracens. The word Anselm uses here is *Saraceni*.[43]

The evidence accumulated so far suggests that Anselm's *pagani*

---

[38] *VA*, i, 30, p. 52 and 52 n. 1, and Osbern, *Vita S. Elphegi Archiepiscopi Cantuariensis*, ed. H. Wharton, *Anglia Sacra*, 2 (London, 1691), pp. 132ff.

[39] *Gesta Normannorum ducum*, ed. J. Marx (Rouen and Paris, 1914), v, 11, p. 86. I am grateful to Dr E. M. C. van Houts of Girton College, Cambridge, who is preparing a new edition of the *Gesta* for *Oxford Medieval Texts*, for this information and for sharing her thoughts with me on Normandy in the eleventh and twelfth centuries.

[40] See Orderic Vitalis, *Hist. ecc.*, ed. M. Chibnall, 6 vols, *OMT* (1969–80), bk v, vol. 3, p. 94 for Muslims, and *ibid.*, p. 304 for Danes.

[41] *Vita Herluini*, sections 3 and 15, ed. G. R. Evans, *The Works of Gilbert Crispin*, pp. 185, 187–8.

[42] London, 1075, canon 8: D. Whitelock, M. Brett, and C. N. L. Brooke, eds, *Councils and Synods with Other Documents relating to the English Church*, 2 (Oxford, 1981), p. 614; M. Gibson, *Lanfranc of Bec* (Oxford, 1978), p. 145.

[43] *Ep.* 263; *S*, 4, p. 178. See also below the reference to *infideles* in letter 235. On Diego, see R. A. Fletcher, *Saint James's Catapult. The Life and Times of Diego Gelmírez of Santiago de Compostela* (Oxford, 1984).

certainly included the Vikings. By Anselm's own day Scandinavia was not yet wholly christened, and the memory of the Viking ancestry of the Normans was still very much alive. It cannot, of course, be entirely ruled out that Anselm had Muslims in mind when he used the term *pagani*. At least the *Cur Deus Homo* and the *Epistola de sacrificio azimi et fermentati* were written at the time of the First Crusade and its aftermath. But if he did, it is inconceivable that he used the term to the exclusion of another category of present-day 'heathen' with which he would have been very much more familiar.

Anselm's repeated use of the trio Christians-Jews-pagans makes it plain, however, that he employed the term *pagani* as a catch-all for all types of non-Jewish 'unbelievers', unrestricted by any element of time or place. We have established that Anselm's writings do not contradict the viewpoints presented in the saying with which we opened this paper. It is, therefore, now time to go back to Anselm's writings and to look carefully at what other terminology he uses for 'unbelievers', and to see whether our simile can help us to determine who they were supposed to be, and why Anselm employed the terms he did.[44]

III

Anselm's works are full of references to those who do not believe or behave as right-minded Latin Christians do, or at least try to. *Graeci*, *gentes*, *philosophi*, *insipientes*, and *infideles* are the terms which will concern us here, and we shall begin with the words which present us with the least difficulties.

Anselm uses the term *Graeci* simply to denote the Greeks of his day and their language, and he does not attach a negative meaning to the word itself. In his treatises against elements of Greek Christian practice, the *De processione spiritus sancti* and the *Epistola de sacrificio azimi et fermentati*, he proceeds from the assumption that Latins and Greeks hold their Christian belief in common ('... Christianam fidem quam Graecis tenemus').[45] And it is this common ground or common religious language that, according to Anselm, will impel the Greeks to accept that what the Latins uphold is actually correct. But it is plain that Anselm was censorious of some Greek beliefs and practices. We have seen how in the matter of the use of leavened bread for the Eucharist, Anselm was convinced the Greeks were

---

[44] For this section and the next I have used *A Concordance to the Works of St Anselm*, ed. G. R. Evans (New York, 1984).

[45] *De proc.*, 14; *S*, 2, p. 215.

behaving in an un-Christian way and were, therefore, acting as *pagani* as far as this point was concerned.

In an equally neutral way, Anselm employs the term *philosophi*. These are clearly the philosophers of classical times. In the *De grammatico* Anselm refers to the ancient philosophers when he discusses whether *grammaticus* is a substance of quality.[46] In the *Cur Deus Homo* he touches on the way in which these philosophers incorporated the concept of mortality in their definition of man.[47]

Anselm usually uses the word *gens* to mean people, without any further specification. For instance, in the *Cur Deus Homo* he says 'every people prays to the God in whom it believes to forgive its sin'.[48] In his letters *gens* will denote the people or followers of a bishop or a king (for example, in letter 270, 'in episcopatu de gentibus Wilfridi episcopi',[49] and in a letter to the king of Scotland, 'gens regni vestri'[50]) or just 'people', as in a letter to some monks of Canterbury telling them not to come to his place of exile: 'via nimis longa, gens extranea'.[51] But *gentes* can also refer to a certain type of 'unbeliever'. In the *Cur Deus Homo*, book i, chapter 18, they are the non-Jews to whom the Gospel was preached when the Jews rejected it.[52] In the light of the fact that Gilbert Crispin wrote a disputation between a Christian and a *gentilis*, it is interesting to note here that *gentilis* is a word which does not occur in Anselm's writings as we have them.[53]

It is when we turn to Anselm's *insipientes* and *infideles* that we come to much rougher terrain. Both terms seem to be employed by Anselm in a technical and non-technical way.

Insipiens and its derivatives can be simply the antonyms of *sapiens*, *sapienter*, and *sapientia*. Thus Anselm will politicly contrast his *insipientia* with the *sapientia* of his former teacher, Lanfranc,[54] or have the pupil of the *De casu diaboli* say, 'non semper facile est insipienter quaerenti sapienter respondere'.[55] Anselm's *Prayer to the Holy Cross* is structured on the presentation of the many antitheses between Christ and those who put

[46] *De gram.*, i; *S*, 1, p. 146.
[47] *CDH*, ii, 11; *S*, 2, p. 109.
[48] *Ibid.*, i, 19; *S*, 2, p. 86.
[49] *S*, 4, p. 185.
[50] *Ep*. 427; *S*, 5, p. 373.
[51] *Ep*. 335; *S*, 5, p. 295.
[52] *S*, 2, p. 78.
[53] *Disputatio Christiani cum Gentili*, ed. A. S. Abulafia, *The Works of Gilbert Crispin*, pp. 61–87; A. S. Abulafia, 'An attempt by Gilbert Crispin, abbot of Westminster, at rational argument in the Jewish-Christian debate', *Studia Monastica*, 26 (1984), pp. 54–74.
[54] *Ep*. 77; *S*, 3, p. 200.
[55] *De casu diaboli*, 27; *S*, 1, p. 275.

him to death. Thus his wisdom finds its opposite in their foolishness.[56] But here *insipientia* is already moving towards a more technical signification, that is, a mindless mode of thinking or behaving which puts a person beyond the pale, or to put it in the language of our simile: a type of folly which will drive a person over the walls of the Christian city. Two of Anselm's letters contain a reference to such mindless behaviour. Letter 385 refers to the folly of the newly elected abbot of Malmesbury when he had his legates offer Anselm a coin: '... ipse in hoc fecit quiddam valde insipienter, quod facere non debuit'. This act laid the abbot open to the accusation of simony, and Anselm writes to Queen Matilda to say he cannot confirm him in his abbacy.[57] Anselm's letter to Eustach, the father of a monk of Bec, speaks even more plainly. Eustach has broken his vow of chastity, and Anselm tells him, 'see even how perilous it is and what folly it is to put off correction in this matter without which you can expect certain perdition'.[58]

The best-known instance of Anselm's use of the term *insipiens* is in the *Proslogion*, where he adopts the fool of Psalm 13(14) and Psalm 52(53) 'who says in his heart there is no God'. Campbell, who has recently reappraised the inner logic of the argument of the *Proslogion*, argues that Anselm starts off the second chapter of the *Proslogion* with the prayer that he might understand that God is just as we believe, and that God is what we believe. By the end of chapter 3 he has reached two conclusions: 1. that God so truly is that he cannot be thought not to be; and 2. that God is 'something-than-which-a-greater-cannot-be-thought'. According to Campbell, the *Proslogion* is, strictly speaking,

> not so much a proof of the existence of God as a demonstration that the whole realm of discourse which admits the believer to speak of God as something-than-which-nothing-greater-can-be-thought rules out the possibility of denying with understanding the existence of God.[59]

---

[56] *Ora.*, 4; S, 3, pp. 11–12.
[57] S, 5, p. 328.
[58] *Ep.* 297; S, 4, p. 217.
[59] *Pros.*, 2–3; S, 1, pp. 101–333; R. Campbell, 'Anselm's theological method', *Scottish Journal of Theology*, 32 (1979), pp. 541–62, esp. 544–6. His book *From Belief to Understanding: a Study of Anselm's Proslogion on the Existence of God* (Canberra, 1976), analyses the logic of the *Proslogion*. This view of the gist of the *Proslogion* does fit in well with Eadmer's summary of what Anselm had set out to do: '... it entered into his mind to investigate whether it was possible to prove in one short argument what is believed and predicated about God'. (*VA*, i.19, p. 29), but see Southern's note giving a somewhat different opinion on the matter.

Barth, Hayen, Charlesworth, and Hopkins and many others have posited
other interpretations of what Anselm did or did not do in the *Proslogion*,
but it would not serve our purpose to discuss this here.[60] It is in chapter 4
that Anselm comes to grips with the problem how the fool can say there is
no God if his conclusion of the previous chapter is valid, that is to say, that
God so truly is that he cannot be thought not to be. The solution is that
although the fool says the words and grasps them as far as their sounds go,
he does not know what his words actually mean. As Anselm puts it: 'for in
one sense an object is thought of when the word signifying it is thought,
and in another when what the object is, is understood'.[61] Thus the fool is
mindless, saying things he would not be saying if he understood what it
was he was actually saying.

A fool's mindlessness does not entail that Anselm will not try to make
him understand what his words mean. This is plain from the fact that in
the *Proslogion* the fool's words are taken at face value in order to refute
them, but this can also be deduced from a passage in the *Cur Deus Homo*.
Book i of the *Cur Deus Homo* closes with an exchange between Anselm
and Boso about whether or not it has been sufficiently proven that man
could be saved by Jesus Christ. According to Anselm, even the so-called
infideles do not deny that man can be saved somehow, and Anselm feels he
has adequately demonstrated that man could not find salvation if one
assumed Christ not to have been. Boso then asks, 'What would you reply
if someone seeing the reason why it could not be otherwise, but not
understanding by what reason it must be Jesus Christ, says it couldn't
happen?' Anselm replies by asking Boso what he would reply to someone
who says something that is necessary is impossible because he does not
know how it is. Boso answers 'that he is an *insipiens* (*quid insipiens est*)';
Anselm rejoins, 'Therefore you say that what he says must be condemned'.
Anselm then has Boso say the significant words, 'True, but all the same he
[that is, the *insipiens*] must be shown by what reason that which he deems
to be impossible is'.[62]

The choice of the term *insipiens* in the *Proslogion* was determined by the
rendering in the Vulgate of Psalms 13 and 52 (the *iuxta Hebraeos* has
stultus), but this does not necessarily mean that Anselm was not using the

[60] K. Barth, *Fides quaerens intellectum, Anselms Beweis der Existenz Gottes im Zusammentrag seines theologischen Programms* (1913, repr. Zurich, 1981); A. Hayen, 'S. Anselme et S. Thomas', *Spicilegium Beccense*, I, pp. 45–93; Charlesworth, *St Anselm's 'Proslogion'*: J. Hopkins, *A Companion to the Study of St Anselm* (Minneapolis, 1972).
[61] *Pros.*, 4: *S*, 1, p. 103.
[62] *CDH*, i, 25; *S*, 2, p. 95.

biblical fool here and elsewhere to personify a type of unbelief with which he was familiar.[63] We have seen that in the *Cur Deus Homo* the terms *insipiens* and *infidelis* appear not to be synonymous. What distinguishes the *insipiens par excellence* is his mindlessness. In Anselm's reply to Gaunilo two more specifications of an *insipiens* are given: he is not a *catholicus*,[64] and an *insipiens* has not received the holy authority [of the Scriptures].[65] And in the first recension of the *De incarnatione verbi*, Anselm reiterates the quality of mindlessness in a fool when he says of Roscelin: 'If he, however, does not understand what he is saying, he is an *insipiens*'.[66]

Anselm's *insipiens* thus emerges as someone who has placed himself outside the Christian community by his mindless thoughts. As long as he remains in his *insipientia*, he cannot be counted as a true Christian, or, to use our simile, he cannot maintain residence in the Christian city. For this reason it is pointless to approach him with arguments coming from the Scriptures. As Anselm says about Roscelin in the second recension of the *De incarnatione verbi* (in a passage parallel to the one in the first recension where he actually uses the word *insipiens*):

> Certainly either he wishes to confess to three gods or he does not understand what he says. But if he confesses to three gods, he is not a Christian. But if he affirms what he does not understand, he is not to be believed. To this man one must not reply using the authority of Holy Scripture, because he does not believe in it or he interprets it in a perverse way. . . . With reason, therefore, with which he strives to defend himself must his error be demonstrated.[67]

In the figure of Roscelin we have someone of whom Anselm—whether rhetorically or not—says that he could be suffering from *insipientia*, and there is no reason to doubt that throughout his life Anselm would have been confronted by many cases of what he would have regarded as mindless thought. Eadmer describes some of William Rufus's ideas in terms which evoke an image of *insipientia*. He says that the King thought it was senseless for anyone to invoke the aid of saints. He also accuses the King of being sceptical of God's judgement ('Dei judicio incredulus fieret'), saying that God either has no knowledge of man's actions or does

[63] *Contra Barth*, pp. 15–16.
[64] *Responsio*, 1; *S*, 1, p. 130: 'Quoniam non me reprehendit in his dictis ille insipiens, contra quem sum locutus in meo opusculo, sed quidem non insipiens et catholicus pro insipiente: sufficere mihi potest respondere catholico'.
[65] *Responsio*, 8: *S*, 1, p. 137.
[66] *De inc. verbi*(1), 5; *S*, I, p. 285.
[67] *De inc. verbi*(2), 2; *S*, 2, pp. 10–11.

not weigh them in an equal balance. The passage concerns Rufus's views on trial by ordeal.[68] Some six years before Anselm wrote the *Proslogion*, Othlo of Saint Emmeram died, leaving among his many works a document full of details about the doubts he had had as a young monk about the existence of heaven and hell and even God himself. Here we have mindless thoughts linked to the phenomenon of doubt. Othlo wrote his work, the *De tentationibus*, to help other monks who were struggling with the same problems.[69] At one point in his composition, Othlo has God say to him,

> ... you think that I, who am God himself, am not omnipotent and that everything you know about me seems to be nothing but idle fancies to you. Recede, unhappy one, from this insanity; for you are being beleaguered by a delusion of the Devil. Heed, O captive, that you are not he about whom the Psalmist says: the fool says in his heart there is no God. ...[70]

I am not suggesting that there is any connection between Othlo's work and that of Anselm, nor that Othlo and Anselm used the term *insipiens* in the same technical way. But we do learn from the *De tentationibus* of a concrete case of doubt about the nature and attributes of God in a monastic milieu roughly contemporaneous with that of Anselm. And we have Othlo using the biblical fool to epitomize the most extreme form of doubt he had been heading for. It is not, I think, unreasonable to suppose that the fool in the *Proslogion* was chosen by Anselm to exercise a comparable function. Whether or not Anselm himself ever struggled with doubt is hard to say: both McIntyre and Campbell imply he did.[71] What can be said is that he seems to have taken doubt seriously enough to quell it to the very best of his ability.

The word *infidelis* can mean one of three things: a non-Christian, a Christian with insufficient belief, or someone who is faithless in the sense of being false or disloyal.[72] Anselm refers to *infideles* or *infidelitas* a

---

[68] *Historia novorum*, 2, pp. 101–2.

[69] I am very grateful to Dr Alexander Murray from University College, Oxford, for allowing me to consult an unpublished paper of his: 'Was religious doubt regarded as a sin in the Middle Ages?' which discusses the case of Othlo.

[70] *Liber de tentationibus suis et scriptis*, I; *PL* 146, col. 41.

[71] J. McIntyre, 'Premises and conclusions in the system of St Anselm's theology', *Spicilegium Beccense*, 1, p. 97 (he refers here to the moving text of the first chapter of the *Proslogion*); Campbell, 'Anselm's theological method', p. 547. Many other scholars would deny this.

[72] H. Schmeck, '*Infidelis*. Ein Beitrag zur Wortgeschichte', *Vigiliae Christianae*, 5 (1951), pp. 129–49, esp. 147; A. Blaise, *Dictionnaire Latin-Français des auteurs chrétiens* (Strasburg, 1954).

number of times in his letters and once in the *De casu diaboli*; but it is especially in the *Cur Deus Homo* that the word plays a significant role. Let us now see in what sense he uses the term.

In his letter to Baldwin congratulating him upon becoming king of Jerusalem, Anselm notes how the land of Jesus had been oppressed for many a long year by *infideles*, that is, non-Christians, who in this case must be Muslims.[73]

In letters 170 and 228 *infidelis* seems to be used especially to indicate disloyalty and falseness. In the first instance, Anselm suggests that the Bishop of London is on his way to becoming a disloyal son (*filium infidelem*) of the Church; in the second letter he begs King Henry not to appoint unsuitable men to head churches, saying that the king has 'pravi et infideles, quantum ad animam vestram, consiliarii (bad and, as far as your soul is concerned, false advisors)', who offer him the wrong advice.[74] In the *De casu diaboli* the word *infidelitas* comes up in a discussion about the seeming paradox between the existence of man's free will and divine foreknowledge. The pupil of the dialogue contrasts those who vacillate between good and evil with those who turn their backs on all that is good. These people will perish in the plunging wave of *infidelitas*.[75] Here *infidelitas* as faithlessness seems to have taken on the ultimate meaning of moral badness in its totality.

In what appears to be his letter of commendation of the *Cur Deus Homo* to Urban II,[76] Anselm writes that after the Apostles the Fathers and Doctors of the Church have said a very great deal 'ad confutandum insipientiam et fragendum duritiam infidelium, and to gratify those who delight in the reason of faith in their hearts which have been cleansed by the same Faith'.[77] Both *insipientia* and *infidelis* seem to be used loosely here in that the terms are not differentiated as elsewhere, but assimilated to one another in order to cover the whole range of attitudes of unbelief with which the Church had been confronted from the beginning of its existence.[78]

Anselm first mentions the *infideles* in the preface, where he explains that the first part of his composition will concern the answers of the *fideles* to the objections of the *infideles* who do not accept the Christian Faith

[73] *Ep.* 235; *S*, 4, p. 142.
[74] *S*, 4, pp. 52 and 133.
[75] *De casu diaboli*, 21; *S*, 1, pp. 266–7.
[76] On the letter see Roques, *Pourquoi Dieu*, p. 194n.
[77] *S*, 2, p. 39.
[78] Roques (*Pourquoi Dieu*, pp. 194–5n) has pointed out the untechnical use of *insipientia* here, but he interprets *infideles* as meaning Jews and Muslims.

because they think it is repugnant to reason.[79] In chapter 1 Anselm describes the genesis of the book, which for all its commonplaces must contain a core of truth: he has written it on the request of those who want to have a written record of his explanations of the reasons of the Christian Faith. He goes on to say that the question, which the *infideles* put to Christians deriding Christian simplicity as if it were silly, is the same question many *fideles* ask, and the question is: by what reason and necessity had God become man and given life back to the world by his death when he could have done this through another person or by his will alone? He then explains that he has cast his book in the form of a dialogue because this would make it more accessible to the less intelligent among his readers. He has chosen his friend Boso, monk of Bec, to be his conversation partner because it was Boso in particular who pressed him to put his thoughts into writing.[80] Obviously, in anything Boso says we have Anselm himself speaking.

Boso's initial step is to state unequivocally that he believes in the profundities of the Christian Faith, and that if there were to be something in that Faith that he did not understand he would in no way be deterred from believing it.[81] Boso is thus represented to us as a real believer. Repeatedly throughout the whole *Cur Deus Homo* we are reminded that Boso knows no doubts. This is in itself an interesting point. For we know from his own *vita* and from the *Vita Anselmi* that Boso was a man with a troubled past. He came to Bec as an educated man much vexed by all sorts of perplexing questions, which were solved for him by Anselm. Once a monk, he went through a crisis which almost drove him out of his mind. As Eadmer puts it, 'The Devil filled with hatred at his conversion and at the manner of his life, swamped him in such a storm of temptation that he could hardly remain sane at all in the many and varied tumults of his thoughts'. Again it is Anselm who helps him to regain his peace of mind.[82] Of course, we have no way of knowing exactly what caused Boso's torment, but it seems unlikely that he had always been quite as stalwart in his faith as he is made out to be in the *Cur Deus Homo*. Anselm's portrayal of him as such must, indeed, have been a great tribute to his present state of mind. Boso went on to become Abbot of Bec (1124–36), and was much loved and venerated by the clergy and laity alike.[83]

---

[79] *S*, 2, p. 42.
[80] *S*, 2, pp. 47–8.
[81] *S*, 2, p. 48.
[82] *VA*, i. 34, pp. 60–1; *Vita Bosonis*, *PL* 150, col. 725.
[83] *Gesta Normannorum ducum*, viii. 24, pp. 298–9.

Chapter 3 of the *Cur Deus Homo* is entitled *Obiectiones infidelium et responsiones fidelium*, and Boso starts by saying that he is going to act as spokesman for the *infideles*:

> For it is proper that when we seek to enquire after the reason of our faith, I posit the objections of those who in no way wish to come to faith itself without reason. For although they seek reason because they do not believe, and we because we do believe, yet it is the same that we ask.

And he goes on to say that

> the *infideles* deride our simplicity and put it to us that we bring injury and shame to God when we assert that he descended into the womb of a woman, was born to a woman, grew up, nurtured by milk and human food, ... suffered weariness, hunger, thirst, lashes and the Cross between thieves and death.[84]

References to these *infideles* are scattered throughout the *Cur Deus Homo*.[85] The last reference occurs in the fifteenth chapter of book ii, where Boso says in a passage similar to the one with which he set off:

> I have no doubts, but I ask that you reveal to me by what reason this must and could happen, this which the *infideles* of the Christian faith think should not and could not happen.[86]

The *infideles* of the *Cur Deus Homo* have commonly been identified with the *Iudei* and *pagani* of the final chapter of the work.[87] We looked at this text before. But because Boso says quite plainly of the *infideles* that they 'nullatenus ad fidem eandem sine ratione volunt accedere',[88] this interpretation immediately presents us with the problem that it posits the existence of Jews and heathen (we have argued that it is most unlikely that the *pagani* are Muslims) combatting Christian teachings on the basis of reason alone. Dahan has quite correctly pointed out that such Jews would not have been forthcoming in Anselm's experience. True, there exists a likely Jewish rational polemic against Christianity, but Jewry cannot be seen as one undifferentiated entity in time and place. The Jews of northern France and England of Anselm's day were not especially engaged

---

[84] S, 2, p. 50.
[85] CDH, i, 4, 6, 8, 25: ii, 8; S, 2, pp. 51, 53, 55, 59, 95, 104.
[86] S, 2, p. 116.
[87] E.g., Schmitt, 'Die wissenschaftliche Methode', p. 354; Roques, *Pourquoi Dieu*, p. 72n.
[88] CDH, i, 3; S, 2, p. 50.

ɹpon questions of philosophy; their interests and their expertise lay in exegetical studies of the Bible and the Talmud.[89] Moreover, the *infideles* of the *Cur Deus Homo* are assumed to have no non-Christian background of their own; reason alone stands in their way of being Christians. Reason certainly was not the only thing which kept Jews from the baptismal font. And the ground Anselm assumes his *infideles* to have in common with Christians is not common ground with Jews. The *Cur Deus Homo* assumes a belief in the doctrine of original sin which Jews do not share.[90] The fact that I do not believe that Anselm's *infideles* are Jews (or pagans) does not mean, however, that I would deny that Jewish rejection of Christianity may well have stimulated the composition of the *Cur Deus Homo*. The objections to the Incarnation which Anselm assigns to his *infideles* are very much the type of criticisms uttered by Jews. Jews were, indeed, the only group of monotheists Anselm would have known to reject every single aspect of Christian teaching about Jesus Christ. The whole question of pairing the dignity of God with the suffering of Jesus Christ was certainly one a Jew of Anselm's day would have happily discussed. The problem is, in fact, touched upon in Gilbert Crispin's *Disputatio Iudei et Christiani*.[91] What I am saying is that the *infideles* are not specifically Jews and pagans, and that the *Cur Deus Homo* was not, in the first instance, addressed to them.

For how are the Jews and pagans precisely mentioned at the end of the book? What Boso seems to be really saying is that Anselm's argument about the necessity of the Incarnation is so very powerful that Anselm has managed to do more than just satisfy the *infideles* for whom he himself had been the spokesman. If a couple of Christian suppositions were removed, the *Cur Deus Homo* would satisfy even Jews and pagans. In other words, the book could satisfy everyone. Jews and pagans are brought in at this point, I believe, to illustrate the presumed universal acceptability of the rational argument of the *Cur Deus Homo*. To call to mind the universe,

---

[89] Dahan, pp. 523–4. It was G. van der Plaas who argued that the *Cur Deus Homo* should be seen as an answer to Jewish objections to the Incarnation: 'Des hl. Anselm *Cur Deus Homo* auf dem Boden der jüdisch-christlichen Polemik Mittelalters', *Divus Thomas*, 7 (Fribourg, 1929), pp. 446–67, and *ibid.*, 8 (1930), pp. 18–32.

[90] D. J. Lasker points out that among the kabbalists there were some who entertained some concept of original sin in that they believed that Adam's sin gave evil an active existence in the world. But the kabbalists believed that every man could overcome the state of corruption by himself with the help of God: *Jewish Philosophical Polemics against Christianity in the Middle Ages* (New York, 1977), p. 226, n. 19. See also G. G. Scholem, *Major Trends in Jewish Mysticism*, rev. edn (New York, 1946), *passim*.

[91] *Disputatio Iudei*, section 153, ed. A. S. Abulafia, *The Works of Gilbert Crispin*, pp. 50–1. See also R. W. Southern's comments and different views in *AB*, pp. 88–91.

or rather its inhabitants, Anselm is using terminology which coincides with that of the simile of God's kingdom, with Christians inhabiting the city, and Jews and pagans the countryside. It cannot be a coincidence that Anselm only mentions pagans together with Jews, and that each time he does, he seems to be trying to cover all religions.[92] So although *pagani* was a term which in itself probably meant something more specific to Anselm, I think he used the term technically when he employed it in conjunction with Jews to denote the entire non-Christian experience. The fact that the term *pagani* originally denoted the population of the *pagus*, that is to say the area outside a city, could well have influenced Anselm's use of the word.

If Anselm's *infideles* are not specifically Jews or pagans, then who are they? I would argue that they are Christians who are no longer considered to be such because they put reason before faith. Their insufficient faith is consciously contrasted to the Faith of the *fideles* who believe in order to understand. Anselm, I would argue, employed the term *infideles* in this way because, on the one hand, he genuinely believed that one could not be a real Christian if one had any doubts or, perhaps I should say, any wilful doubts,[93] about any aspect of the Christian Faith, even if one lacked an understanding of the reason of faith. On the other hand, I think that his encounter with Roscelin made him wake up to the dangers which the new learning could present to Christians if at any time reason were allowed to take precedence over faith.[94]

Much of what underlies the *Cur Deus Homo* can, I think, be related to Anselm's fulminations against Roscelin in a letter to Bishop Fulk of Beauvais[95] and in the *De incarnatione verbi*. In the letter in which Anselm asks Fulk to defend him against Roscelin's slander at the Council of Rheims, Anselm states that in his eyes Roscelin is not a Christian as long as he persists in his error.

> Although he has been baptized, and has been brought up among Christians, he should not be listened to; nor should the reason of his error be asked for, nor should the reason of our truth be shown to him.

[92] Besides *CDH*, ii, 22; *S*, 2, p. 133; *De inc. verbi*(1), 5: *S*, 1, p. 285; *Ibid.*(2), 2; *S*, 2, p. 10; *EpSac*, 4; *S*, 2, p. 227; see above.
[93] See n. 69 above.
[94] See *AB*, pp. 78–82 on the influence of the controversy with Roscelin on Anselm's development.
[95] *Ep.* 136; *S*, 3, pp. 279–81.

Anselm goes on to say that

> it is mindless and senseless to the extreme (*insipientissimum et infrunitum*) to introduce again the doubt of wavering questions on account of someone who does not understand what has been founded most solidly on firm rock. For the Christian faith must be defended rationally against the impious, not against those who say they rejoice themselves in the honour of the name of a Christian. Of Christians it can be justly demanded that they firmly adhere to the obligation taken on at baptism, to the impious it must be shown rationally how irrationally they condemn us. For a Christian must proceed to understanding through faith, and not come to faith through understanding, nor must he leave faith behind if he cannot understand. If he can reach understanding he rejoices; if he cannot, he venerates what he cannot grasp.[96]

The antithesis here is not between Christians and non-Christians, such as Jews or pagans, but between true Christians and impious Christians who have withdrawn themselves from their co-religionists by over-emphasizing the need to understand what they believe. So doing, they no longer believe in sufficient measure, because belief on condition of understanding is not true belief. To reword the situation using the terminology of our simile, as long as Christians investigate their Faith on the basis of firm and unwavering belief, they can remain inhabitants of the Christian city. As soon as they will only believe what they understand, they are on their way out of the city: they have forfeited their permit of residence. As Anselm puts it in the *De incarnatione verbi*:

> No Christian may debate how what the Catholic Church believes in her heart and bears witness to by her mouth could not be; but as long as he always holds the same Faith without doubt, loves it and lives humbly according to its precepts, he may seek the reason why it is, to the extent he is capable. If he can understand, he thanks God; if he cannot, he does not grab a horn to vent it about: he bows his head in awe.[97]

And what is it exactly one must believe? In his letter to Fulk, Anselm makes plain that a Christian needs to believe in the principles of the Creed, that is to say, belief in one God, Father omnipotent and Creator,

---

[96] *S*, 3, pp. 280–1.
[97] *De inc. verbi*(2), 1; *S*, 2, 6–7.

and belief that whoever wishes to be saved must before all else adhere to the Catholic Faith.[98] Thus Anselm lays down clear guidelines for how the Christian Faith could be debated. And legitimate debate differed from illicit debate only in that its participants, such as Boso and Anselm in the *Cur Deus Homo*, believe so rightly that no lack of understanding can alter that belief. Thus Anselm can repeat again and again in the *Cur Deus Homo* and in the *De incarnatione verbi* that the questions *infideles* (or Roscelin and his ilk) put are the same questions which *fideles* ask: 'Many labour in the same question, even if in them faith overcomes reason which seems to contradict faith'.[99]

This is the reason why Anselm will not discuss Roscelin's trinitarian ideas as if he were still a member of the fold; he will do so only after having made quite plain that Roscelin is, as far as he is concerned, no longer a Christian. It is not without meaning that the *De incarnatione verbi* was not written as a dialogue. Anselm's dialogues are between Christians, not between a Christian and a non-Christian. The *Cur Deus Homo* could be a dialogue because Boso, who has established his credentials as a true Christian, acts as a spokesman for those who are not.

Anselm makes it plain in the *De incarnatione verbi* that those who use dialectic incorrectly (in the second recension of the work he says very precisely 'nostri temporis dialectici, immo dialecticae haeretici'), that is, those who cannot abstract their thoughts from concrete matter, have no business concerning themselves with spiritual issues.[100] Plainly, Anselm was no enemy of dialectic; he happily employed it. But one of the things he learned from the controversy with Roscelin was that dialectic needed to be carefully handled—perhaps more carefully than he had at first thought necessary.[101]

So to return to the *Cur Deus Homo*, it seems to me that Anselm is forcefully putting across his views about the line of demarcation between

[98] *Ep.* 136; *S*, 3, p. 280: ' "credo in unum Deum, patrem omnipotentum, creatorem"; et "Credo in unum Deum, patrem omnipotentem, factorem"; et quicumque vult salvus esse, ante omnia opus est ut teneat catholicam fidem'. Schmitt points out that the Apostolic, Nicean-Constantinopolitan, and Athanasian creeds are being used here.

[99] *De inc. verbi*(2), 1; *S*, 2, p. 6.

[100] *De inc. verbi*(2), 1; *S*, 2, p. 9; on this passage see D. P. Henry, 'Saint Anselm as a logician', *Sola Ratione. Anselm-Studien für . . . F. S. Schmitt* (Stuttgart-Bad Cannstatt, 1970) p. 16; R. W. Southern. 'St Anselm and his English pupils', *MRSt*, 1 (1941), p. 20; Campbell, 'Anselm's theological method', p. 553. See also *De inc. verbi*(1), 10; *S*, 1, p. 289; *Ibid.*(2), 4; *S*, 2, pp. 17–18. Anselm does not employ the word *haeretici* anywhere else in his *oeuvre*. He uses the word *haeresis* once in both recensions of the *De Incarnatione Verbi* ([1], 7; *S*, 1, p. 287; [2], 3; *S*, 2, p. 15) when he compares Roscelin's ideas to the *haeresis Sabellii*, a trinitarian heresy.

[101] See *AB*, p. 79.

permissible theological inquiry and the illicit kind which expelled its participants from the Christian fold. The *infideles* are those who 'credere nihil volunt nisi praemonstrata ratione';[102] the *fideles* believe in order that they may understand. Thus Boso can put to Anselm all sorts of questions which were probably being discussed in the schools and even among monks. R. W. Southern has most convincingly linked passages of the *Cur Deus Homo* concerning the rights of the Devil to an extant fragment of work done at the School of Laon. We recall that Boso came to Bec as a *clericus*, puzzling over questions for which he has not been able to find satisfactory answers. It is more than likely that he had been studying at one of the schools, and Laon does present itself as a strong possibility.[103]

Just as Anselm took the mindless words of the *insipiens* seriously enough to counter them, so he challenged the views of *infideles*. To Anselm, understanding could only come through faith, so Anselm could not hope to bring any type of 'unbeliever' to faith or understanding in only one step. What Anselm would seem to be attempting to do is to present to the *insipientes* and *infideles* of his time arguments of such inherent rational cohesion that they could offer no alternative arguments and thus be compelled to grasp what it is they should believe. Once they knew what to believe they could, if they willed rightly and if they received God's grace, hope to come to faith.[104]

Finally, if I am right that Anselm's *infideles* are specifically Christians who put reason above faith, it is possible that Anselm chose the term in part for rhetorical reasons. For every occurrence of the term could be seen as a warning as to where a preference for reason could lead. And because there were real non-Christians about in the persons of flesh-and-blood Jews, the warning would have gained that extra edge which would have made it appear not very far-fetched at all.

IV

In this paper, I have not at all been concerned with the problem whether or not Anselm's *credo ut intelligam*[105] can be deemed a valid

[102] *CDH*, i, 10; *S*, 2, p. 67.
[103] *AB*, pp. 82–8 and 37–67; *VA*, i.34, pp. 60–1. See also G. R. Evans, *Anselm and Talking about God* (Oxford, 1978), pp. 165, 178.
[104] On believing and willing rightly see, e.g., *De concordia*, III. 2, 6: *S*, 2, pp. 265 and 270. See also, R. A. Herrera, 'The Foolish of the *De Utilitate credendi*: a parallel to Anselm's *insipiens*?', *Analecta Anselmiana*, 5 (1976), pp. 133–40 for an original view on the benefit an *insipiens* could draw from Anselm's argument.
[105] *Pros.*, 1; *S*, 1, p. 100.

method of inquiry in terms of the study of philosophy. I have not addressed myself to the question whether Anselm should be seen as a rationalist, a fideist, or a mixture of both. Nor have I studied Anselm as a logician or paid any real attention to his theory of knowledge. And I have not delved into the writings of the Church Fathers to discover to what degree Anselm was indebted to his predecessors. What has concerned me here is to discover why and how Anselm refers to 'unbelievers' and who those 'unbelievers' were.

Karl Barth, I think, would argue that Anselm had nothing to do with real 'unbelievers'[106] other scholars have gone, as it were, to the other extreme. Julia Gauss, for instance, sees in Anselm a keen interest in missionary activity among Jews and Muslims. She would have crusaders snatch copies of the unfinished *Cur Deus Homo* to take with them to the Holy Land to convert their enemies there.[107]

I have argued that there is no evidence for any knowledge on Anselm's part or of any interest in Muslims. We have two letters which Anselm wrote to the King of Jerusalem. There is not one word in either of them which betrays any concern for who the non-Christian inhabitants of the kingdom are and how best they could be converted to Christianity. What concerns Anselm is that Baldwin prove himself to be a good king as an example to other kings and a dutiful son to the Church.[108] Nor is there a hint in the *Vita Anselmi* that Anselm was much disturbed by the fact that Roger did not want his Muslim soldiers to be converted.[109] As far as Jews are concerned, Anselm seems to have been aware of, and seems to have been affected by, their wholesale rejection of Christian teaching. But of Jewish practice or belief Anselm can have known but little.

What emerges from a careful analysis of Anselm's use of terms for unbelievers is, I think, an overriding concern for the members of his own religion. Anselm did care about unbelievers, but the unbelievers he cared about most were those who were nominally Christians. They were the ones who were plagued by doubts; they were the ones who had been tempted away from belief by the lures of reason.

I think Anselm really did see the world in the terms of the simile with which he used to educate his monks. His first concern was to keep monks

---

[106] Barth, pp. 15–16 and 59–72.
[107] Gauss, 'Anselmus', p. 363 and *passim*.
[108] *Epp.* 235 and 324; *S*, 4, pp. 142–3; *S*, 5, p. 255. See also, J. F. A. Mason, 'St Anselm's relations with laymen', *Spicilegium Beccense*, 1, pp. 556–9; J. A. Brundage, 'St Anselm, Ivo of Chartres and the ideology of the First Crusade', *Les Mutations socio-culturelleas au tournant des XIe–XIIe siècles*, p. 178.
[109] *VA*, ii, 33, pp. 111–12.

safe behind the imaginary walls of their castle. His second was to bolster those living outside the castle, exposed as they were in their flimsy abodes. To do so necessitated action against dangerous ideas breaching the walls of the Christian city in the guise of the tools of the new learning, and strengthened by the presence of vociferous non-Christians beyond the city walls. Keeping himself and his fellow Christians secure within the city of 'right' belief and true obedience to God, that is surely what moved Anselm most. And the opportunity this presented him to quench his own thirst for understanding what he believed must have made the task seem more than worth his effort.

Clare Hall, Cambridge

NATIONS AND LOYALTIES:
THE OUTLOOK OF A TWELFTH-CENTURY SCHOOLMAN
(JOHN OF SALISBURY, *c.* 1120–1180)

by JOHN McLOUGHLIN

B
Y the twelfth century literate Europeans—and probably a far wider range of the population—were well aware of the differences between nations.[1] The word most commonly used by twelfth-century writers to indicate nations or ethnic groups was *gens*.[2] R. Bartlett in his work *Gerald of Wales* has observed that *gens* was a fluid concept: Gerald of Wales regarded the Welsh and Bretons as belonging to a single *gens* because of their ethnic relationship; the Irish and English were *gentes*; and the inhabitants of the Welsh Marches were also a *gens*—'a *gens* raised in the Marches'.[3]

It has traditionally been a commonplace that even if one allows that medieval people may have been aware of national and ethnic differences, these did not play a major part in shaping loyalties or self-identity. In some respects that interpretation is untenable. As Bartlett's study and the researches of historians working on Welsh and Irish medieval history have shown, self-identity and political loyalties were extremely complex in frontier regions and were frequently shaped to a large degree by awareness of nation.[4] Nevertheless, the main thrust of the traditional interpretation

---

[1] The term 'nation' is used here to mean a people which has, or is perceived to have, a common origin as well as a culture and perhaps language, which are common and distinctive. For these concepts see V. H. Galbraith, 'Nationality and language in medieval England', *TRHS*, ser. 4, 23 (1941), pp. 113–28; R. C. Hoffmann, 'Outsiders by birth and blood: racist ideologies and realities around the periphery of medieval European culture', *Studies in Medieval and Renaissance History*, 6 (1983), pp. 1–34, which uses the terms 'race' and 'racist' in a clearly defined and precise way; G. A. Loud, 'The *gens Normannorum*—myth or reality?', *Proceedings of the Battle Conference on Anglo-Norman Studies IV: 1981*, ed. R. A. Brown (Woodbridge, Suffolk, 1982), pp. 104–16, which is more wide-ranging than its title suggests, and which develops issues raised by R. H. C. Davis, *The Normans and their Myth* (London, 1976).

[2] See R. Bartlett, *Gerald of Wales, 1146–1223* (Oxford, 1982), p. 187; see the discussion *de gentis moribus*, pp. 187–94.

[3] Bartlett, pp. 187–8.

[4] For Ireland see especially J. F. Lydon, ed., *The English in Medieval Ireland: Proceedings of the First Joint Meeting of the Royal Irish Academy and the British Academy, Dublin 1982*, Royal Irish Academy (Dublin, 1984); J. F. Lydon, 'A Land of War', *A New History of Ireland* II: *Medieval Ireland, 1169–1534*, ed. A. Cosgrove (Oxford, 1987), pp. 240–74 (esp. pp. 241–3 setting out the argument); J. F. Lydon, *The Lordship of Ireland in the Middle Ages* (Dublin, 1972), *passim*; J. A. Watt, *The*

appears to be correct. There were other compelling factors which shaped people's loyalties and their sense of identity: personal ties to a lord through homage and fealty, loyalty to kin, and—increasingly important in the twelfth century—obligations incurred through pragmatic forms of *amicitia*, which were being practised by school-trained churchmen, who did not have the backing of important kin, and who therefore had to rely on their specialist training and on their range of contacts for advancement within the Church.[5]

The object of this paper is to look at a single schoolman—John of Salisbury (*c.* 1120–80) and to see how his awareness of nation fits into the framework of the other ties which shaped his loyalties and sense of self-identity.[6] John of Salisbury makes a particularly interesting case-study because he was very much an international figure. He spent over a decade in the schools of northern France, travelled to the papal Curia on at least five occasions, and had a network of friends in northern France through his closest friend, Peter of Celle, successively abbot of Montier-la-Celle and of Saint-Remi in Rheims. During the 1150s John was one of the leading administrators in the household of Theobald Archbishop of Canterbury; he spent six years in exile in Rheims during the Becket dispute; during the last four years of his life he was bishop of Chartres. He had a wide range of correspondents in England, the Angevin Continental lands, and in the kingdom of France.[7]

Church and the Two Nations in Medieval Ireland (Cambridge, 1970); R. Frame, *English Lordship in Ireland, 1318–1361* (Oxford, 1982), *passim*. For Wales, issues of national identity and political loyalty are discussed in R. R. Davies, 'Colonial Wales', *PaP* 65 (1974), pp. 3–23; 'Race relations in post-conquest Wales; confrontation and coexistence', *Transactions of the Honourable Society of Cymmrodorion*, (1974–5), pp. 32–56; *Lordship and Society in the March of Wales, 1282–1400* (Oxford, 1978), cap. 14, pp. 302–18; *Conquest, Coexistence and Change: Wales, 1063–1415* (Oxford, 1987) cap. I, esp. pp. 12–20.

[5] It is clear from John of Salisbury's correspondence (*The Letters of John of Salisbury*, 1: *The Early Letters*, ed. W. J. Millor and H. E. Butler, rev. C. N. L. Brooke, OMT, 10 (1) (1986) [hereafter *Letters JS*, 1] and *The Letters of John of Salisbury*, 2: *The Later Letters*, ed. W. J. Millor and C. N. L. Brooke, OMT, 10 (2) (1979) [hereafter *Letters JS*, 2]) that *amicitia* was pragmatic and involved mutual obligations and service (*obsequium*). For the *officia amicitiae*, see, for instance, *Letters JS*, 2, ep. 262, p. 530; ep. 264, p. 534; ep. 273, p. 370. Other explicit references occur, e.g., in *Letters JS*, 1, ep. 39, p. 72, *Letters JS*, 2, ep. 263, p. 534.

[6] See M. Wilks, ed., *The World of John of Salisbury*, SCH.S, 3 (1984); for outlines of his career see C. N. L. Brooke, 'John of Salisbury and his world', *ibid.*, pp. 1–20, and *John of Salisbury's Entheticus Maior and Minor*, ed., J. van Laarhoven, *Studien und Texte zur Geistesgeschichte des Mittelalters*, 17, 3 vols (Leiden, 1987), 1, pp. 3–13.

[7] For John's correspondents see the Indexes of Recipients to *Letters JS*, 1 and 2. His two letter collections contain 213 letters written in his own name to 92 correspondents, and 112 letters written in other persons' names to 36 correspondents. 12 correspondents fall into both categories.

The awareness of national differences developed in two ways—first, by interaction within the confines of feudal Europe. Examples of such awareness occur in John's writings when he speaks of the *Franci* or *Galli* living within the domain of the Capetians, the people of Lisieux, who were famed for their eloquence, the Poitevins, who were in conflict with King Henry II, and the *Normanni*, who lacked the urbanity of the *Franci*.[8] The second way in which awareness of national differences developed was through colonization on the frontiers of feudal Europe. Alien societies lying beyond the frontiers of feudal Europe were described in detail and viewed as 'barbaric' by a number of writers, such as Gerald of Wales, writing about the Irish and Welsh, and Helmold of Bosau, writing about the Slavs in the 1170s. During the previous century Adam of Bremen had described the societies of the Slavs and Scandinavians in similar terms.[9]

John's perceptions of two frontier nations—the Welsh and the Irish— were similar to Gerald of Wales's observations on both nations and to Bernard of Clairvaux's remarks on the Irish: these nations were unruly, barbarous, and irreligious.[10] Writing to Becket in July 1166, John compared England with Wales and Scotland:

> God yet spares the island [that is, England] from being destroyed with its sisters whose riotous living and ungodliness it copies.[11]

John's perceptions of the Germans have been discussed by Timothy Reuter, who suggests that when John used literary classical topoi, such as the Germans being like the Parthians, 'these were not rhetorical devices which stood in the way of objective understanding of a strange and rather incomprehensible world'.[12]

The contrast between *Anglici* and *Franci* occurs occasionally in John's

[8] For *Franci* see *Letters JS*, 1, ep. 13, pp. 21–2; for *Galli*, *ibid.*, ep. 17, p. 28, ep. 33, p. 58. For the *Lexovienses: Letters JS*, 1, ep. 110, pp. 175–8 (to Master Ralph of Lisieux). For the *Pictavenses* (or *Pictaves*): *Letters JS*, 2, ep. 272, pp. 566–70; ep. 277, p. 598; ep. 279, pp. 602–6; ep. 280, p. 614. For the contrast between Normans and French see *Entheticus*, lines 135–40: 'Hoc onus, ecce iugum, quod vitans nostra ieuventus/ad summum currit prosperiore via:/admittit Soloen, sumit quod barbarus affert,/inserit haec verbis, negligit arte loqui./Hoc ritu linguam comit Normannus, haberi/dum cupit urbanus, Francigenamque sequi'. For the changing meanings of the word *Francia* see M. Bloch, *The Ile-de-France: the Country around Paris*, trans. J. E. Anderson (London, 1971), cap. 1, pp. 1–15 and the references cited there.

[9] Discussed by Bartlett, p. 158.

[10] *Vita Sancti Malachiae*, in *Sancti Bernardi Opera Omnia*, ed. J. Leclercq, C. H. Talbot, and H. M. Rochais, 8 vols (Rome, 1957–77), 3, p. 325.

[11] *Letters JS*, 2, ep. 175, pp. 161–3.

[12] T. Reuter, 'John of Salisbury and the Germans' in Wilks, ed., *John of Salisbury*, pp. 415–25 at p. 425.

writings. It is of course true that northern France and England formed in some senses a single cultural entity in the twelfth century.[13] The contrast between the English and French was a source of playful teasing between John and his friends. In a letter to John, his closest friend, Peter of Celle, depicted the English as greedy drinkers:

> I know about your people (*gens*) and their customs: always filling their bellies and lungs with wine as much as with honeyed wine, just as the Hebrews circumcise themselves as a sign that they are the untainted seed of Abraham.[14]

Writing to Peter, in the late 1150s, John touches on the same theme: 'But your experience shows that "man does not live by bread alone" and that your assiduity in drinking has made the English famous among foreign nations (*exteras nationes*).'[15] In a later letter John remarks: 'I therefore beg you give me a good quantity of wine, or at least a dole (*misericordia*), provided always it be enough to satisfy an Englishman and drinker (*potor*)'.[16] John goes on to assert that the *Galli* are more restrained than the English: 'It is the custom of the Gauls to dismiss their guests often sober but never dry'.[17]

Having spent almost twelve years studying in northern France, John had a deep affection for the region. The theme of *dulcis Francia* occurs in John's earliest extant letter written in exile—a report to Becket composed in early 1164. He praises Paris and its region:

> And there I saw such quantity of food; a people so happy; such respect for the clergy; the splendour of the whole Church; the tasks so diverse of the students of philosophy—saw and marvelled at it, as Jacob marvelled at the ladder whose summit reached to Heaven, which was the path of angels going up and down.[18]

This idealistic vision of *Francia* was almost certainly intended to heighten the contrast with England, where by implication the Church's authority was being undermined. For John, the kingdom of France was a repository of virtue and goodness.[19] Not only did it display intellectual and economic

---

[13] See R. M. Thomson, 'England and the twelfth-century Renaissance', *PaP* 101 (1983), pp. 3–21.
[14] Peter of Celle, *Epistolae*, *PL* 202, cols 574D–75A.
[15] *Letters JS*, 1, ep. 33, p. 56.
[16] *Ibid.*, p. 58.
[17] *Ibid.*, p. 58.
[18] *Letters JS*, 2, ep. 135, p. 7.
[19] *Ibid.*, ep. 225, p. 394.

riches, but it was ruled in a civilized manner (*civiliter*) rather than in the manner of the Germans, whose ruler, according to John, travelled like a barbarian and tyrant, surrounded by armed guards.[20] For John, the French were the most gentle and civil of nations ('omnium mitissima et civilissima nationum').[21]

Some of the same enthusiasm for *Francia*—a schoolman's enthusiasm—is to be found in a passage in Herbert of Bosham's *Vita* of Thomas Becket.[22] Writing at characteristic length, Herbert used the words *Gallia* and *Francia* interchangeably. Elaborating on the phrase *dulcis Francia*, he contrasts the sweetness (*dulcedo*), humanity (*humanitas*), and kindness (*benignitas*) of the *Franci* with the English ('propria quippe gens nostra'), who had offered the Becket exiles 'a chalice of sorrow and bitterness (calice maeroris, calice amaritudinis)'. The French kings are depicted as exercising their power with gentleness (*mansuetudo*): though warlike, according to the ancient *gesta*, they had rarely been tyrants.

While in exile during the Becket dispute, John sometimes described himself as *Francus*, when playing on the theme of the contrasting drinking habits of the English and French. Thus in a letter to one of his friends at Canterbury, John declares:

> For you to think us French (*nos Francos*) drunk is as if the bandy-legged should ridicule the straight-legged, or the Ethiopian the white man.[23]

We cannot read into these lines an argument that John saw 'Frenchness' and 'Englishness' as depending on where one lived. Here there is some affectation on John's part. He is, as Christopher Brooke suggests, indicating that he is happy and feels at home in *Francia*.[24] Because John was a cosmopolitan churchman, it is perhaps easy to overlook the fact of his strong pride in the place of his birth, Salisbury. He was a canon of the cathedral, which he described as *mater mea*, and he held benefices within the diocese.[25] Through his career John considered himself bound in loyalty to Jocelin, Bishop of Salisbury, who had promoted him. Thus, during the Becket dispute, John energetically argued on Jocelin's behalf

[20] *Ibid.*, ep. 277, p. 592.
[21] *Ibid.*, ep. 225, p. 394.
[22] *MHTB*, 3, pp. 407–8.
[23] *Letters JS*, 2, ep. 270, p. 547.
[24] Brooke, 'John of Salisbury and his world', p. 9, n. 44.
[25] John's attachment to Salisbury is brought out well in Brooke, 'John of Salisbury and his world'. For revenues from benefices: *Letters JS*, 2, ep. 152, p. 52; as a canon of Salisbury see *MHTB*, 3, p. 46; for the cathedral as *mater mea* see *Letters JS*, 2, ep. 137, p. 16.

when the Bishop had fallen foul of the Becket circle.[26] John seems to have taken a delight in claiming a link between his native town and ancient Rome. Twice in the *Policraticus* he suggests that Salisbury derived its name from the Emperor Severus.[27] In one of these passages, John uses the word *gens* to mean the inhabitants of Salisbury.[28] John's fascination with the ancient origins of towns and his speculations on the origins of town names are worth noting. Towns could have a link with classical antiquity in ways which regions could not. Rheims is depicted as being a twin city of Rome, for drawing on a tradition going back at least to the ninth century, John suggests that the origin of the name 'Remensis' can be traced to Remus.[29] John was intrigued by the origins of the city of Siena. He suggested in the *Policraticus* and in one of his later letters that it was established by Brennus, the leader of the Senones, who overthrew the Capitol in Rome.[30]

The highly educated person of the twelfth century could feel proud of the town in which he was born, proud of the cathedral city of his diocese, and he could add lustre to it by discovering or conjecturing links between the town and the ancient past.

The strength of loyalty to one's *ecclesia* is a bond which can easily be overlooked when dealing with someone as cosmopolitan as John. His loyalty to Salisbury was matched by a strong attachment to Canterbury. This is hardly surprising as John's first long-term employment, after his penurious years as a student, was in the household of Archbishop Theobald of Canterbury. As one of the leading advisers to Theobald, from the early 1150s until Theobald's death in 1161, he was deeply involved in protecting and furthering the interests of the see of Canterbury. The strength of this loyalty can be judged from two examples. John had special responsibility for dealings with the papal Curia. In the collection of John's early letters are forty-three dealing with appeals from the court of Canterbury to the papacy.[31] Twelve of these contain some reference to serious problems posed by litigants evading justice in Theobald's court by

---

[26] *Letters JS*, 2, epp. 216–18. For Jocelin's activities during the dispute see D. Knowles, *The Episcopal Colleagues of Archbishop Thomas Becket* (Cambridge, 1951), pp. 17–22.

[27] *Policraticus*, ed. C. C. J. Webb, 2 vols (Oxford, 1909), 2, p. 47, line 14 to p. 48, line 3, and 2, p. 371, lines 14–19.

[28] *Policraticus*, 2, p. 371, line 16: '. . . a quo genti meae nomen est . . .'.

[29] *Letters JS*, 2, ep. 225, p. 394.

[30] *Policraticus*, 2, pp. 44–6.

[31] This is suggested by the fact that 43 of the 136 letters from the early letter collection (*Letters JS*, 1) deal with appeals, and 59 are addressed to the Pope. For a discussion of these, and for what follows, see cap. 5 of J. P. McLoughlin, 'John of Salisbury (*c.*1120–1180): The career and attitudes of a schoolman in church politics' (Dublin Ph.D. thesis, 1988).

appealing to Rome.[32] In one letter John expressed his disquiet quite strongly when depicting one litigant as threatening the unity of the Church by persistently evading settlement in Theobald's court by appealing to the papal or royal court.[33] John's serious reservations about appeals fits into what we know of Theobald's policy. In 1150–1, in his dispute with Christ Church, Canterbury, and again in 1155–6, in his dispute with St Augustine's, Canterbury, Theobald had tried to block appeals going to Rome, resorting to force in 1151 in his efforts to prevent representatives of Christ Church setting out for the Curia.[34] On both occasions Theobald provoked considerable opposition at the Curia.[35]

The strength of John's loyalty to Canterbury is also evident in a surprising source, the *Historia pontificalis*.[36] In the prologue to the work John claimed that it was intended as a defence of papal *privilegia*. He was, he insisted, writing to counteract the pro-imperial and anti-papal bias of Sigebert of Gembloux's *Chronicon*.[37] However, when one looks at the contents of the *Historia* one sees a very different set of motives lying behind the rhetoric of John's introduction. When we remove the detailed account of the conflict between Gilbert of Poitiers and Bernard of Clairvaux at the Council of Rheims in 1148,[38] it is evident that the dominant theme is an *apologia* for Archbishop Theobald.[39] John shows that Theobald was prepared to go into exile because of his loyalty to the Apostolic See,[40] and that he supported the Angevin succession,[41] but nevertheless he fulfilled all his obligations as archbishop to King Stephen. Thus he fended off the Pope's threat to excommunicate Stephen at the Council of Rheims, and he defended the right of Gilbert Foliot, newly appointed Bishop of Hereford, to take an oath of fealty to Stephen rather than to Henry.[42] Given that in its present form the *Historia pontificalis* was probably composed in the early 1160s, when John was in exile in Rheims and when the papacy was locked in struggle with Frederick Barbarossa

---

[32] *Letters JS*, 1, epp. 51, 53, 56, 58, 62–5, 73, 77, 84–5.

[33] *Letters JS*, 1, ep. 51.

[34] See A. Saltman, *Theobald, Archbishop of Canterbury* (London, 1956), p. 60.

[35] *Ibid.*, p. 58.

[36] Ed. M. Chibnall, *The 'Historia Pontificalis' of John of Salisbury*, NMT (London 1956).

[37] *Ibid.*, pp. 2–3.

[38] *Ibid.*, caps 8–14.

[39] The 'Theobald theme' dominates the following chapters: 2 (most), 15, 17–20, 22, 40 (part), 42–3, 45, 46 (fragment, final extant chapter).

[40] *Historia*, cap. 15, p. 42.

[41] *Ibid.*, cap. 19, pp. 47–9.

[42] *Ibid.*, cap. 2, p. 7; cap. 19, pp. 48–9.

and with the successive anti-popes,[43] it is remarkable that the *Historia* was written as an *apologia* for an archbishop of Canterbury rather than a defence of the papacy. Throughout the 1160s, John, like Becket's other propagandists, was interested in the struggle between empire and papacy not only because it impinged directly on the Becket dispute—for the more successful the pope was, the more he was in a position to deal effectively with Henry II—but also because Becket's supporters were vigorously propagating the view that Becket's dispute with Henry II had parallels with the dispute between Alexander III and Frederick Barbarossa.[44] Despite strong reasons to write a defence of the papacy, John chose instead to write an *apologia* for Theobald.

The picture which emerges is that John was indeed a schoolman very much aware of the differences between *gentes*, actively involved for about a decade in dealings with the papal Curia, and belonging to an international élite of schoolmen and churchmen. However, he had very strong ties to his place of birth and promotion, Salisbury, and it was loyalty to his local *ecclesia* which shaped his chief loyalties and his sense of identity as a churchman.

London School of Economics

---

[43] Chibnall's hypothesis (*Historia*, p. xxv) of 1164 as the probable date of composition has no supporting evidence. The date cannot be convincingly narrowed down further than to the years 1164–70. The dating is reviewed in McLoughlin, 'John of Salisbury', cap. 3:3.

[44] For example, *Letters JS*, 2, ep. 181, p. 201, *MHTB*, 5, p. 138.

THE CHURCH AND THE NATION: THE EXAMPLE OF THE MENDICANTS IN THIRTEENTH-CENTURY POLAND

by JERZY KŁOCZOWSKI

I

LET us briefly recall the point of departure for the history of the relations between the Church and the Polish nation in the ninth and tenth centuries, that is, at the time when a strong monarchy had been formed between the Vistula and the Oder rivers, within the borders approximating to those we see today. These centuries were decisive not only for Poland, but also for other central and east European countries—for Bohemia, Hungary, Kiev, Ruthenia, and also for Scandinavia. In all these countries the emergence of the state structure went together with the official adoption of Christianity by the rulers and the social élites. The authorities also saw to it that at least the minimum requirements of the new religion were introduced and observed throughout the population. Around AD 1000 the borders of European Christianity had expanded to a fairly impressive size, and therefore this is a moment of special significance in the history of the European community. Only relatively small areas of heathendom remained unaffected, particularly the region of the Baltic coast—and it was in this region where the last stage of European Christianization took place, namely, the baptism of Lithuania in 1386–7, whose six-hundredth anniversary we celebrated recently.[1]

The relations between the local churches and the monarchies, in Poland as well as in other countries of the 'new Christianity' were—in the course of the first few centuries—very intimate in all cases. There was a perceptible tendency to identify the State with a church province. Here Poland led the way with its metropolitan see in Gniezno, formed in 999–1000 by the Pope, in close co-operation with the Emperor Otto III.[2] The

---

[1] Among the attempts, written since 1945, to approach the history of central eastern Europe we shall mention: O. Halecki, *Borderlands of Western Civilization* (New York, 1952), and by the same author *Millenium of Europe* (St Louis, 1963); F. Dvornik, *The Slavs in European History and Civilization* (New Brunswick, 1958), and by the same author, *Les Slaves. Historie et civilisation de l'Antiquité aux débuts de l'epoque contemporaine* (Paris, 1970).

[2] Regarding the history of Christianity in Poland see the relevant chapters and the bibliography in *Histoire religieuse de la Pologne*, (Paris, 1986), a collective work by the Lublin historians, with

47

few bishops—the dioceses were everywhere enormous, particularly as compared with the Mediterranean regions—were among the king's closest advisors. Around the bishops, in turn, circles of clerical élites were formed, in which secular (diocesan) clergy often met with Benedictine monks, active in the first generations, engaged in the mission of Christianization. What is striking about the Poland of the second half of the eleventh century is that practically every diocese obtained its 'own' Benedictine monastery.

The social, ecclesiastical, and political élites, by virtue of being connected with the monarchy and with the entire state ecclesiastical structure, more rapidly and deeply assimilated the process of Christianization. At the same time, it was in them that the national consciousness became crystallized, the consciousness of belonging to a fatherland in the sense of one's own country, one's own monarchy. In all cases historiography, national chronicles that concentrate on the rulers, expressed this phenomenon in a very distinct manner. In the Polish context, there are two fundamental texts about the beginnings of the history of our country: the so-called *Chronicle of Gall Anonim*, written in the second decade of the twelfth century, and the *Chronicle of Master Wincenty Kadłubek*, written at the end of the same century. Anonim, a foreigner of considerable literary culture, perhaps a monk from France (according to an old tradition), based himself on informers from a circle of clergymen and secular men close to Duke Bolesław Krzywousty; he also knew the country, probably having stayed there for some time.[3] Words indicative of love for the country, and of the case for its independence and liberty feature prominently in the *Chronicle*, especially in reports concerning the campaigns against foreign invasion. Master Wincenty was a Pole descended from a knightly family from Little Poland: he was a priest with university education, acquired most probably in Paris; and was bishop of Cracow in the years 1207–18. Along with a strong sentiment for his country, this educated author is endowed with European horizons, and presents us with an ancient genealogy of the Poles, which he intends to serve as their powerful credentials for a significant position in the European community. Hence we have the stories of victorious battles fought by ancient Polish rulers against—among others—such famous historical figures as Alexander the Great or Julius Caesar.[4]

J. Kłoczowski as chief editor. N. Davies, *God's Playground. A History of Poland*, 1–2 (Oxford, 1981) is an English-language introduction to the history of Poland.

[3] The text is in *Monumenta Poloniae Historica*, ns, 2 (Cracow, 1952), ed. K. Maleczyński.

[4] So far we have no fully critical edition of Wincenty's *Chronicle*, one that would take into

Throughout the eleventh and twelfth centuries the position of the Church became stronger and stronger; gradually the Church became more and more independent of the monarchy. By its struggle for 'liberty'—in conformity with the tendency prevalent in the days of Gregorian reform—the Church in Poland also paved the way for the acquisition of privileges and of a greater degree of independence by other social groups, particularly the knights, the nobility, and the burghers. A decisive point in the struggle, which extended over many generations, came at the beginning of the thirteenth century when cathedral chapters (among others) won for themselves the right to elect bishops. In the generation of Polish bishops at the Fourth Lateran Council—which they attended for the first time in significant numbers—outstanding men were not rare. We may also safely maintain that the bishops accepted the Council programme as the programme of the Polish Church, intended for long-term introduction during subsequent generations. Also, the programme was to be gradually applied by the Polish Church in the course of the thirteenth century, in the context of transforming social and state structures in the context also of the formation of a basis for an estate society which closely imitated the models and laws of the West.

II

At a significant moment, in the first post-conciliar years, the Dominicans arrived in Poland as the first Mendicant Order, opening up the way for the others to follow.[5] This initiative was connected with the most distinguished Polish bishop of the day (*c.*1220), Iwon, of the powerful Odrowaz family, who, starting in 1218—after his predecessor, Master Wincenty, left the office to join the Cistercians—was Bishop of Cracow, Poland's capital since the eleventh century. It is possible that, by an agreement between Iwon and Dominic, a few men from the Bishop's closest circle, among them his relative, the future saint, Jacek Odrowaz, lived for some time in Bologna, learning the basic principles of life in the Order. That group, now already the Preaching Brothers, sent out on a

---

account about thirty manuscripts scattered throughout the world. The available edition is by A. Bielawski in *Monumenta Poloniae Historica*, 2 (Lvov, 1872) [offset reprint Warsaw, 1961]; a Polish translation with an excellent introduction and textual commentaries, by B. Kurbis, *Kronika Polska* (Warsaw, 1974) (cf. a paragraph in the introduction on pp. 67–8 about the influence of John of Salisbury on Wincenty).

[5] J. Kłoczowski, 'Dominicans of the Polish Province in the Middle Ages', in *The Christian Community of Medieval Poland*, ed. J. Kłoczowski (Wroclaw, 1981), pp. 73–118.

mission by Dominic, arrived in Cracow probably in the autumn of 1222. Once in Cracow, they soon obtained from the bishop the parish church of the Holy Trinity—the parish itself was transferred to another church—in which they were destined to remain (a unique occurrence in Poland) without intermission to the present day. The Cracow church soon became the source of a dynamic expansion across the territories of historical Poland and Bohemia, with perceptible—especially at the beginning— support from the bishops. Soon afterwards, in the years 1225–8, the Polish Dominican province was formed; only at the beginning of the fourteenth century was Bohemia to leave this structure to form its own. After the separation, there remained in the Polish province thirty-two monasteries, plus three convents formed at the end of the thirteenth century. One ought to remember that simultaneously with the Polish province two other Dominican provinces were formed in territories considered peripheral to Western Christianity: the Hungarian province, and the Danish province covering all of Scandinavia. Esztergom, the capital of the Hungarian metropolitan, and Lund, the seat of the oldest Scandinavian metropolitan, became the first centres of the new provinces.[6]

The expansion of the Friars Minor into our territory took a slightly different course from that of the Dominicans.[7] The crucial factor in this context was the strengthening of the position of the Franciscans in the 1220s in the German territories. In 1230, two provinces were formed there, the Rhenish and Saxon provinces; and it was from these territories that the Friars Minor went north and east in the 1230s. It was also then that four or even five other provinces were formed: Danish (Scandinavian), Bohemian, Polish, Austrian, Hungarian, and probably Slavonic (Dalmatian). Prague became the centre of the Bohemian-Polish province—just as Cracow was the centre of the Dominican province—and the first houses in Poland were founded c. 1237–8 in Cracow and in Wrocław. Soon afterwards a rapid expansion of the province took place, especially in Silesia, and many new houses were established. A considerable number of these, from the western and northern region, became separated from the Bohemian-Polish province and joined the Saxon province. This process was completed in 1272. This was to provoke, in the coming years, a sharp protest by the Polish Church against attaching Polish houses to the

---

[6] Cf. J. Kłoczowski, 'The Mendicant Orders between the Baltic and Adriatic Seas in the Middle Ages' in *La Pologne au XVe Congrés International des Sciences Historiques á Bucarest* (Wrocław, 1980), pp. 95–110.

[7] J. Kłoczowski, 'Friars Minor in Medieval Poland' in *Franciscan Orders in Poland*, ed. J. Kłoczowski, I, part 1, pp. 13–108 (pp. 94–108 summary in English).

German province. Within the borders of the Polish Kingdom, renewed at the beginning of the fourteenth century, there were ultimately seventeen monasteries belonging to the Bohemian-Polish province, and a few convents of the nuns of St Clare of Assisi.

Over the whole territory of historical Poland, including Silesia and Posnan—as it was covered by the Polish Dominican province—there were founded about eighty houses of Mendicant Orders—Dominicans, Francis cans, and a small number of the hermits of St Augustine. Their basic role, conforming to the principles and character of the entire mendicant movement, consisted in a thorough Christianization of society. It was the mendicants and not the monks—as was the case to a greater degree in the countries of the old Christianity—who, in Poland, and, to a larger extent in other countries of the eastern and Scandinavian peripheries, had to take up the task of strengthening Christianity and giving it a final and definitive shape. In contemporary historiography we can see clearly such a role of the Mendicants, although there is much left to be done in order to demonstrate this role convincingly in the context of the 'new' Christianity, whose traditions were different from those of the 'old'. What this means here is a Christocentric Christianity, one which concentrates on God-Man, a Christianity of the Incarnation, which does full justice to the world of man and of nature. We should especially recognize and appreciate the success with which the Brothers adjusted to the countries and situations in which they worked. They showed not only an ability to reach the élites—about whom we know more because the sources are connected with the courts or mention princesses fascinated by initiatives and projects, but also an ability to reach society at large. In this connection we know a good deal about the Brothers' concern for the development of local cults and pilgrimages, in which all social groups began to participate vigorously.

III

Within this general framework let us now look at the phenomenon connected directly with the theme of our symposium, that is, the question of the relations between things religious and things national, between religious and national consciousness. The role played by the Mendicants in the cult of St Stanislaus and in his canonization is a perfect example. The Bishop of Cracow, Stanislaus, was murdered in 1079, on the orders of, or maybe even personally by, King Bolesław the Bold, who was soon removed from the country as a direct result of a rebellion by his subjects.

The facts of these events themselves have for a long time been debated vividly in Polish historiography. Here, however, we are concerned with the cult itself, which—and there is much to suggest it—was fairly well established in thirteenth-century Cracow.[8] The *Chronicle of Master Wincenty*, mentioned above, gives strong evidence of this cult among the ecclesiastical élite of Cracow at the end of the twelfth century, while the registered miracles performed at the grave—recorded in connection with the canonization procedure—testify to the cult's deep penetration of society.[9] It is well known that the Mendicants, the Dominicans and Franciscans of Cracow, along with the canons of the Cracow chapter, were very active in preparing the solemn canonization of the Bishop-martyr.[10] This canonization was finally performed by Pope Innocent IV in 1253; it was probably no accident that the ceremony took place in Assisi.[11] The canonization was celebrated solemnly in the following year, 1254, in Cracow, with the Piast princes and many guests from all over Poland participating.

The gifted Dominican scholar, Wincenty of Kielce, wrote in connection with the canonization a long biography or *vita* of Stanislaus. This work contained also a total vision of Poland's history, with Stanislaus as the central figure in the historical drama.[12] One has to keep in mind the extremely difficult situation of Poland at the moment of the canonization of the first Pole, in the mid-thirteenth century. It was a time of progressive internal disintegration into small dukedoms, often at war with each other and all too willing to seek their neighbours' support. In 1241 the Tartar invasion rolled over southern Poland, laying it waste and inspiring terror. The Mongols created a huge empire stretching from eastern Poland to China, and the threat of invasion was constantly looming over

[8] The basic text nowadays is M. Plezia, 'Regarding the case of St Stanislaus. A study in sources' in *Analecta Cracoviensia*, 11 (1979), pp. 251–412 (pp. 410–12 summary in French).

[9] These have been critically analysed and used, from the point of view relevant to our purposes, by M. H. Witkowska, 'The problem of religious mentality in the light of *miracula* from the thirteenth and fourteenth centuries' in *The Church in Poland*, 1 (Cracow, 1968), pp. 585ff.

[10] Cf. the valuable contemporary note in the Cracow Chapter's Yearbook, in the entry for 1251: '. . . magister Jacobus doctor decretorum et magister Gerardus can/onici/Crac/ouienses/cum Predicatoribus et Minoribus pro canonizacione beati Stanyzlai certi nuncii et procuratores eiusdem negocii ad Romanam curiam destinantur', *Monumenta Poloniae Historica* [hereafter *Mon. Pol. Hist.*], ns. V (Warsaw, 1978), pp. 83–4.

[11] A contemporary description exists in *Mon. Pol. Hist.*, IV, pp. 436–8.

[12] The life of St Stanislaus has been preserved in two versions: *Vita S. Stanislai episcopi Cracoviensis/ Vita Minor/* ed. W. Ketrzynski, *Mon. Pol. Hist.*, IV (L'vov, 1884) [offset reprint, Warsaw, 1961], pp. 238–85; *Vita Sancti Stanislai Cracoviensis episcopi/Vita Maior/* ed. W. Ketrzynski, *ibid.*, pp. 319–438. Concerning Vincenty and his work, cf. Plezia, 'Regarding the case of St Stanislaus', pp. 357ff.

this and subsequent generations. The Mendicants in Poland faced in those years a situation of great danger, fear, and a feeling of helplessness. The canonization and the cult of Stanislaus were intended to provide an element of hope connected with a holy compatriot. The Dominican, Wincenty, therefore expatiates on the grand splendours of the old royal Poland, especially in the days of Bolesław the Brave (992–1025), already a character surrounded with an aura of legend. He also has much to say about the figure of his hero, who is portrayed as the model bishop, according to the formulas prescribed by contemporary (mid-fourteenth century) ecclesiastical reform. Of central importance is the detailed, and very clearly outlined, depiction of Stanislaus's martyrdom, one which was destined to be so firmly inscribed in the national memory. The sinful king, Bolesław, did not want to obey the admonitions of the Bishop, who defended subjects wronged by the King. Stanislaus irritated the King so much that Bolesław issued orders to dispatch him. However, when the assassins did not dare to approach the Bishop-priest, who was just celebrating the Mass, the King himself stepped violently forward and killed him at the altar. 'Thus the cruel villain', writes Wincenty, 'with his murderous hands kills the innocent one making him a glorified martyr, and tearing his body to pieces, still butchers the separated members and scatters them in all directions . . .'.[13]

But God intervened immediately and

> sent forthwith earthly and celestial creatures, that they should find the remnants of his glorified martyr and guard them. Because in the vicinity there appeared—from the four corners of the world—sent by God—four eagles, which, hovering high above the site of the martyrdom prevented vultures and other birds of prey from coming close to the saint's body. . . .

At last, when the Bishop's friends had the courage to collect his remnants, 'they found the body intact, strewn with blood, but without any traces of scars . . .'.[14]

The consequences of the murder were terrible, both for the King himself, who was banished from the country and finally committed suicide, and well as for his Kingdom.

---

[13] *Mon. Pol. Hist.*, IV, p. 387, Polish text translated by J. Pleziowa in *Analecta Cracoviensia*, 11, p. 181.
[14] *Mon. Pol. Hist.*, p. 388.

JERZY KŁOCZOWSKI

And as he had cut the body of the martyr into numerous parts and
scattered them around, even so the Lord divided his kingdom and
permitted that many princes rule in it and, as because of our sins we
see now, he gave the kingdom—divided against itself—over to be
trampled and destroyed by the neighbouring robbers ... Because
God, who knows the future, punishes the sins of the fathers even
unto the third and fourth generation. . . .[15]

However, together with the punishments—our author is making here
an explicit reference to the experiences of his generation—God began to
manifest his grace and favour by the mediation of Stanislaus. Wincenty
also describes the multitude of miracles performed by him. The canonization is also the visible sign of forgiveness.

Just as God's power has made the holy body of the bishop and the
martyr as it had been, without traces of scars, and just as it had
revealed his saintliness by signs and miracles, even so in the future, by
virtue of his merits, it shall restore to the previous condition the
divided kingdom, it will fortify it with truth and justice, it will dress
it with the radiance of glory and honour. . . . And because he himself
only knows when he is to have mercy on the nation and to lift it up
from its ruin, therefore even unto our days ... he keeps all the royal
insignia, that is the crown, the sceptre and the spear, hidden in the
cathedral treasury in Cracrow, which is the capital and the royal see,
until the one comes who is called by God, like Aaron was called, and
for whom these insignia are there put for keeping. . . .[16]

In such an image there was infused a powerful charge of hope, eschato-
logical as well as temporal and national; a charge well suited to the
basically optimistic vision of Christianity represented by the Mendicants.
Stanislaus soon became, side by side with St Adalbert—also a bishop-
martyr, killed in 997 and canonized in 999—the chief patron saint of the
country.[17] The Mendicants, engaged in the canonization, certainly made
their contribution, through their sermons, to the propagation of the cult,
and also to the concrete hopes linked with it. For a few centuries the image
of Polish history presented by Wincenty was to have, in basic outline, a

[15] *Ibid.*, pp. 391–2.
[16] *Ibid.*, p. 392.
[17] The studies collected in the volume already quoted of *Analecta Cracoviensia*, 11 (Cracow,
1979) present the diverse aspects of this cult.

firm grip on the Polish historical tradition. One may safely assume that the Polish Mendicants not only left a special imprint on Polish religious culture, but also had their own considerable share in strengthening national consciousness.

Catholic University of Lublin

LE MOUVEMENT HUSSITE DEVANT LES PROBLÈMES NATIONAUX

by STANISŁAW BYLINA

L E médiéviste tchèque connu František Šmahel a développé récemment la thèse précédemment déjà formulée sur 'les anomalies historiques' du hussitisme dans lequel il voit 'une réforme avant les réformes et une révolution avant les révolutions des Temps modernes'.[1] Dans la perspective comparative de l'Europe centrale et occidentale, était également selon lui une 'anomalie' la maturité précoce, la grande extension et le sentiment ailleurs inconnu de communauté ethnique en Bohême. Il serait difficile de préjuger dès maintenant la stabilité des 'anomalies tchèques' dans les recherches ultérieures sur le hussitisme et l'époque hussite. Il est toutefois certain que les conclusions de F. Šmahel ont présenté dans un nouvel éclairage tout ce que l'on a coutume d'appeler aspects nationaux du mouvement hussite.[2]

Celui-ci, en tant que mouvement de réforme radicale du christianisme, accordait de toute évidence la primauté aux affaires de la foi par rapport aux affaires de la communauté ethnique. Ce principe avait déjà été formulé par Jean Hus, qui accentuait la priorité du 'droit divin' face aux autres valeurs hautement prisées par lui: le bien de la nation (*árod*) et du pays (*země*).[3] Le calice hussite, symbole commun du mouvement idéologiquement divisé, contenait des valeurs religieuses et universelles; ses confesseurs croyaient qu'il dépasserait les frontières ethniques et étatiques. Mais c'est en Bohême justement que se sont spécifiquement fondus les contenus religieux et nationaux: 'le calice' est devenu le signe de 'la foi tchèque'. Le Tchèque émigrant en revanche, quand il accentuait son attitude orthodoxe, catholique, disait de lui-même: 'ego sum Bohemus nacione, sed errore non sum'.[4] Il subissait la pression du stéréotype étranger en voie de formation par exemple en Pologne voisine

---

[1] F. Šmahel, *La révolution hussite, une anomalie historique* (Paris, 1985) *passim*.

[2] Voir en particulier: F. Šmahel, 'The idea of the "Nation" in Hussite Bohemia', *Historica*, 16 (1969), pp. 143–247; 17 (1969), pp. 93–197; *idem*, *Idea národa v husitských Čechách* (L'idée de 'nation' dans la Bohême hussite) (České Budějovice, 1971); *idem*, 'Antytezy czeskiej kultury późnego średniowiecza' (Les antithèses de la culture en Bohême dans le bas Moyen Age), *Kwartalnik Historyczny*, 90, 4 (1983), pp. 710ff.

[3] Voir: *idem*, 'Udea internacionální spolupráce v husitství' (L'idée de la collaboration internationale dans le mouvement hussite), *Husitský Tábor*, 4 (1981), p. 37.

[4] *Idem*, 'The idea of the "Nation"', *Historica*, 17, p. 183.

de la Bohême, selon lequel le mot 'Bohême' devenait synonyme du mot
'hérétique'.[5] Les partisans de 'la nouvelle foi' en Bohême ne se con-
sidéraient évidemment pas comme hérétiques, ils repoussaient aussi les
termes offensants de 'hussites' et 'wicléfistes'. Devant les étrangers ils
étaient tout simplement des Tchèques. Ils conservaient la tradition de
l'orthodoxie tchèque: les adeptes des sectes hérétiques dans le Royaume
tchèque étaient en effet presque exclusivement des colons allemands.

Les recherches plus récentes apportent un correctif au substrat et à la
portée des antagonismes tchéco-allemands au siècle préhussite.[6] Faisant
apparaître la coexistence en général pacifique des deux nations dans un
même pays, elles permettent cependant de voir nettement le phénomène
de formation du sentiment de la communauté ethnique tchèque dans les
conditions du contact et de la rivalité croissante des Tchèques avec le
dynamique élément étranger. Elles projettent un éclairage nouveau sur les
témoignages d'articulation vivante de la conscience nationale tchèque
doublée d'une violente hostilité à l'encontre de l'élément germanique (la
chronique dite de Dalimil du début du XIVe s. et le pamphlet anti-
allemand ultérieur *De Teutonicis bonum dictamen*).[7]

Dans la période préhussite, des changements essentiels s'étaient
produits dans les notions touchant à la nation et liées au sentiment du lien
national. Depuis le milieu du XIIIe s. env., le terme *terra Bohemiae* a
commencé à désigner non plus seulement l'État tchèque (*regnum
Bohemiae*), mais aussi la collectivité ethnique tchèque qui l'habitait, tout
d'abord limitée à la seule 'nation politique' (identifiée au territoire
tchèque et à ses intérêts).[8] Cependant la 'nation politique' qui englobait le
clergé, la noblesse et les habitants des villes qui aspiraient à y participer,
cessait, d'être identique à une partie de la communauté ethnique en
absorbant de nombreux éléments germaniques.[9] Plus tard, l'étendue de la
communauté s'élargissait pour englober au seuil du hussitisme, du moins
en théorie, tous les Tchèques. Dans la chronique de Dalimil et dans les

[5] S. Bylina, 'Wizerunek heretyka w Polsce późnośredniowiecz-nej' (Le portrait de l'hérétique dans la Pologne du bas Moyen Age) *Odrodzenie i Reformacja w Polsce*, 30 (1985), pp. 12–15.
[6] Cf. F. Graus, 'Die Bildung eines Nationalbewusstseins im mittelalterlichen Böhmen (Die vorhussitsche Zeit)', *Historica*, 13 (1968), pp. 30 *et seq.*; *idem, Die Nationenbildung der Westslawen im Mittelalter* (Sigmaringen, 1980), pp. 89 *et seq.*; Šmahel, 'Idea národa', pp. 20 *et seq.*
[7] Cf. R.Ch. Schwinges, '"Primäre" und "sekündäre" Nation. Nationalbewusstsein und sozialer Wandel im mittelalterlichen Böhmen', *Europa slavica–Europa orientalis, Festschrift für H. Ludat* (Giessen, 1980), pp. 512–30.
[8] S. Russocki, *Protoparlamentaryzm Czech do początku XV w.* (Les formes pré-parlémentaires en Bohême jusqu'au début du XVe s.) (Warsaw, 1973), p. 61.
[9] B. Zientara, 'Struktury narodowe średniowiecza' (Les structures nationales au Moyen Age), *Kwartalnik Historyczny*, 74, 2 (1977) p. 307.

sources ultérieures, le terme *zeme česká* (terre tchèque) est employé alternativement avec le terme *jazyk český* (langue tchèque). La *lingua bohemica* était devenue l'équivalent le plus essentiel de la notion de *natio bohemica*: 'de bohemica lingua seu nacione', lisons-nous dans un document de la première moitié du XIVᵉ s.[10] Dans ce siècle, mais aussi au suivant, on parle du bien, du respect ou de l'infamie de 'la langue tchèque', et, disant cela, on a à l'idée la nation comprise d'une manière vague, ou, suivant le contexte, sa partie la plus privilégiée. Continuaient à être employés les termes *gens*, *pleme* (tribu), mais prédomine *lingua*, *jazyk*—témoignage du fait que la langue commune déterminait dans son essence la cohésion de la nation. C'était d'ailleurs un phénomène général chez les Slaves occidentaux à la recherche de leur identité nationale pour se distinguer de la population étrangère en voie d'installation, utilisant une langue étrangère; de même en Pologne le mot *jezyk* (langue) était devenu le synonyme du mot *narod* (nation).[11] A une autre catégorie appartiennent évidemment des termes tels que *regnum Bohemiae* se rapportant au territoire de la Bohême et *Corona regni Bohemiae*, désignant le royaume tchèque avec ses fiefs.[12] Au XIVᵉ s. ils étaient les composantes et les signes du pariotisme étatique (et non plus dynastique), qui englobait surtout les couches supérieures de la société.

Les sources de la période préhussite témoignent que l'on se demandait en ce temps: qui est Tchèque? La distinction *regnicolae–extranei*[13] était vague n'expliquait pas grand-chose. L'évêque de Prague Jean de Dražice avertissait que personne ne soit admis au noviciat du monastère des chanoines réguliers qu'il avait fondé à Roudnica, qui ne fût Tchèque ayant hérité la langue de ses deux parents.[14] On voit donc apparaître le phénomène du purisme ethnico-généalogique de portée certainement assez élitaire. L'important c'est que le seul terme *Bohemus*, *Čech*, suffisait de plus en plus rarement. Il sera accompagné de toutes sortes de compléments, les plus essentiels d'entre eux expriment des liens et des dépendances entre l'idée nationale et les idéologies de communautés d'autre type.

L'une des conclusions les plus importantes des recherches sur l'époque hussite est la constatation d'une rapide généralisation du sentiment

[10] Graus, *Die Nationenbildung*, p. 174.
[11] B. Zientaru, *Świt harodów europejskich* (L'aube des nations européens) (Warsaw, 1985), p. 340.
[12] J. Prochno, 'Terra Bohemiae, Regnum Bohemiae, Corona Bohemiae', dans *Corona Regni. Studium über die Krone als Symbol des Staates im späteren Mittelalter*, (Weimar, 1961), pp. 198–224; F. Graus, *Die Nationenbildung*, pp. 167–8.
[13] F. Seibt, *Hussitica. Zur Struktur einer Revolution*, (Köln-Graz, 1965), p. 61.
[14] *Ibid.*, p. 62; Graus, *Die Nationenbildung*, p. 174.

STANISŁAW BYLINA

d'appartenance à la communauté ethnique englobant, selon de nombreux auteurs, une partie importante de la société tchèque.[15] Reste discutable le problème de la distinction d'une collectivité pilote, le principal agent et porteur de l'idée nationale. Un rôle incontestable incombait au clergé hussite, à commencer par Jean Hus et le groupe des intellectuels de Prague. Ces derniers avaient déjà plus tôt été témoins de la scission de la communauté universitaire en deux camps hostiles, quand la querelle des universaux a crûment départagé les positions des nominalistes et des réalistes des partisans de réforme radicale de l'Église et de ses adversaires, Tchèques et Allemands. Extrêmement important était ici le rôle de la noblesse hussite qui gardait la mémoire de l'exécution de Jean Hus considérée comme un abaissement de toute la 'langue tchèque'. Particulièrement remarquable était l'explosion du sentiment national parmi les habitants des villes. La résistance nationale des hussites au temps de la lutte contre les forces de la croisade se fondait justement sur l'union des villes tchèques, et 'la grande ville de Prague' appelait au combat toute la nation.[16] L'on souligne le rôle joué dans l'intégration de la société tchèque par la menace extérieure dans la première période hussite et au temps des combats contre les armées de la croisade. Ceci provoquait la montée d'une nouvelle vague d'antagonisme à l'encontre des Allemand en qui on voyait à présent à la fois des ennemis de la 'langue tchèque' et du 'calice' hussite.

La période hussite a été marquée par la généralisation et la rapide promotion de la langue nationale dans la littérature. Le latin était resté, il est vrai, la langue des polémiques confessionnelles intellectuelles (catholico-hussite et taborites–utraquistes), mais les genres nouveaux, idéologiquement les plus engagés de la littérature: chants d'actualité, satire invectives, feuilles volantes et manifestes, se développaient principalement dans la langue tchèque. Depuis Jean Hus, le tchèque pénétrait dans les recueils de sermons, le principal instrument d'action sur les masses, et, plus rarement, dans les traités sur les questions de la foi. La promotion de la langue nationale assumait à un certain degré une fonction intégratrice dans la société, mais en même temps, servant les buts idéologiques et la propagande, elle renforçait les particularismes confessionnels et les divisions au sein de la communauté tchèque.

Quand on parle de problématique nationale à l'époque hussite il est absolument nécessaire de distinguer les niveaux de conscience, d'idéologie

---

[15] Cf. Šmahel, *La révolution hussite*, p. 91.
[16] *Výbor z české literatury husitské doby* (Antologie de la littérature tchèque de l'époque hussite), t. l, éd. B. Havránek, J. Hrabák et J. Daňhelka (Prague, 1963), p. 322.

et de propagande. Il faut aussi distinguer les niveaux de savoir: savant et populaire. Au seuil du hussitisme, à l'époque des querelles sur la répartition des voix entre les 'nationes' universitaires (1409), chez les intellectuels d'orientation wicléfiste est apparue une nouvelle manière d'entendre la communauté nationale, dépassant de beaucoup l'ancienne sphère de la 'nation politique'. Selon maître Jérôme de Prague proche de Hus, *'sacrosancta communitas boemica'* est la communauté de 'tous les hommes: (*universorum hominorum*) depuis le roi jusqu'au paysan, depuis l'archevêque jusqu'au plus petit presbytre, depuis le bourgmestre jusqu'au plus modeste journalier de la ville'.[17] L'exposé de la structure de la société rapporté en abrégé est ici pour nous moins important. Plus essentiel est le fait que la communauté ethnique traitée avec un pieux respect a été subordonnée au critère de l'orthodoxie religieuse: aucun de ceux qui en font partie n'est ni ne peut être hérétique.[18] Les représentants de toutes les catégories sociales énumérées doivent en outre répondre au critère spécifique exprimé dans le terme *purus Bohemus*. Mais *purus Bohemus* (ou dans d'autres textes *verus Bohemus*) c'est celui qui non seulement appartient à la communauté linguistique tchèque et est d'origine tchèque par ses deux parents: c'est aussi celui qui appartient à la communauté idéologique élue—les partisans de l'enseignement de Hus et de Wiclef. Quiconque en effet est son adversaire s'oppose aux intérêts fondamentaux de la nation tchèque.[19] Dans la conception du monde hussite, extrêmement essentielle sera l'importance de la triade mentionnée de notions *lingua–sanguis–fides*, quoique pas toujours conscientisée avec une précision égale.

L'on a remarqué que la définition de Jérôme de Prague a vite perdu son actualité et sa signification. Elle a été éliminée par la notion *fideles Bohemi*, *věrni Česki*, fondamentale pour la terminologie nationale de l'époque hussite.[20]. A sa généralisation avait contribué Hus lui-même quand il s'adressait dans ses écrits, surtout ses lettres, de la prison de Constance, aux 'Tchèques fidèles'—amis, disciples, hommes proches sur le plan des idées.[21] Par la suite ce terme, constituant la catégorie centrale de la

---

[17] *Magistri Hieronimi Pragensis Recommendacio arcium liberalium*, ed. A. Molnár, (Výbor), t. l, p. 244. Cf. Šmahel, 'The idea of the "Nation"' *Historica*, 16, pp. 175 *et seq*.; *idem*, *La révolution hussite*, p. 91.

[18] Cf. les observations de Šmahel, 'The idea of the "Nation"' *Historica*, 16, pp. 176 *et seq*.

[19] *Ibid*.

[20] *Ibid.*, *Historica* 17, pp. 122 *et seq*.

[21] *Sto listu M. Jana Husi* (Cent lettres de Maître Jean Hus), éd. B. Ryba (Prague, 1940), pp. 174, 190, 194, 229.

nouvelle manière de penser et de sentir, intervenait avec une netteté
particulière dans les textes destinés au récepteur massif. Il fonctionnait
dans le chant religieux hussite au sens de société privilégiée par Dieu.[22] Il
possédait aussi un sens idéologique d'union et de mobilisation. Les 'fidèles'
désignaient en effet les 'croyants fidèles à la foi élue, la seule vraie, donc
appartenant à la communauté hussite tchèque. Selon les hussites, eux seuls
sont des 'Tchèques fidèles'. Ce ne sont évidemment pas les catholiques:
l'ont est conscient, il est vrai, qu'eux aussi appartiennent à la *natio
bohemica*, mais cette conscience est étouffée. Le parti catholique fera
également sienne la notion de 'Tchèques fidèles', par laquelle il opposera
sa communauté aux hussites. Un texte écrit dans le camp catholique dit:
'fidelis Bohemus plangit, omnes wiklefistas tangit'.[23] 'Les wikléfistes' ont
en effet projeté l'ombre de l'hérésie sur toute la communauté tchèque.[24]
Les scissions au sein du mouvement hussite continuaient cependant à
briser le sentiment de communauté idéonationale. Selon les auteurs
utraquistes, les taborites ne sont pas des 'Tchèques fidèles'. Le principal
idéologue des calixtiniens, Jean de Pribram, intervenait contre les
taborites au nom des 'Tchèques fidèles', les seuls héritiers légitimes de
l'enseignement de Jean Hus. Mais dans ses polémiques contre les
étrangers: Wiclef et Peter Payne, il prenait en défense 'tous les
Tchèques';[25] la xénophobie traditionelle avait raison du rigorisme des
critères de la communauté ethnico-confessionnelle.

La question se pose de savoir dans quelle mesure le sentiment de ce type
de communauté était enraciné dans la société tchèque. Il semble qu'il faut
tenir compte surtout du facteur temps. On peut admettre que ce
sentiment, né dans le milieu de l'élite réformatrice intellectuelle, a ensuite
été partagé par les groupes idéologiquement les plus engagés (surtout le
clergé hussite), et encore plus tard il a connu une extension plus large, se
manifestant le plus nettement dans la collectivité urbaine (la Prague
hussite).

Des fois, au travers de la couche d'agitation idéologique dans les sources
de l'époque hussite, on réussit à parvenir jusqu'à la couche de la conscience. Une telle possibilité est par exemple offerte par les manifestes

---

[22] *Husitské písně* (Les chants hussites), éd. J. Daňhelka (Prague, 1952), pp. 77, 180.
[23] Šmahel, 'The idea of the "Nation"', *Historica*, 17, p. 12.
[24] *Traktát Mistra Ondřeje z Brodu o púvodu husitů* (Tractatus [Andreas de Brod] de origine
hussitarum), éd. J. Kadlec (Tábor, 1980), p. 21.
[25] J. Boubín–A. Misková, 'Spis M. Jana Příbrami "Vyzání věrnych Čechů"' (Un traité de Maître
Jean de Příbram "Confession des Tchèques fidèles"), *Folia Historica Bohemica*, 5 (1983),
pp. 262–74.

provenant des première années du hussitisme, destinés aux masses sociale-ment très différenciées.

On peut supposer qu'à l'époque précédant la proclamation de la croisade contre les Tchèques (mars 1420), les chefs et les idéologues hussites, quand ils s'adressaient aux habitants de la province (y compris la population rurale), ne comptaient pas sur la résonance des mots d'ordre nationaux.[26] On s'adressait plus souvent aux 'fidèles de Dieu', plus rarement aux 'Tchèques fidèles', on opérait plus volontiers avec la terminologie religieuse qu'avec la nationale, sans doute encore trop peu généralisée et accessible.

Dans les prophéties chiliastes populaires des années 1419–20,[27] se référant aux visées temporelles des couches inférieures de la société (également les paysans) les contenus universels: vision de l'anéantissement des adversaires de la 'vérité divine' hussite, des désastres et malheurs universels ainsi que la vision du triomphe des élus et de la compensation sociale tangible, n'ont absolument pas laissé de place aux affaires ethniques. Cet universalisme eschatologique avait été inscrit, il est vrai, dans des cadres régionaux (cinq villes tchèques choisies qui seront sauvées, Prague—la nouvelle Babylone criminelle qui sera vouée à la perdition), mais l'on a affaire à l'adoption, du modèle biblique et à une concrétisa-tion, caractéristique des prophéties chiliastes du bas Moyen Age en Europe.[28]

Des contenus quelque peu autres apparaissaient dans le courant eschatalogique praguois où l'on peut retrouver de nets éléments d'ethnocentrisme messianiste.[29] On y voyait apparaître l'élévation de la nation tchèque élue par Dieu et de la terre tchèque sur laquelle doit descendre le Christ.[30] Aucune nation n'est aussi grande que la tchèque, car Dieu descend vers elle, disait le prédicateur de la Nouvelle Ville de Prague Jean de Želiv. C'est en Bohême justement que triomphera la vérité divine et elle commence alors à conquérir les pays limitrophes.[31] Dans ce

---

[26] Voir par exemple le texte d'une proclamation hussite, publiée dans Výbor, t. l, pp. 442–3.
[27] Voir en particulier: J. Macek, *Ktož jsú Boží bojovníci* (Ceux qui sont les combattants de Dieu) (Prague, 1951), pp. 57 *et seq.*; *idem, Jean Hus et les traditions hussites* (Paris, 1973), pp. 117 *et seq.*; F. Machilek, 'Heilserwartung und Revolution der Taboriten 1419–1421,' dans *Festiva lanx. Studien zum mittelalterlichen Geistesleben* (München, 1966), pp. 67–94 (cf. n. 13).
[28] S. Bylina, 'La chute de l'antéchrist', dans *The Church in a Changing Society. Conflict–Reconcilia-tion or Adjustment?* (Uppsala, 1978), p. 91.
[29] Šmahel, 'The idea of the "Nation"', *Historica* 16, pp. 200 *et seq.*: *idem, La révolution hussite*, pp. 93 *et seq.*
[30] R. Urbánek, 'Český mesianismus ve své době hrdinské' (Le messianisme tchèque dans son temps héroïque), *idem, Z. husitského věku* (Prague, 1957), pp. 72–8.
[31] *Dochovaná kázání Jana Želivského z roku 1419* (Sermons de Jean de Zeliv conservés pour l'année

courant messianiste il n'est pas difficile de déceler sous la notion de nation élue de Dieu la collectivité hussite des 'défenseurs de la vérité divine', mais l'inculcation à la société de la croyance en la position exceptionnelle, privilégiée, de la terre et de la nation tchèques dans l'Église et dans le monde, pouvait favoriser la consolidation du sentiment de la communauté et de la fierté nationale. Prague pécheresse, condamnée par les chiliastes provinciaux, a été élevée dans les idées de ses prédicateurs à la dignité de ville sainte, de centre de la 'cause divine' et de la cause de la nation. Elle vivait le temps de sa sacralisation: le Christ en effet est l'"invictissimus miles et bellator Pragensis'.[32]

La conviction sur la situation exceptionnelle des Tchèques vis-à-vis de Dieu persistera longtemps encore après la période du messianisme eschatologique des années cruciales. Jean de Rokycany, un dignitaire de l'Église utraquiste tchèque et prédicateur, considérait que les victoires sur la croisade numériquement et militairement supérieure étaient le fruit du privilège particulier des Tchèques et de l'assistance accordée aux Tchèques par Dieu.[33] Le camp catholique en revanche traitait la révolution hussite et les guerres hussites comme une manifestation de la colère divine contre la nation tchèque pécheresse: c'est le négatif de la vision précédente, mais lui aussi attaché à la communauté des destins nationaux.

Au-delà de la frontière nord de la Bohême hussite, dans le Royaume de Pologne où l'Église et l'État avaient suffisamment tôt pris de sévères mesures préventives contre les infiltrations de l' 'hérésie tchèque', s'était fait jour l'idée de la mission particulière dévolue au pays et à la nation. Conformément à l'intention des cercles ecclésiaux influents, on mettai l'accent sur le dévouement de la Pologne au Siège Apostolique, sur l'orthodoxie confessionnelle des habitants du pays et leur aversion des Tchèques hérétiques.[34] Il se formait, destinée pour une grande part à la réception étrangère, l'image d'une Pologne catholique, encerclée par des hérétiques (les hussites) et des schismatiques (les orthodoxes). L'attitude

---

1419), éd. A. Molnár (Prague, 1953), p. 192. Cf. aussi les textes cités par F. M. Bartoš, *Dvě studie o husitských postilách* (Deux études sur les Postilles hussites) (Prague, 1955), p. 21.

[32] F. Graus, 'Prag als Mitte Böhmens 1346–1421', dans *Zentralität als Problem der mittelalterlichen Stadtgeschichtsforschung*, éd. E. Meynen, (Cologne and Vienna, 1979), p. 44.

[33] Voir les textes cités par A. Molnár, 'Aktywność ludu w ruchu reformatorskim. Świadectwo kazań husyckich' (L'activité du peuple dans le mouvement de la réforme. Le témoignage des sermons hussites) dans *Kultura elitarna a kultura masowa w Polsce późnego średniowiecza*, éd. B. Geremek (Wrocław, 1978), pp. 108–10.

[34] Cf. U. Borkowska, *Treści ideowe w dziełach Jana Długosza* (Les idées des oeuvres de Jean Długosz) (Lublin, 1983), pp. 145–70 Cf. aussi les observations de J. Kłoczowski, *Europa słowiańska w XIV–XV w.* (L'Europe slave aux XIVᵉ–XVᵉ s.) (Warsaw, 1984), pp. 315 *et seq.*

hostile envers la Bohême hussite consolidait les communautés régionales et locales. En Silésie, pendant le violent conflit opposant Wrocław (Breslau) au roi de Bohême Georges de Poděbrady—à propos de la question de l'hommage exigé de la ville—les prédicateurs appelaient la population locale au combat dans lequel Dieu et les anges les aideraient à vaincre les étrangers et les hérétiques.[35]

En Bohême, le recours au sentiment de la communauté nationale intervenait surtout quand, face à la croisade antihussite les manifestes, appels et autres textes de diffusion massive étaient adressés à la collectivité socialément différenciée. Les arguments puisés dans l'arsenal de l'idéologie religieuse trouvaient alors des compléments dans des contenus 'nationaux'. Le manifeste de Prague d'avril 1420 apporte un large éventail de notions et de formules se référant à diverses sources et visant différents niveaux de conscience nationale. Il recourt notamment au traditionnel antigermanisme (quand il parle des Allemands—'nos ennemis naturels'), à la formule la plus courante de communauté ethnique (la défense de 'la langue tchèque' contre la menace venant de l'extérieur), au patriotisme ethnico-territorial et étatique (le profit pour toute notre patrie le Royaume de Bohême), au très ancien culte de saint Venceslas (l'appel de l'aide de Dieu et de l'illustre saint Venceslas, notre seigneur), enfin aux notions tirées de la tradition universaliste et étatique du temps de Charles IV (quand on parle du 'royaume le plus chrétien').[36] Cet extraordinaire éclectisme dans le recours à la terminologie 'nationale' ne peut s'expliquer que par l'intention de parvenir jusqu'à la conscience de différents récepteurs. Le manifeste était destiné aux habitants de la Vieille Ville de Prague, mais il faut se rendre compte qu'elle était peuplée par différents groupes de la noblesse et de la chevalerie, et qu'il fallait les gagner tous. Il faut aussi tenir compte de l'attitude des auteurs du document qui représentaient plutôt la droite hussite.

Quand les appels visaient tous les états de la société, l'idée nationale devenait—transitoirement, il est vrai—une composante du programme hussite général. Un manifeste, autre que celui qui vient d'être présenté, s'adressant aux seigneur à la noblesse, aux chevaliers, aux bourgeois et à toute la société du royaume de Bohême, formule les fondements idéologique de la communauté hussite: la réception de l'Eucharistie sous les deux espèces, la proclamation libre de la parole de Dieu, le mode de vie

---

[35] Voir par exemple J. Drabina, *Rola argumentacji religijnej w walopolitycznej w późnośrednio-wiecznym Wrocławiu* (Argumentation religieuse et les querelles politiques à Wroclaw à la fin du Moyen Age) (Cracow, 1984), p. 76.

[36] Výbor, t. l, p. 444.

apostolique du clergé, et enfin le bien universel et la purification de l'infamie du royaume et de 'la langue tchèque'.[37] C'est alors que les notions de la sphère de l'idée nationale sont pour la première fois entrées dans le mouvement hussite au programme de réforme de l'Église et de la communauté chrétienne.[38] Cela venait cependant des conditions concrètes existant en ce temps. Plus tard, quand la situation a changé et que s'est établi un certain rapport de forces dans les camps catholique et hussite, le postulat à teneur nationale a disparu du programme général de l'idéologie hussite—les quatre articles de Prague. La cause de la défense de la gloire du royaume et de la langue tchèque a cédé la place à la revendication d'une teneur universelle: que le pouvoir temporel châtie les péchés mortels.[39] Nous y avons toutefois affaire à l'idéologie d'une communauté religieuse déterminée, et non à de la propagande. C'est un facteur également important que les références sociales mentionées plus tôt.

Le rattachement par programme de l'idée nationale à l'idée religieuse était caractéristique surtout de la période du hussitisme combattant à main armée. Jean Žižka comprenait la nécessité d'utiliser les contenus nationaux: dans l'appel adressé aux chefs militaires et à la société hussite d'une des villes tchèques, invoquant l'exemple des vaillant aieux les 'vieux Tchèques', il appelait au combat contre les Allemands 'ennemis de Dieu et destructeurs de la terre tchèque'. Et les prêtres devaient, selon lui, stimuler le peuple dans leurs sermons à se dresser 'contre cet Antéchrist'.[40] Dans les chants commémorant les victoires armées des hussites, la notion de la 'foi tchèque' associait des contenus religieux, idéologiques, nationaux et éthiques. S'y associaient les idéaux du triomphe du 'calice de la défense de la patrie (*vlast*)' de l'humiliation des étrangers, de l'éthos chevaleresque, de l'imitation des vertus des aieux.[41]

Dans les polémiques théoriques entre taborites et utraquistes du début des années trente du XVe s. sur le culte et la liturgie, on puisait parfois dans l'argumentation faisant appel au bien de la nation et de la 'langue tchèque'.[42] Cependant dans les querelles des élites intellectuelles, les mots d'ordre nationaux nétaient plus qu'une étroite marge des problèmes hantant les deux communautés hussites, dont l'une (l'utraquiste) se

---

[37] Voir le texte d'une proclamation publiée dans *Archiv český*, t. 3, pp. 210–11. Cf. Šmahel, 'The idea of the "Nation"', *Historica*, 16, pp. 231 *et seq*.

[38] *Ibid*., p. 232.

[39] *Ibid*., p. 245.

[40] Výbor, t. l, p. 450.

[41] *Husitské písně*, pp. 158–65.

[42] *Confessio Taboritarum*, éd. A. Molnár et R. Cegna (Rome, 1983), pp. 163, 289.

constituait une Église distincte. La coexistence future de l'idée nationale avec les principes de la foi devait se manifester surtout dans les polémiques entre hussites et catholiques. Dans ce dialogue se répètent les accusations de contribuer à la perte et à la désolation de 'la terre tchèque' de 'la langue tchèque', à la profanation de la patrie, etc. Du côté catholique, la propagande prend pour instrument (et à la fois un élément de l'idéologie de sa communauté) le culte une fois de plus rénové du seigneur de la terre tchèque saint Venceslas, propagé pour une grande part en réponse au culte de Hus, martyr de 'la vérité divine' et à la fois martyr de la nation tchèque.[43] Il est significatif que les utraquistes ont fait leur le culte de saint Venceslas, considérant sans doute qu'il était nécessaire de renforcer le sentiment de la communauté nationale chez leurs adeptes.

Les unes et les autres, catholiques et utraquistes, voulaient réunifier les Tchèques autour de leurs communautés confessionnelles. La nation tchèque cependant restait fortement désintégrée. Les liens confessionnels unissant les confesseurs des communautés religieuses particulières divisaient la société ethniquement tchèque, en dépit de la coexistence ultérieure, en principe tolérante, des catholiques et des utraquistes jusqu'à la Réforme. La situation confessionnel-nationale de la Bohême hussite se résume bien dans la formule de F. Šmahel 'double foi, double nation'.[44]

University of Warsaw

[43] Voir par exemple Šmahel, *Idea národa*, p. 207, illustr. XV.
[44] *La révolution hussite*, pp. 85–104.

THE MERGING OF RELIGIOUS ELEMENTS WITH NATIONAL CONSCIOUSNESS IN THE HISTORICAL WORKS OF JAN DŁUGOSZ

by URSZULA BORKOWSKA

THE fifteenth century was a very important period in the history of the Polish State and nation. It had a particular significance for the development of national consciousness. The union of the Polish kingdom with the Grand Duchy of Lithuania (1385) changed not only the boundaries of this new and unified state called the Polish-Lithuanian Commonwealth, but also created new and specific conditions for the development of the nation. The different nationalities of the Jagiellonian state, Poles, Ruthenians, Lithuanians, Germans, Jews, and Armenians played an important role in the lively exchange of cultural experience on the basis of a sometimes uneasy partnership. Poland guaranteed privileges to the lords, both spiritual and temporal, to the gentry, and to the patricians, estates that had emerged in the course of the fourteenth century. These were united by common sentiment and desire for a strong political foundation. The urban and rural populations of both Polish and non-Polish speakers were bound together by loyalty to the Crown and its territory. Like other groups in late-medieval Europe they saw such a political union as advantageous.[1]

In comparison with any earlier period in Polish history, the fifteenth century is more richly documented. Of special value in historical research is historical writing, which by this time had developed beyond the mere recording of events, providing more evidence about contemporary attitudes and opinions.[2] Such historical writing was produced with the reader in mind. And although we must always be mindful of individual

---

[1] For relevant general histories of late-medieval Poland, see especially A. Gieysztor and S. Kieniewicz, eds., *A History of Poland* (Warsaw, 1968), pp. 133–207; O. Halecki, *A History of Poland* (London, 1978), pp. 65–127; N. Davies, *God's Playground: A History of Poland*, 2 vols (Oxford, 1982), 1, pp. 115–55; N. Davies, *Heart of Europe. A Short History of Poland* (Oxford, 1986), pp. 291ff. For a more specific topic and detailed bibliography, see U. Borkowska, 'The funeral ceremonies of the Polish kings from the fourteenth to the eighteenth centuries', *JEH*, 36 (1985), pp. 513–34.

[2] Most accessible for European historical writing up to the fifteenth century is B. Smalley, *Historians in the Middle Ages* (London, 1974), which provides a comprehensive bibliography. Also B. M. Lacroix, *L'Historien au Moyen Age* (Montreal and Paris, 1971), B. Guenée, *Historiens au Bas Moyen Age* (Paris, 1977), and A. Gransden, *Historical Writing in England*, 1, *c.550–c.1307* (London, 1974); 2, *c.1307 to the Early Sixteenth Century* (London, 1982).

traits in the writer's personality, his work is nevertheless deeply rooted in the age and society in which he lived. The most important Polish historical writer in the fifteenth century was Jan Długosz, whose literary legacy seems particularly valuable in the context of this paper.[3]

Jan Długosz (1415–80), secretary to Bishop Zbigniew Oleśnicki (of Cracow), then canon of the cathedral chapters of Cracow and Gniezno, diplomat and tutor to the sons of Casimir Jagiellon, was the most important Polish chronicler and historian of the later Middle Ages. He studied at the University of Cracow and later was closely connected with many famous scholars of that university milieu. Długosz belonged to the intellectual, political, and religious elite of fifteenth-century Poland, using the language and expressing the ideas and opinions of these groups. His works present a very rich and many-sided testimony to the problems of political, religious, and social consciousness and reflect the views current in late-medieval Poland. His major work was a history of Poland, *Annales seu cronicae incliti regni Poloniae*. Fashioned after Livy in both style and technique, and based on extensive research in documentary and oral primary sources, the work in twelve books, brought up to the year 1480, is a monument to patriotism and historical knowledge.[4]

Studies of the historical method, language, and sources of inspiration of Jan Długosz are still a long way from providing a basis for firm conclusions, even taking account of what has already been accomplished by historians who devoted themselves to years of patient study of his work.[5] It may, however, be worthwhile to attempt to discover those convictions, opinions, and attitudes that are implicit in his writings. His ecclesiological views surely deserve closer analysis, because they held a

---

[3] An older work covering the position of Długosz as historian and writer is M. Bobrzyński and S. Smolka, *Jan Długosz. His Life and Position as a Writer*, (Cracow, 1893). See also U. Borkowska, *Treści ideowe w pismach Długosza: Kościół i świat poza Kościołem* (The Ideology of John Długosz: the Church and the World *extra Ecclesiam*) (Lublin, 1984).

[4] J. Długosz, *Annales seu cronicae incliti regni Poloniae*, lib. I–VIII, ed. J. Dabrowski, 4 vols, (Warsaw, 1964–75) [hereafter *A* with the number of the volume]. Since not all of Długosz's *Annales* have been re-edited, the earlier edition is also quoted in the present paper: *Historiae Poloniae*, lib. xii, vols 1–5 in *Opera Omnia*, vols 10–14, ed. A. Przezdziecki (Cracow, 1873–9) [hereafter *H*]. Other works used as the basis of the present study are *Liber beneficiorum dioecesis Cracoviensis*, vols 1–3 in *Opera Omnia*, ed. A. Przezdziecki, vols 7–9 (Cracow, 1863–4) [hereafter *LB*]; *Vita beatae Kunegundis*, ed. I. Polkowsi and Z. Pauli, *ibid*, vol 1 (Cracow, 1887), pp. 183–336 [hereafter *VK*]; *Vita sanctissimi Stanislai Cracoviensis episcopi, ibid.*, pp. 1–180 [hereafter *VS*]; *Vitae episcoporum Poloniae, ibid.*, pp. 337–547 [hereafter *VE*]; *Epistolae ... ab anno 1447–1448, ibid.*, pp. 597–638 [hereafter *E*]; also *Vitae episcoporum Plocensium*, ed. W. Ketryzyński in *Monumenta Poloniae Historica*, vol. 6 (Lvov, 1893), pp. 592–619.

[5] For progress in research see the review by M. Koczerska, 'État et perspectives des recherches sur Jan Długosz', *Acta Poloniae Historica*, 52 (1985), pp. 171–219.

specific relevance to the fifteenth century, with its three ecumenical councils, its long theological treatises seeking to define the nature of the Church, its polemics with the Hussites, and its efforts to resolve the problem of the Eastern Schism. Poland, with its vital centre of scholarly thought emanating from the University of Cracow and extending its influence to a growing circle of the population, entered with greater vigour than ever before into the mainstream of discussion on the nature of the Church, its institutions and reform programme, and especially on conciliarism. Now, not only the University of Cracow, but perhaps also wider circles of enlightened clerics became conscious of the distinctive character of the Polish Church, of its links with the State, and of its specific role within Christendom. Długosz was the first historian to describe this distinctive role, and devoted his greatest work, the *Annales*, to the history of the Church and its relations with the kingdom of Poland.

The writing of history which bound together Church and State had been cultivated from the time of Eusebius of Caesarea and his continuators, both in Byzantium and in Western Europe.[6] Polish historiography followed this tradition in the Middle Ages.[7] Długosz recognized the particular role of his predecessor, Wincenty of Kielce, in bringing together ecclesiastical and political history and built his *Annales* on this previous work.[8] Yet no one before Długosz had presented the history of the Polish Church in such a broad geographical and chronological perspective or with such careful attention to a wealth of detail. Długosz was interested in the organisation and administration of the Church, in the succession of bishops to Polish dioceses, papal legations and other instances of contact with Rome, and in the development of the regular Orders within Polish territories. He was also the first historian to compile a complete list of Polish saints. Furthermore, he turned his attention to the economic affairs of the Church, to the evolution of ecclesiastical privileges in the face of opposition from the king and gentry alike.

All these questions, combined in a cohesive whole with the political history of Poland, may be found in the pages of Długosz's *Annales*. He was also the author of other, closely related works, most notably his *Liber*

---

[6] See R. Gustaw, *Rozwój pojęcia historii Kościoła od I do XVII wieku* (The Evolution of the Concept of the History of the Church from the First to the Seventeenth Century) (Poznań, 1964), p. 86.

[7] On the historiography of the Church in the Wielkopolska Chronicle see B. Kurbis, *Dziejopisarstwo wielkopolskie XIII i XIV wieku* (The Historiography of Great Poland in the Thirteenth and Fourteenth Centuries) (Warsaw, 1959), especially p. 251.

[8] G. Labuda, 'Twórczość hagiograficzna i historiograficzna Wincentego z Kielc' (The hagiographic and historiographic works of Wincenty of Kielce) in *Studia Źródłoznawcze. Commentationes*, 16 (1971), p. 136.

beneficiorum dioecesis Cracoviensis, the *Vitae* of St Kinga and St Stanisław, and the *Vitae episcoporum Poloniae*. These last are introduced by short prefaces and dedicatory letters, which in themselves constitute what we may call a concise history of the Polish Church, containing nearly all the main elements of Długosz's thought. He was convinced that Church and State had evolved simultaneously, believing that state boundaries should be coterminous with dioceses, and emphasizing the separation of the *ecclesia Poloniae* as an independent unit in the *Ecclesia Universalis*. This chronicler's concept of history reveals a local Polish patriotism which is manifested in his special attachment to the church of Cracow. Yet, in common with other historians of the period, he shares the view of the inherent deterioration of mankind. From his preface to the *Vita episcoporum Poloniae*, we discover his conviction of a 'golden age' in the early years of the Polish Church, sharply contrasted with the dark pictures painted of his own time.

When we analyse those texts which reveal most clearly his view of the Church, Długosz is seen as heir to the decretalists by moving away from a mystical concept of the Church towards the acknowledgment of the *corpus iuridicum*. For Długosz, the Church was an hierarchical body, powerful, rich, playing an important role in the Kingdom, and occupying a privileged position within society.[9] When he speaks of the Polish Church it is *corpus ecclesiae Poloniae*, while the kingdom of Poland is *corpus regni*, one of his favourite synonyms.[10] The formation of these two bodies took place, he tells us, during the reigns of Mieszko I (*c.*965–92) and Bolesław the Brave (992–1025). These two rulers are described as the cornerstones of both the *regnum* and of *ecclesia Poloniae*. The struggles of Mieszko to secure the crown are, in the account given by Długosz, implicitly bound to the fruition of these aspirations under Bolesław.[11] The two rulers appear bound together as the founders of two metropolitan and seven episcopal sees.[12] Długosz thus not only restored to Mieszko I his role in establishing Christianity, underplayed by earlier writers of history, but also ascribed to him an equal importance with Bolesław the Brave,

[9] This topic is discussed in the first chapter of the examination of Długosz's ecclesiological views in U. Borkowska, *Treści ideowe*.

[10] Highly significant in this context is the manner in which Długosz describes Poland in the period of feudal disintegration. He speaks of the country as if it were a sick and torn body. Having united part of the territories in 1295, Przemysław deliberated with his Council as to how 'tenerum et molle Regni Poloniae corpus coalesceret et in virile robur evaderet', *A*, IV, p. 287.

[11] *A*, I, pp. 218–20, 233.

[12] *VE*, pp. 338, 379, 440, 443, 480, 482; *LB*, III, p. 449; *A*, I, pp. 178, 194, 215, 283.

making both of them co-founders of the first ecclesiastical organization in Poland. The link between the two founders of the Polish State and the origins of the Polish Church, in its fullest and most perfect form, took on a specific significance, consonant with Długosz's conviction that God's own will was revealed through the will of the founders. This explains his strong view that the pattern imposed on the Church by Mieszko I and Bolesław was unalterable for all time, any subsequent attempt to change the established boundaries becoming a grave crime and irregularity.[13]

The distinction between the terms *corpus regni* and *corpus ecclesiae* is often obscured by the manner in which Długosz expresses himself, particularly in those passages which speak of boundaries.[14] In his *Annales* Długosz upheld the myth of the boundaries established by Bolesław the Brave, bordering on the Sala river in the west, and extending as far as Kiev in the east.[15] The Church which Bolesław established developed within these boundaries. The myth of the demesne ruled by Bolesław, coupled with the myth that this demesne fell under ecclesiastical jurisdiction, represents in the work of Długosz sufficient motivation for his claim that these territories thus belonged to the *corpus regni Poloniae* and were inviolable. Długosz scrupulously records the territorial losses over the centuries, describing them as a crime perpetuated on the living bodies, the *regnum et ecclesia Poloniae*.[16]

Much of the turmoil of the Later Middle Ages in Europe was the result of squabbles over diocesan boundaries, which were not always co-terminous with political frontiers. The intervention of popes, who peremptorily introduced changes to ecclesiastical boundaries without any reference to national tendencies, was one of the causes of disaffection towards the Holy See. Nor was Długosz slow to express similar sentiments of disaffection. Invoking the established ecclesiastical boundaries of the past, he also demanded restoration of those territories which, in his own time, had no political ties with Poland. He did not hesitate to speak out

---

[13] This was a significant trait of Długosz's mentality. For instance, he blames the bishops of Kamień for harming themselves and the Kingdom 'fraudendo et primarium ecclesiae Caymenensis fundatorem et dotatorem, Boleslaum videlicet Chabri Poloniae Regem, et eius piam et devotam ordinationem adulterando', *VE*, p. 341. He sharply criticizes the religious Orders, which have departed from the intentions of their founders, and have thus brought the wrath of God upon themselves, *LB*, III, pp. 103, 106–7, 222.

[14] *VE*, pp. 341–2, 518, 519, 528; *LB*, I, p. 616; III, p. 449.

[15] *A*, I, p. 262.

[16] *LB*, I, p. 633; *A*, III, p. 171; *A*, IV, pp. 142–3, 292, 294; *H*, III, pp. 79–80, 244; V, pp. 459–60.

against the popes who detached dioceses from the metropolitan see of Gniezno.[17]

Długosz considered the payment of Peter's Pence, the *denarius Petri*, a decisive argument in equating ecclesiastical boundaries with the political frontiers of Poland. As an authority on the suits brought against the Teutonic Knights, he knew full well the decisive role the *denarius Petri* had played in the defence of Poland's rights to the territories seized by the Teutonic Order in the fourteenth and fifteenth centuries. He also recognized that the same payment had saved the diocese of Wroclaw from being separated from the metropolitan see of Gniezno in the fourteenth century. It is no wonder then that Długosz argued with such fervent zeal that Peter's Pence be also paid from Lithuania, Ruthenia, and Prussia, since this would secure for the future those territories united with Poland in the fourteenth and fifteenth centuries.[18]

The thought of restoring to the Polish Church the territories on which, according to Długosz, it had been established by the first two Piasts, occurred frequently in the historian's works. In his sketches of the bishops of the Polish dioceses he did not fail to praise those who defended their diocesan boundaries against the Teutonic Knights and Brandenburg. Nor did he fail to disparage those who did not fight for the principle of inviolate ecclesiastical territory.[19]

Długosz clung to the idea of a Poland founded by the first two Piasts and applied it to prove the validity of ancient rights over the territories of Silesia and Pomerania and their continued adherence to the Church. He further argued that the territories acquired in the fourteenth and fifteenth centuries fell under the Church and were thus forever united with the kingdom of Poland. This programme brought the concept of a great Polish kingdom into close association with the idea of the greatness of the Church. Długosz's ideas are here contained in the fragment of his *Liber beneficiorum dioecesis Cracoviensis*, devoted to the history of the Dominican Order in Poland. The model of the political territory is 'Regnum Poloniae corpus, quod sub primo rege Poloniae Boleslao Chabri stabilitus et adunatum fuit'. The Dominican province had grown up within these

---

[17] *VE*, p. 341; *H*, p. 252, e.g., Prague, 1345.

[18] *VE*, p. 518; *A*, II, pp. 28–9, 51–2; *H*, III, pp. 86, 107, 243.

[19] Among the first were the Archbisops of Gniezno: Borzysław and St Jarosław, and the Bishops of Włocławek, Gerwardus and Jan Gruszyński, *VE*, pp. 351, 359–62, 528, 540. Among the second, also from Włocławek, Bishops Maciej and Jan Kropidło, *VE*, pp. 529, 532, 534. See also, C. Eubel, *Hierarchia Catholica medii aevi* (Monasterii, 1898–1913), I, pp. 2, 265, 533; 2, p. 270.

boundaries. Długosz praises the provincials of this Order, whose main concern over the centuries was that this province should continue to follow the example of Poland, 'ad instar corporis Poloniae', that no part should fall under foreign domination, and that the territories of Ruthenia, Lithuania, Samogitia, and Wallachia be part of it.[20]

In another related work, the *Chorographia*, a kind of geographical introduction to his *Annales*, Długosz describes the cities of Poland as if through a prism of ecclesiastical organization. Although Cracow heads the list, as the capital of the country, it is followed by the two metropolitan sees, Gniezno and Lvov. The bishoprics are arranged according to Długosz's version of the order in which they were founded. In the archdiocese of Gniezno—Poznań, Wrocław, Włocławek, Płock, Kamień, and Lubusz: in his archdiocese of Lvov—Przemyśl, Kamieniec, Kiev, Vilna, Miedniki, Łuck, Chełm, and Suczawa. After these cities, 'pontificale habentes decus', Długosz mentions 'ceteras ... minus vulgatas ... collegiatarum ecclesiarum nomine aliis prestantes'.[21] He thus arranges these Polish towns not in ascending order of economic importance, but according to their rank in the ecclesiastical hierarchy, and under the heading of *Civitates et oppida Poloniae*. These 'Polish cities' listed by Długosz are scattered over a far wider area than we usually understand by the term 'Poland', and he includes towns in Lithuania, Ruthenia, and Wallachia. Those same areas have been occupied by the Dominican province of Poland, for which Długosz had so much praise in his *Liber beneficiorum*. It seems that these territories were included in Poland on the principle that they represented ecclesiastical units, especially that easternmost part of Christendom where *corpus regni Poloniae* merged into and became synonymous with *corpus ecclesiae Poloniae*.[22]

The expression *ecclesia Polonica (Poloniae)*, so frequently used by Długosz, describes a certain organic whole at the head of which stands *mater ecclesiae Polonicae*, the archbishopric of Gniezno.[23] Even after the

[20] *LB*, III, pp. 449–50. For the Dominican province in the fifteenth century, see J. Kłoczowski, 'Zakony na ziemiach polskich w wiekach średnich' (The Religious Orders in Poland in the Middle Ages) in *Kościół w Polsce* (The Church in Poland) I (Cracow, 1966), pp. 516–22, 528–39.

[21] *A*, I, pp. 109–14. This list based on diocesan organization was extended by Długosz through the addition of a further three cities which were seen by him as playing an important economic role. He placed Gdańsk, Toruń, and Elblag at the end of his list.

[22] For the medieval concept of the West as an ecclesiological whole, *republica christiana*, as contrasted with the East, which was a political entity, see W. Ullmann, *Principles of Government and Politics in the Middle Ages* (London, 1961), pp. 113–20.

[23] *VE*, pp. 345, 519. The terms 'the Polish Church', 'the Polish episcopate', which appear countless times in the writings of Długosz, deserve all the more attention because they appear

creation of the metropolitan see of Lvov in 1375 Gniezno retained its primacy, while its archbishops secured their title of Primate of all Poland.[24] Although *ecclesia Poloniae* was part of the wider *Ecclesia Universalis*, yet the interests of the two institutions were often in conflict. We may take the case of the diocese of Kamień, founded in the twelfth century to serve West Pomerania. Długosz refers several times to the decision, taken in Rome, to detach this diocese from Gniezno, of which it had been a part for many years. The chronicler clearly believed that the Bishop of Kamień 'seeking freedom, sold himself to the Roman Church to his own sorrow and to the detriment of the clergy, instead finding himself bound in servitude to the Apostolic See'. By thus cutting himself off from that unity of the church of Gniezno and the Polish kingdom, he brought upon his clergy the inconvenience of delays and enormous expense in settling suits at the Curia, matters, claimed Długosz, that could easily have been resolved in Gniezno.[25]

We should not be surprised at the note of displeasure in the writings of Długosz at the foreign element in the Polish episcopate. We see it particularly in the manner in which he compiled the *Vitae episcoporum*. His own common sense as well as his source material must have told him that the first bishops were of foreign extraction. Indiscriminately defining their nationalities, he introduced Italians, Frenchmen, and Germans in the *Vitae*. But had the papal practice of installing foreigners in Polish cathedrals gone on too long it would probably have been, according to Długosz, a mark of disrespect towards the Polish clergy. He therefore introduced in his text of the *Vitae episcoporum* the precise moment when foreigners were definitely excluded from presentation to bishoprics, describing in dramatic terms the intervention of Polish rulers who objected to the decisions of Rome, or the opposition of the chapters to foreign bishops.[26] Długosz also viewed with distaste the presence of foreign bishops in the Polish Church of his own day.[27] He believed that a

---

so rarely in earlier chronicles such as Gallus Anonymous, Wincenty Kadlubek, the Wiekopolska Chronicle, and the Silesian sources. Attention to the emphasis placed on the national character of the Church was drawn by B. Guenée, *L'Occident aux xiv* et xv* siècles* (Paris, 1971), p. 238.

[24] *A*, I, p. 179; *VE*, p. 369; *H*, IV, p. 206.

[25] *VE*, p. 341.

[26] Długosz has Bolesław the Bold explain himself before the Wrocław chapter thus: 'in Ecclesia Poloniae ... Polonum ... eligi oportet: sufficiere ... Italis ... indignum et dedecorum ratus forenses propriis et indigenis aneferri', *VE*, p. 449. Also see, *VE*, pp. 485, 488.

[27] *VE*, pp. 469, 472; *H*, III, p. 501. There are exceptions such as Rudolph of Rüdesheim, whom Długosz supported as a candidate to the see of Wrocław [Eubel, 2, p. 270]. The chronicler

bishop should be dedicated, not only to his church, but also to his country, and one could not always expect that from a foreigner.

Długosz was irritated that papal nominations were made under pressure from the emperors, and that episcopal offices were sold by the Curia.[28] To him, this was a flagrant violation of the rights of the chapters. He also criticized the papal custom of appropriating the income of a diocese following the death of its bishop and of delaying the nomination of a new bishop in order to extend this period.[29] While he approved the necessity of paying Peter's Pence for the political benefits which accrued from these payments, he looked disapprovingly upon all additional financial exactions made by Rome.[30] It seems that not only in his disapproval of these financial burdens, but also in his annoyance at bishops of foreign extraction appointed by the Holy See, Długosz was expressing that public opinion prevalent in the Poland of his day, an opinion as clearly formulated by Jan Ostroróg (1436–1501) in his work, *Momentum pro Republicae ordinatione conquestum, c.* 1475. Jan Ostroróg, the Castellan of Posnan, waged a life-long campaign against papal power, demanding the abolition of annates, of juridical appeals to the Court of Rome, and of clerical exemption from royal taxation.[31] These sentiments were also shared by the envoy sent in 1479 by King Casimir Jagiellon to negotiate with the Prussian diet over the question of the bishopric of Warmia. He reminded the diet that if it were not the King, then the Pope would decide on who should fill the episcopal vacancy, and he would most certainly appoint an Italian. Money would then flow out of the diocese to the detriment of all save Rome.[32]

Długosz saw a real link between the living cult of Polish saints and his love for his country, and considered it his religious as well as his patriotic duty to write about these saints.[33] Indeed, like no one else before him, he

---

must here have been convinced that the papal legate had a positive attitude towards Poland. Possibly he viewed his candidature solely through the prism of the positive resolution of the Polish-Teutonic conflict which Rudolph helped to bring about in 1466.

[28] *VE*, pp. 365, 377, 503, 506, 532; *A*, III, pp. 158, 395–6; *A*, IV, p. 202: *H*, III, 265–9, 501; *V*, p. 561.

[29] *H*, III, pp. 364–5.

[30] *H*, III, p. 366; IV, pp. 333–4.

[31] See A. Pawiński, *Jan Ostroróg, Żywot i pismo 'O naprawie Rzeczypospolitej'*, (Life and Work 'On the Reform of the Commonwealth') (Warsaw, 1884), pp. 126–8, 136–40.

[32] K. Górski, 'Rządy wewnętrzne Kazimierza Jagiellończyka w Koronie', (The Internal Government of Kazimir Jagiellończyk in the Kingdom of Poland), *Kwartalnik Historyczny*, 66 (1959), p. 742.

[33] See Bobrzyński and Smolka, *Jan Długosz*, p. 206.

diligently recorded the names of Polish saints and beatified persons, based on written sources as well as on oral tradition. Moreover, he surrounded with an aura of sanctity a whole host of persons appearing in his works, thus creating a kind of pantheon of national saints in Polish historiography. No wonder then that these works served the hagiographers as a rich source of reference for centuries to come. They were also cited in canonization procedures as the main argument for the so-called *ex traditione* cult and in support of their claim for a place on the altar.[34] Długosz mentions twenty-six out of the thirty-six persons who lived before his time, but who were later recognized as saints or beatified.[35]

Being himself a fervent worshipper of Polish saints, a point he proved not only by his pen, but also by the numerous foundations he established in their honour,[36] he upbraided the Poles for their negligence in seeking the canonization of Polish saints.[37] The long accounts he gives of the canonization processes of St Stanisław and St Jadwiga of Silesia are proof of the importance he attached to this act. Pride and joy are reflected in his description of the canonization celebrations.[38] Długosz saw the saints as jewels in the crown of Poland, enhancing the splendour of that country.[39] First amongst the saints was St Stanisław, overshadowing even St Adalbert, and these two, together with St Florian and St Wenceslaus, are described by Długosz as the special patrons of the kingdom of Poland. Now no longer local saints, they have become the powerful guardians of the whole country.[40]

St Stanisław plays a major role in Długosz's historical and philosophical approach to Polish history as a central figure and continual presence. From the chronicler's pen, the eleventh-century conflict between the Bishop of Cracow and King Bolesław the Bold becomes the archetype of all later clashes between secular and ecclesiastical authority. As presented by Długosz that conflict was to influence the whole course of later Polish history. As a punishment for Bolesław's crime, numerous disasters befell the kingdom: enemy invasions, the denial of the crown to Poland in the thirteenth century, and the breaking up of the country.

[34] See U. Borkowska, 'Hagiografia polska wiek XVI–XVIII' (Polish hagiography from the sixteenth to the eighteenth centuries) in *Dzieje teologii katolickiej w Polsce* (The History of Catholic Theology in Poland) 2, pt 1 (Lublin, 1975), p. 477.

[35] See *Hagiografia polska* (Polish Hagiography), ed. R. Gustaw, 2 vols (Poznań, 1971).

[36] See Bobrzyński and Smolka, *Jan Długosz*, p. 206.

[37] *V*, pp. 189, 240; *A*, IV, p. 117.

[38] *VS*, pp. 131–51; *A*, IV, pp. 155–6, 158–9.

[39] *VS*, p. 172; *VK*, p. 185.

[40] *VS*, p. 83.

Finally, in Długosz's own time, Bolesław's punishment continued with the loss of the Polish crown by the Piasts, 'the natural rulers of Poland' to those 'alien strangers', the Jagiellonian dynasty from Lithuania.[41]

Belief in the dogma of 'the communion of the saints' was similarly merged with patriotic elements in the history of the defence of the fortified town by St Adalbert against the Prussians,[42] and the support of the Polish forces in two major battles: the battle of Płowce, in 1331,[43] and the Battle of Grünwald, in 1410, in which St Stanisław appeared in the sky and defended the whole Polish army. Długosz preceded his description of the Battle of Grünwald with a dramatic scene depicting the arrogant and overbearing manner of the Teutonic envoys who brought two swords to Jagiello and his brother, the Duke of Lithuania. Długosz makes the envoys say, 'Understand, King and Witold, that this very hour we shall also do battle with you, and to this end we send you these swords for your assistance'.[44] Replying to these words, the Polish King expressed his deep faith in the assistance of 'his own and his kingdom's patrons, Stanisław, Adalbert, Wenceslaus, Florian, and Jadwiga'.[45] Długosz thus gives a realistic account of one of the most significant battles of the late Middle Ages, yet remains convinced that its outcome had been decided by supernatural forces. The Poles were indeed fighting for a just cause and therefore they deserved the protection of national patrons who tipped the scales of victory in their favour. Patriotic overtones such as these may also be detected in the prayer with which Długosz closes the first part of the *Vita* of St Stanisław. Here he expresses his deepest conviction that the territories of Poland had been united at the end of the fourteenth century at the express intervention of the Saint.[46]

Throughout Europe by the fifteenth century, national awareness was beginning to take on more concrete forms and was seeking support from, amongst others, the saint-protectors of the nation. Długosz emerges as an exponent and propagator of this particularly 'national' aspect of the cult of the saints. Indeed, his whole corpus of historical writing must be seen as highly significant for the Polish Church and kingdom. Although he was

---

[41] See U. Borkowska, 'Święty Stanisław w concepcji historii narodowej Jana Długosza' (The role of St Stanisław in Długosz's concept of national history), *Znak*, 31 (1979), pp. 4–5, 298–9.

[42] Gallus Anonymous, lib. 2, p. 6, *Monumenta Poloniae Historica*, ns, 2 (Cracow, 1952), p. 3. Długosz repeats the text faithfully in his own words. *A*, II, p. 193.

[43] *H*, III, p. 151.

[44] *H*, IV, p. 51.

[45] *H*, IV, pp. 61–2.

[46] *VS*, p. 92.

not the originator of the Polish tradition of historical writing, no one
before him had advanced the view that the two institutions founded by
the Piasts, the 'natural lords' of Poland, shared a common beginning. He
saw the lands of the *corpus regni Poloniae* as coextensive with the lands of
the Church. His own deep knowledge of both civil and canon law and his
personal involvement in diplomacy gave his major work, the *Annales*, a
clear and well-defined purpose. His aim was the defence of the whole of
the Polish royal rights and patrimony as well as those of the Church.
Convinced that he was serving the Polish Church as well as his beloved
patria with his pen and with his life, [47] he was perhaps typical of those
clerics within the court circle of Zbigniew Oleśnicki, Chancellor of the
Kingdom and Bishop of Cracow, enjoying royal favour and strongly tied
to the milieu of the University of Cracow. It is within this group, with its
highly developed religious and political awareness, that we may seek the
roots of the belief that the Polish Church was a quite distinct entity within
the Universal Church. Jan Długosz, historian, diplomat, and cleric,
played a major role in blending together religious and political elements
to advance the view of one Polish State and one Polish Church.

Catholic University of Lublin

[47] This aspect underlines the arguments of S. Gawlas in 'Świadomość narodowa Jana Długosza'
(Jan Długosz's national consciousness), *Studia źródłoznawcze. Commentationes*, 27 (1983), p. 14.

ONE CHURCH AND TWO NATIONS: A UNIQUELY IRISH PHENOMENON?

by KATHERINE WALSH

T HE Reformation in the sixteenth century brought with it the complex and—for contemporary religious and political groupings—unacceptable phenomenon of religious plurality. In the Middle Ages citizenship as an independent concept scarcely existed, and tacit assumptions about the function of Church–State relations rested on the view that all inhabitants of the polity were members of the Christian *respublica*. There were, of course, some specific, necessary, and therefore tolerable exceptions, such as Jews in many, but not in all countries. Heretics and infidels, who did not conform to these specifications, were therefore regarded as legitimate targets for repression, even for physical violence, in the complex machinery of the Inquisition and in the ideology of the crusades.[1] The Reformation brought about a reversal of this monolithic thinking about the nature of the Christian polity. Faced with plurality of religious ideas and organizations, various solutions were attempted. The earliest, and that which was to have the most widespread and long-lasting effect in pre-Enlightenment and pre-Emancipation Europe, was that formulated in the Religious Peace of Augsburg (1555).[2] Here the decree of *cuius regio, ejus religio*—with a deliberate retrospect to the Emperor Constantine[3]—guaranteed the continuation of the medieval principle, whereby the good and loyal citizen was one who conformed in religious as well as political sentiment with the ruling authority. Like the

---

[1] Suspicion of the outsider, who did not conform to the established norm, took many forms and has been the subject of wide-ranging studies. A good starting-point is to be found in L. Schmugge, 'Über "nationale" Vorurteile im Mittelalter', *DA*, 38 (1982), pp. 439–59. Cf. R. C. Schwinges, *Kreuzzugsideologie und Toleranz. Studien zu Wilhelm von Tyrus — Monographien zur Geschichte des Mittelalters*, 15 (Stuttgart, 1977); *Zur Geschichte der Juden im Deutschland des späten Mittelalters und der frühen Neuzeit*, ed. A. Haverkamp — *Monographien . . .*, 24 (Stuttgart, 1981); R. Kieckhefer, *Repression of Heresy in Medieval Germany* (Liverpool, 1979), esp. pp. 77ff. on the perception of heresy as civil disorder.

[2] Cf. E. W. Zeeden, *Die Entstehung der Konfessionen. Grundlagen und Formen der Konfessionsbildung im Zeitalter der Glaubenskämpfe* (Munich and Vienna, 1965); *idem, Konfessionsbildung. Studien zur Reformation, Gegenreformation und katholischen Reform — Spätmittelalter und Frühe Neuzeit. Tübinger Beiträge zur Geschichtsforschung*, 15 (Stuttgart, 1985); S. Skalweit, *Reich und Reformation* (Berlin, 1969), esp. pp. 391ff.: M. Heckel, *Deutschland im konfessionellen Zeitalter — Deutsche Geschichte*, 5 (Göttingen, 1983), esp. pp. 67ff.

[3] Cf. S. G. Hall, 'Constantine and the Church' in the present volume.

medieval heretic, the religious deviant was stigmatized as a social and political outsider, no longer entitled to the protection of the State, and faced with the alternatives of forced emigration or physical punishment—or conversion to the majority religion. An alternative solution, necessitated by political and dynastic change in France at the end of the sixteenth century, sought to pursue the concept of bi-confessionalism by detaching the idea of citizenship from the necessity of religious conformity. In between these two extremes, that formulated at Augsburg (1555) and the Edict of Nantes (1598), lay the ideal of a religious 'open area' (*Freiraum*) on Erasmian lines, such as had existed in Poland before the collapse of the consensus of Sandomierz—the *via media*, which could not survive the increasing polarization into religious camps.[4]

A medieval antecedent of this dilemma arose from an opposing tendency: from the conflict between common membership of a Christian *respublica* on the one hand, and on the other the emotive, cultural, economic, and political dictates of belonging to different *nationes*, 'national' groupings within a particular secular polity.[5] Such was the case in medieval Ireland and in pre-Hussite Bohemia. In the centuries following the Anglo-Norman annexation of Ireland, with the help of a papal legitimation enshrined in the bull *Laudabiliter*,[6] the country's development in both the secular and ecclesiastical spheres was determined by the—often less than peaceful—coexistence of two *nationes*. These consisted of two totally divergent linguistic groups, with differing cultural and political allegiances and aspirations: the older Gaelic inhabitants and the newcomers of Norman-French extraction, who reached Ireland via the Marcher lordships on the borders of England and Wales. Although—analogous to the situation in Bohemia—neither group was initially homogenous, circumstances helped to make them so, and it

---

[4] Cf. L. Hein, *Italienische Protestanten und ihr Einfluss auf die Reformation in Polen während der beiden Jahrzehnte vor dem Sandomirer Konsens (1570)* (Leiden, 1974); in her—albeit controversial— interpretation, *The Valois Tapestries* (rev. edn London, 1975), pp. 67–71, the late Dame Frances A. Yates drew attention to the openness of Polish society in the 1570s. Cf. also F. Heer, *Die Dritte Kraft. Humanismus zwischen den Fronten des konfessionellen Zeitalters* (Frankfurt am Main, 1959).

[5] Cf. H. Beumann and W. Schröder, ed., *Aspekte der Nationenbildung im Mittelalter. Ergebnisse der Marburger Rundgespräche — Nationes. Historische und philologische Untersuchungen zur Entstehung der europäischen Nationen im Mittelalter*, 2 (Sigmaringen, 1978).

[6] Modern Irish research has shown the extent to which the traditional description, used by Irish nationalist and British historians alike, of an 'Anglo-Norman invasion of Ireland' is a misnomer. For a balanced account see that of F. X. Martin, *A New History of Ireland*: II. *Medieval Ireland, 1169–1534*, ed. A. Cosgrove (Oxford, 1987), pp. 43ff.

soon became customary to speak of Ireland as a country of two distinct parts, that *inter Anglicos* and that *inter Hibernicos*.[7]

In both cases the opposing groups—the Gaelic and Anglo-Norman elements in Ireland, and the German and Slav *nationes* in the lands of the Crown of St Wenceslaus[8]—professed their allegiance to a common religious ideal. But they nevertheless sought and found expression for their 'differentness' in a claim to a better and truer perception of Christian values and of the teachings of the Bible. It is certainly no accident that structural and social divergencies played an important part in the course of events in both countries. The Gaelic element in Ireland was a largely rural and agricultural one, with a highly developed capacity for violence, but without a radical ideology.[9] Elsewhere, possible reasons have been discussed why both Lollardy and the sort of agrarian unrest that spread across western Europe in the later fourteenth and fifteenth centuries, and which culminated in the German Peasants' War (1525), left Ireland virtually untouched.[10] Here their absence is merely noted. The Anglo-Norman community on the other hand was, like the German element in Bohemia, strongly centred on the towns and on new mercantile methods, with a corresponding structure of ethics, appropriate pastoral practice, and a somewhat different catalogue of sins. Here the proper question in the confessional was not: did you move your neighbour's fence, so that your cows could get at the best grass? Instead it was: did you tamper with the account books in order to show no trading profit at the end of the year, and thus avoid paying tithes?[11]

---

[7] Cf. J. Watt, '*Ecclesia inter Anglicos et inter Hibernicos*: confrontation and coexistence in the medieval diocese of Armagh' in *The English in Medieval Ireland. Proceedings of the First Joint Meeting of the Royal Irish Academy and the British Academy, Dublin 1982*, ed. J. Lydon (Dublin, 1984), pp. 46–64. The same author developed this theme further in the presidential address read to the Ecclesiastical History Society on 21 July 1987 at St Patrick's College Maynooth: 'The Church and the two nations in late medieval Armagh', *SCH*, 25 (1989), pp. 37–54.

[8] That is, the kingdom of Bohemia, together with the margravate of Moravia and the two Lusatias.

[9] An outstanding recent study is K. Simms, *From Kings to Warlords. The Changing Political Structure of Gaelic Ireland in the Later Middle Ages* (Woodbridge, Suffolk, 1987).

[10] In an Aubrey Gwynn memorial lecture under the title 'Preaching, politics and social tension in later medieval Ireland'. This series of lectures is in press. For comparable material for the rest of Europe cf. *Europa 1400. Die Krise des Spätmittelalters*, ed. F. Seibt and W. Eberhard (Stuttgart, 1984).

[11] This moral theological dilemma figures frequently in the sermons preached by Archbishop FitzRalph to the merchant communities in Drogheda and in his native Dundalk, cf. K. Walsh, *A Fourteenth-Century Scholar and Primate: Richard FitzRalph in Oxford, Avignon and Armagh* (Oxford, 1981), esp. pp. 322ff.; cf. T. N. Tentler, *Sin and Confession on the Eve of the Reformation* (Princeton, 1977), and the stimulating essay by A. Murray, 'Confession as a

At first glance the structural similarities and parallels between the Irish and Bohemian situations are striking: in both cases the existence of two *nationes* or ethnic-cultural-linguistic groups, whereby the Gaelic and Slav elements among the older inhabitants regarded themselves as oppressed and alienated by a foreign upper strata of society. This sense of injustice and exploitation sharpened the edge of other potential occasions of conflict, for example, differences between town and country, agrarian and commercial society, old nobility and new urban mores. Both countries had a native, landowning oligarchy, which could provide a focus for discontent. Incentives to assimilation were consequently limited—among the laity almost non-existent, while among the Irish clergy J. A. Watt has noted differing pressures to conform,[12] and a similar pattern also has relevance for Bohemia.[13] The secular diocesan clergy, and especially the episcopate, found an accommodation with the Crown both useful and desirable. This need not have been mere opportunism. Churchmen saw themselves as members of an international institution and as such members of a supra-regional privileged class. *Ipso facto* they were, or should have been, better equipped to deal more judiciously with the conflicts and tensions of the *nationes* at local level.[14] The extent to which they succeeded in doing so is a useful barometer, and shows whether the individual cleric or prelate succeeded in identifying first and foremost with his function as a churchman, or whether he placed greater stress on the regional and societal ties of kinship. In Gaelic Ireland the pressures not to neglect the latter were considerable.

---

historical source in the thirteenth century' in *The Writing of History in the Middle Ages. Essays presented to Richard William Southern*, ed. R. H. C. Davis, J. M. Wallace-Hadrill, *et al.* (Oxford, 1981), pp. 275–322.

[12] J. A. Watt, *The Church and the Two Nations in Medieval Ireland — Cambridge Studies in Medieval Life and Thought*, ser. 3, 3 (Cambridge, 1970), p. 174.

[13] A good general survey is that by F. Seibt, in *Handbuch der Geschichte der Böhmischen Länder*, ed. K. Bosl, 1 (Stuttgart, 1967), pp. 351–568. Cf. further F. Šmahel, 'The idea of the nation in Hussite Bohemia. Study on the ideological and political aspects of the national question in the Czech lands from the end of the 14th century to the 1470s', *Historica*, 16 (1968), pp. 143–247; 17 (1979), pp. 93–197. Cf. also the literature cited in K. Walsh, 'Wyclif's legacy in central Europe in the late fourteenth and early fifteenth centuries' *SCH.S*, 5 (1987), pp. 397–417, and S. Bylina, 'Krisen–Reformen–Entwicklungen. Kirche und Geistesleben im 14.–15. Jahrhundert in den neueren tschechischen und polnischen Forschungen' in *Europa 1400* (as n. 10 above), pp. 82–94.

[14] Cf. K. Simms, 'The archbishops of Armagh and the O'Neills 1347–1471', *Irish Historical Studies*, 19 (1974–75), pp. 38–55; *idem*, 'The concordat between Primate John Mey and Henry O'Neill (1455)', *Archivium Hibernicum*, 34 (1976–77), pp. 71–82. Watt's sample (as n. 7 above) also indicates a willingness to mediate in the interests of peace. *Idem*, 'John Colton, Justiciar of Ireland (1382) and Archbishop of Armagh (1383–1404)' in J. F. Lydon, ed., *England and Ireland in the Later Middle Ages* (Dublin, 1981), pp. 196–213.

When we turn to the regular clergy, not merely to the older Cistercian Order,[15] but also to the friars in Ireland, we find these to have been more divisive in terms of the two nations. They reflected more accurately the prevailing order. This was understandable, as their allegiances were also different—especially in the case of the friars, who were dependent on their immediate environment both as an audience and as a source of financial support: it was to be expected that they would identify politically and culturally with their 'clients' in each region, and that they would recruit from among the sons of those who supported them. This also proved to be the case among the Franciscans in mixed communities of Germans and Slavs.[16] Here the German element became dominant in the fifteenth century. But the ethnic-cultural clash was still relatively frequent and cut across the already bitter divisions between Observant reformers and Conventuals, with the result that the larger units of provinces and Observant vicariates became ungovernable, and the major centre of the Bohemian Observance within the Franciscan Order shifted to Silesia.[17]

Unlike Ireland, Bohemia enjoyed for a brief period of about half a century at least one unifying element. In the more rarified atmosphere of the University it was easier to overcome the difficulties caused by racial and ethnic strife within a religious order. It has been shown in the case of the University of Prague that the colleges of regular clergy, which functioned as *studia* for members of a particular monastic or mendicant order (and which in several cases had antedated the foundation of the University) were less conducive to strife between the *nationes* than was the case, for example, of the militant Bohemian-Moravian colleges founded

---

[15] The strife between the two nations within the Cistercian Order has been carefully studied by B. W. O'Dwyer, *The Conspiracy of Mellifont* (Dublin, 1970); 'The crisis in the Cistercian monasteries in Ireland in the early thirteenth century', *ACi*, 31 (1975), pp. 267–304; 32 (1976), pp. 3–112.

[16] Cf. K. Kantak, 'Die Ostmission der polnischen Observanten und die lithauische Observantenprovinz (1453–1570)', *FS*, 14 (1927), pp. 135–68; *idem*, 'Les données historiques sur les bienheureux Bernardins (Observants) polonais du XVe siècle', *AFH*, 22 (1929), pp. 433–61; J. Kłoczowski, 'Les ordres mendiants en Pologne à la fin du moyen âge', *Acta Poloniae Historica*, 15 (1967), pp. 5–38; K. Minarik, 'Die Provinzvikare der österreichisch-böhmisch-polnischen Observantenprovinz von 1451 bis 1567', *FS*, 1 (1914), pp. 328–36; J. Hofer, *Johannes Kapistran. Ein Leben im Kampf um die Reform der Kirche*, 2 vols, 2nd edn (Heidelberg, 1964), esp. 2, pp. 255ff.

[17] Cf. L. Teichmann, 'Der deutsche Charakter der böhmischen Observantenprovinz im Mittelalter', *FS*, 34 (1952), pp. 61–87, whose interpretation of the German-Slav problem among the Silesian Franciscans differs significantly from that of F. Doelle, *Die Observanzbewegung in der sächsischen Franziskanerprovinz (Mittel-und Ostdeutschland) bis zum Generalkapitel von Parma 1529* (Münster, 1918).

by King Wenceslaus.[18] However, after the heavy concentration of opposition to John Wyclif among the (German) Dominicans in Prague became evident, this state of affairs could no longer prevail.[19] Allegiance or opposition to Wyclif's teaching became a hallmark of the division between the Bohemian and German *nationes*, and after the German secession realism (Wycliffite or otherwise) came to be regarded as something peculiarly characteristic of the *natio Bohemica*. By contrast, the reaction both to academic Wycliffitism and to popular Lollardy among both *nationes* in Ireland is one of deafening silence. Despite previous attempts to establish one, Ireland had no university[20] and therefore lacked an academic framework for scholastic debate. And for a variety of reasons which cannot be elaborated here, Lollardy had little appeal and found no missioners. In practice, therefore, the presence or absence of a (heretical) movement, which attempted to establish an alternative ecclesiastical and social order distinguishes the Irish case from the Bohemian. Similarly tensions between Poles and Teutonic Knights, or between Poles and Germans in Silesia[21]—which have specific relevance for the present discussion—showed on the whole more similarity with the Irish situation than with the Bohemian one. However, one important difference must be noted: in Poland, despite vehement opposition to Wycliffite teaching at the University of Cracow, and despite the reserve with which its masters

[18] Cf. J. Kadlec, 'Das Augustiner-Generalstudium bei Sankt Thomas zu Prag in der vorhussitischen Zeit', *Augustiniana*, 17 (1967), pp. 389–401; J. Hemmerle, 'Nikolaus von Laun' in *Lebensbilder zur Geschichte der böhmischen Länder 3, Karl IV und sein Kreis*, ed. F. Seibt (Munich and Vienna, 1978), pp. 175–197, with extensive bibliography; R. Schmidt, 'Begründung und Bestätigung der Universität Prag durch Karl IV und die kaiserliche Privilegierung von Generalstudien', *Kaiser Karl IV 1316–1378. Forschungen über Kaiser und Reich*, ed. H. Patze – *Blätter für Deutsche Landesgeschichte*, 114 (1978), pp. 695–719; on Wenceslaus see most recently J. Spěváček, *Václav IV, 1361–1419 k predpokladum husitské revoluce* (Wenceslaus IV 1361–1419 and the Beginnings of the Hussite Revolution), and on his collegiate foundation, R. R. Betts, 'The University of Prague: the first sixty years' in *Essays in Czech History* (London, 1969), pp. 13–28, esp. 22f.
[19] For detailed references cf. literature cited in Walsh, 'Wyclif's legacy' (as n. 13 above), esp. nn. 23–7.
[20] Cf. A. Gwynn, 'The medieval university of St. Patrick's, Dublin', *Studies*, 27 (1938), pp. 188–212, 437–54. On 13 July 1312 Clement V issued a bull permitting the establishment of a *studium generale*, and further steps to implement this decree were taken during the pontificate of John XXII, but to no avail. The bull of 1312 is located in ASV, *Reg. Vat*. 59, fol. 196v, and a faulty text is printed in W. H. Monck Mason, *History and Antiquities of the Collegiate and Cathedral Church of St. Patrick, near Dublin* (Dublin, 1820), appendix, pp. ix–x.
[21] In addition to the vast literature on the circumstances surrounding the battle of Grünwald/ Tannenberg (1410), cf. M. Burleigh, *Prussian Society and the German Order. An Aristocratic Corporation in Crisis c.1410–1466* (Cambridge, 1984); also numerous historical essays in the exhibition catalogue: *Polen im Zeitalter der Jagiellonen 1386–1572, Schallaburg 8. Mai–2 November 1986 – Katalog des Niederösterreichischen Landesmuseums*, Neue Folge, 171 (Vienna, 1986).

viewed developments in Prague, popular Hussitism found substantial pockets of support.[22]

A striking feature of the problem of nations in the medieval period is that they are regularly taken for granted, but rarely defined, and even less frequently the subject of theoretical discussion. Despite its obvious relevance for both university and conciliar organization in the Middle Ages, the topic did not merit an entry in 1962 in the widely-consulted *Lexikon für Theologie und Kirche*. Although the title of this paper is derived from a—probably provocative—interpretation of J. A. Watt in *The Church and the Two Nations in Medieval Ireland*,[23] he addressed himself to a slightly different question. He very properly pointed out that in medieval Ireland the distinction between the two nations was identified as one of language—the determining factor of their difference was their *lingue*—but he accepted the two groups as foreordained antitheses. Contemporary observers of the communities under discussion did likewise. Richard FitzRalph's convictions about the inevitability of racial strife in Ireland were widely publicized in a sermon preached before Clement VI in August 1349. According to his account, the Irish reputation for violence had travelled widely throughout Europe, and had reached the ears of, among others, the Cistercian scientist and cardinal, Johannes de Toledo, generally known as the Necromancer of Toledo.[24] The latter claimed to have been informed by the Devil that the Irish were the best-represented nation in Hell, and this was because of their irreconcilable hatred and violence. The context within which FitzRalph publicized this dramatic claim was his attempt to have the Jubilee indulgence of 1350 extended to his flock, by which he invariably meant those *inter Anglicos*, without the obligation of personal pilgrimage to Rome. He argued that these dared not go on pilgrimage for fear of jeopardizing the safety of family, lands, and livestock left behind. Either because he was personally convinced, or because it was expedient to do so, FitzRalph gave the impression that he

---

[22] M. Schlauch, 'A Polish vernacular eulogy of Wyclif', *JEH*, 8 (1957), pp. 53–73, esp. p. 56 concerning the Czechs in Cracow from 1418 onwards. Polish interest in the teachings of Wyclif and Hus derived less from criticism of a wealthy endowed church than did that of the Lollards. Hence Jan Długosz, even when writing on behalf of the anti-Hussite cardinal Zbigniew Oleśnicki, could use the example of Constantine with fewer reservations than might otherwise have been the case: cf. U. Borkowska in the present volume.

[23] As n. 12 above.

[24] Cf. H. Grauert, 'Meister Johann von Toledo', *SBAW.PPH* (1901), pp. 111–325; A. Paravicini Bagliani, 'Medicina e scienze della natura alla corte di Bonifacio VIII: uomini e libri', *Roma anno 1300. Atti della IV Settimana di Studi di Storia dell'Arte medievale dell'Università di Roma "La Sapienza"*, a cura di A. M. Romanini (Rome, 1983), pp. 773–89.

regarded the violence in Ireland as racially and culturally conditioned. The evidence does not always bear him out, but he was in distinguished company. Little more than half a century later, Jerome of Prague was saying much the same thing, when he elevated tension between Germans and Slavs to something like a law of nature.[25]

This self-conscious emphasis on ethnic, cultural, and linguistic differences, expressed in the division of the polity into *nationes*, had both negative and positive causes. On the one hand we cannot ignore the prevailing aversion to the stranger, the fear and suspicion of all that is different from the familiar and accepted. The cosmopolitanism of Pentecost (Acts 2.7–12) was an ideal that had little place in medieval popular thinking. This negative attitude was to be found in all regions and at all levels of society—from the eleventh-century inhabitants of Lower Austria, who executed the Gaelic pilgrim Coloman as a spy, because they could not understand the strange sounds he made,[26] to the Estates of Prussia in the middle of the fifteenth century, who bluntly told the Portuguese papal legate Bishop Louis Perez to go home and mind his own business. He should not meddle in the private quarrel between the Bishop of Ermland and the German Knights—at home in Portugal there were enough unbelievers, Jews, and religious deviants to occupy his attention.[27]

In the positive sense a concept of *natio*, with all its subsequent implications for ecclesiastical and social organization, was widespread from about the twelfth century, and John of Salisbury was familiar with it.[28] But it was not an innovation of Gaelic *v.* Anglo-Norman, of Germans

---

[25] Cf. Jerome's statement at his trial in Constance 1416, cited in Betts (as n. 18 above), pp. 26f. Betts saw the importance of Hussitism essentially in the fact that it was the first body of heretical thought to become identified with a successful experiment in national independence: 'National and heretical religious movements from the end of the fourteenth to the middle of the fifteenth century', in *Essays in Czech History*, esp. pp. 117f. But see also F. Graus, 'Die Bildung eines Nationalbewußtseins im mittelalterlichen Böhmen (Die vorhussitische Zeit)', *Historica*, 13 (1966), pp. 5–49.

[26] *LThK*[2] 3, cols 7–8.

[27] Cited in Burleigh (as n. 21 above), p. 163, and *idem*, 'Anticlericalism in fifteenth-century Prussia: the clerical contribution reconsidered', *The Church in Pre-Reformation Society. Essays in honour of F.R.H. Du Boulay*, ed. C. M. Barron and C. Harper-Bill (Woodbridge, Suffolk 1985), p. 45, from *Acten der Ständetage Preussens unter der Herrschaft des Deutschen Ordens*, ed. M. Toepen, 3 (Leipzig, 1882), no 85, p. 213. A papal protonotary, Perez (Pires), held successively the sees of Silves, Porto, Evora and died in 1480 as archbishop of Braga: cf. *Hierarchia Catholica medii aevi . . . per Conradum Eubel*, 2 (Monasterii, 1914), pp. 110, 149, 218, 227.

[28] J. McLoughlin, 'Nations and loyalties' in the present volume has drawn attention to this, though it would appear not to have attracted much attention in other recent research: cf. D. Luscombe's 'A bibliography 1953–82', in *The World of John of Salisbury — SCH.S*, 3 (1984), pp. 445–57.

against Slavs, or of Poles, Silesians and the German Knights in east central Europe. It was a concept born, not of conflict in the political or military sense, but partly of the organization of schools and universities, from which it was then grafted on to the voting practice of the councils of the Church. Whereas the composition of the *nationes* in the university of Paris—French, Picard, Norman, and the mixed bag grouped together as Alamanni, including English, Germans, Poles, Hungarians, Bohemians, and Scandinavians—reflected no contemporary political realities, the form of organization was to prove influential. As a sentiment rather than an institution the concept of *natio* was to be even more decisive. Here it was largely determined by those feelings of solidarity for one's fellow countrymen that a long sojourn at a university far from home frequently generated. This *natio* meant not just fellow countrymen in the sense of those who shared a common statehood or citizenship, but embraced the untranslatable term *Landsmannschaften*, or even the Gaelic word *muintir*, which includes family, clan, and neighbourhood.

The organization of universities and their students into nations appears to have presented few insurmountable problems for the small number of Gaelic-Irish ecclesiastics who found their way to a medieval university. They came mainly to Oxford, where they joined their fellow countrymen of the other Irish *natio*, the Anglo-Normans, and with the Scots and the men from north of the river Nene formed the northern nation.[29] Here we see how the concept of *natio* is already becoming blurred, or at least ambiguous in its application. A man who saw himself as a member of a *natio* or *lingua*, separate and different from that of the Anglo-Norman intruder in Gaelic Ireland, found himself sharing membership of the same nation with his Anglo-Norman fellow student within the more exclusive university context at Oxford. Even fewer Gaelic students got as far as Cambridge, and education at a Continental university, even in the fifteenth century, remained largely a privilege for members of religious orders, mainly friars. Within this wider framework, as members of a single order in a *studium generale* or *particulare*, the *nationes* issue lost much of its bite.[30]

[29] A. B. Emden, 'Northerners and Southerners in the organization of the University to 1509', *Oxford Studies Presented to Daniel Callus* = OHS, ns, 16, (1964), esp. pp. 4–5, drew attention to the implausibility of the older view, whereby the border was located at the river Trent—the men of Lincolnshire were reckoned as Northerners.

[30] There is no comprehensive study of the *studia* of the religious Orders in the later medieval universities, but the impression gained from a random sample of piecemeal evidence is that—unlike their secular counterparts—they did not seek the society of their fellow countrymen within the *natio*.

The situation in later fourteenth-century Prague was very different. Here the organization was composed of four nations on the Paris model, but with more crucial political implications. The Polish nation was composed of Poles and Silesians, but was largely depleted after the re-foundation of the University of Cracow on a more secure financial and intellectual basis under the patronage of King Władisław Jagiełło II in 1397.[31] The latter's development in the fifteenth century is also of relevance for any consideration of the dual problem of *natio* in university circles. On the one hand, *a priori* assumptions about irreconcilable differences between German and Slav elements there must be rejected. The level of academic co-operation was too high to permit the conclusion that Cracow was then an anti-German cradle of Polish intellectual nationalism.[32] On the other hand, Cracow's enthusiasm for the aspirations of the Council of Basel led to a distinguished series of reflections on the broader issue of the *nationes*.[33]

The second and third nations in Prague were the Bavarian and the Saxon, both of which included large numbers of Slavs, because the boundaries of the nations had been drawn under Charles IV on an *ad hoc* basis, which did not anticipate the future crisis. The fourth, the *natio Bohemica*, included a mixed gathering from Bohemia, Moravia, and the remaining crown lands, all regardless of their ethnic origins, and therefore including sons of the richest German families in Prague and in the towns of northern Bohemia. Such procedures were a clear indication that the architect of the Charles University did not think in 'national' terms. He thought in terms of geographical regional varieties, and divided the *nationes* accordingly, with scant respect for ethnic susceptibilities and a—presumably autobiographic[34]—assumption that these did not matter

[31] The standard work is still C. Morawski, *Histoire de l'Université de Cracovie: Moyen Âge et Renaissance*, 3 vols (Paris and Cracow, 1900–5). It appeared simultaneously in French and Polish. A brief survey by L. Hajdukiewicz, 'Bildungswesen und Wissenschaft in der Epoche der Jagiellonen', appeared in *Polen im Zeitalter der Jagiellonen* (as n. 21 above), pp. 77–85.

[32] Cf. K. Walsh, 'Ein Schlesier an der Universität Krakau im 15. Jahrhundert. Zu Biographie, wissenschaftlichen Interessen und Handschriftenbesitz des Laurentius von Ratibor', *Archiv für schlesische Kirchengeschichte*, 40 (1982), pp. 191–206.

[33] In addition to the work of Jan Długosz cited by U. Borkowska, a number of *determinationes* and *conclusiones* now extant in MSS in Cracow indicate that the questions of authority raised in Basel were enthusiastically discussed in the Polish university: cf. Morawski (as n. 31 above), 2, pp. 62ff.

[34] He united in his person—and consciously—the heritage of the Přemyslid dynasty with the French cultural assumptions of the House of Luxembourg: cf. *Vita Caroli quarti. Die Autobiographie Karls IV. Einführung, Übersetzung und Kommentar von E. Hillebrand* (Stuttgart 1979); *idem*, 'Die Autobiographie Karls IV. Entstehung und Funktion' in *Kaiser Karl IV* (as n. 18 above), pp. 39–72.

very much. In his Wenzel-Karl dual vision[35] of a Bohemia in which Slav and German elements would be reconciled and integrated, in which all three languages (German, Latin, and Czech) were legitimate media for cultural expression, the hardened lines which emerged after the Wycliffite condemnations in 1403 had no place.

Not surprisingly, in view of the nature of medieval university education, the organization of *nationes* developed its own self-perpetuating logic. Because of the university's dependence on legitimation through ecclesiastical approval, its function as training ground for the clergy and for the (quasi-clerical) élite of administrators, lawyers, chancery officials, and medical doctors, it could extend its area of application into the non-academic world.[36] In the everyday thinking of all those who had been exposed to the system at university, it became a convenient form of categorization of friend and foe for the late-medieval intelligentsia, and that still meant for the most part clerics. The system received further support from generations of university-trained Roman lawyers, who began to give legitimation to the idea of the sovereignty of the nation-state.[37]

A further indication that later medieval clerics in pursuit of higher education had adopted the notion of their own *natio* and had distanced themselves from the earlier ideal of an international community of scholars, such as had attracted the best minds of previous generations to Paris, is the changing personal composition of the four *nationes* in Prague at the turn of the fourteenth to fifteenth centuries. As soon as other alternatives became available nearer home, both the Polish and the German contingents in Prague diminished dramatically. Poles and Silesians went to Cracow[38]—even if some present-day historians from

[35] Cf. R. Schneider, 'Karolus, qui et Wenceslaus', *Festschrift für Helmut Beumann zum 65. Geburtstag.*, ed. K.-U. Jäschke and R. Wenskus (Sigmaringen, 1977), pp. 365–87.

[36] Cf. most recently the important publication: *Die Rolle der Juristen bei der Entstehung des modernen Staates*, ed. R. Schnur (Berlin, 1986); on the sense of corporate professional solidarity which emerged among the academic community, and especially among those who became administrators and learned advisors in lay and ecclesiastical principalities, cf. L. Boehm, 'Libertas Scholastica und Negotium Scholare: Entstehung und Sozialprestige des Akademischen Standes im Mittelalter', *Universität und Gelehrtenstand, 1400–1800*, ed. H. Rössler and G. Franz = *Deutsche Führungsschichten der Neuzeit*, 4 (Limburg an der Lahn, 1970), pp. 15–61.

[37] In addition to the extensive literature on the French jurists around King Philip the Fair, cf. O. Hageneder, 'Weltherrschaft im Mittelalter', *MIÖG*, 93 (1985), pp. 257–78, esp. 273; W. Stelzer, *Gelehrtes Recht in Österreich. Von den Anfängen bis zum frühen 14. Jahrhundert* = *MIÖG*, Ergänzunsband, 26 (Vienna, 1982).

[38] Cf. G. Bauch, 'Schlesien und die Universität Krakau im XV und XVI Jahrhundert', *Zeitschrift des Vereins für Geschichte und Alterthum Schlesiens*, 41 (1907), pp. 99–180.

Silesia are reluctant to accept that fifteenth-century Cracow attracted substantial numbers of students from Wrocław and Ratibor. The remaining Germans, on the other hand, divided according to their region of origin. Those from the Rhineland preferred to go to Cologne or Heidelberg.[39] The latter acquired additional prestige after 1400, when the election of Count Ruprecht of the Palatinate as King of the Romans—as anti-candidate to Wenceslaus IV—made Heidelberg briefly that which Prague had been during the first decades of that university's existence— the leading university at court.[40] By the same token, the Habsburg university foundation in Vienna acquired a similar function as the intellectual centre for the German-speaking lands of the south-east. Again here it is no coincidence that the student from Ingolstadt, the eighteen-year-old Kaspar Weinberg—who owes his place in history to the evidence he gave at the trial of Jerome of Prague in Vienna 1410[41]—made the predictable choice for a member of the Bavarian *natio*. After the Kuttna Hóra decrees and the German migration from Prague he continued his studies, not in Leipzig—which came to be dominated by the secessionists from the Saxon nation—but in Vienna.

Another feature of later medieval life, in which both the Church and the element of *nationes* predominated, can be crudely described as 'the path to Rome'. This was far from being a marginal matter. It concerned more than a clerical and/or aristocratic élite, which made a visit *ad limina apostolorum* either in fulfilment of ecclesiastical obligations or in search of office, or in the case of prosperous pilgrims, who came in search of spiritual benefits and a whif of adventure.[42] Especially after the Black Death and the increased travel for the Jubilee indulgence, Rome-consciousness impinged on an ever-widening segment of the population.

[39] G. Ritter, *Die Heidelberger Universität im Mittelalter (1386–1508). Ein Stück deutscher Geschichte* (Heidelberg, 1936, reprinted 1986), pp. 506–7, drew attention to this.

[40] Cf. P. Moraw, 'Heidelberg: Universität, Hof und Stadt im ausgehenden Mittelalter', *Studien zum städtischen Bildungswesen des späten Mittelalters und der frühen Neuzeit*, ed. B. Moeller, H. Patze, and K. Stackmann = *AAWG.PH* III, Folge 137 (Göttingen, 1983), pp. 524–52.

[41] Cf. L. Klicman, 'Processus iudiciarius contra Jeronimum de Praga habitus Viennae A. 1410–1412', *Historický Archiv*, 12 (Prague, 1898), p. 29; *idem*, 'Der Wiener Process gegen Hieronymus von Prag, 1410', *MIÖG*, 21 (1900), pp. 445–57; the student's criticism clearly centred on Jerome's teaching on universals, and in this context it is worth noting that the Polish eulogist cited in n. 22 above propounded the view that nobody should presume to lecture on universals without being familiar with Wyclif's writings—not those of Hus or Jerome of Prague!

[42] On the rapid increase in travel in the later Middle Ages and the various motives for it cf. *Unterwegssein im Spätmittelalter*, ed. P. Moraw = *Zeitschrift für historische Forschung*, Beiheft 1 (Berlin, 1984), with extensive bibliographies.

Even those who never got the opportunity to travel there in person knew of somebody who had been there or was eager to go. They heard sermons from bishops, friars, and members of the beneficed secular clergy who had been there, and who knew how to hold an audience's attention with *exempla* and stories—tales of travel to exotic places were firm favourites, and Rome was guaranteed to please most listeners. But the major point at issue here concerning the marked increase in later medieval travel is linked with the question: where did all these travellers live, once they arrived in Rome? Their stay was usually longer than that of the modern tourist. Either they had business at the papal court, which might take many months to complete, or they were pilgrims who—having undertaken the hardship and expense of the journey—were not content with a round trip of the major basilicas before setting out for home. The pilgrims' hostels and hospices, in which they lived, increased and multiplied at a remarkable rate in and after the Jubilee year, 1350, and they did so on a 'national' basis. These were not erected at official level, but on private initiative, and with private money. It was clearly regarded as desirable to have a centre in the *urbs aeterna*, to which pilgrims of a particular nationality or regional affiliation could resort for support, for lodging, and for the security that he was still among his own people, even when he was far from home, in a strange city, and surrounded by people whose language he did not understand.[43]

The famous hostel of the English nation, dedicated to St Thomas of Canterbury, needs little introduction.[44] Equally well known are those of the German 'national' element, which set up its quarters in the Roman church and college of Santa Maria dell'Anima, and of the French, who did likewise at San Luigi de'Francesi.[45] What is perhaps less familiar is the assiduity with which many smaller *nationes*—with or without the *de iure* character of an autonomous territorial state—tried to follow suit. The Poles, Bohemians, and Scots soon had foundations for their own fellow

[43] Cf. *Gastfreundschaft, Taverne und Gasthaus im Mittelalter*, ed. H. C. Peyer = *Schriften des Historischen Kollegs, Kolloquien*, 3 (Munich, 1983); L. Schmugge, 'Die Entstehung des organisierten Pilgerverkehrs', *QFIAB*, 64 (1984), pp. 1–83; C. W. Maas (†), *The German Community in Renaissance Rome, 1378–1523*, ed. P. Herde = *Römische Quartalschrift*, Suppl. 39 (Rome, 1981).

[44] Cf. 'The English Hospice in Rome', *The Venerabile*, sexcentenary issue, 21 (Rome, 1962); G. B. Parks, *The English Traveller to Italy*. I, *The Middle Ages* (Rome, 1954).

[45] On the early history of the Anima cf. J. Schmidlin, *Geschichte der deutschen Nationalkirche in Rom, Santa Maria dell'Anima* (Freiburg im Breisgau and Vienna, 1906); J. Lohninger, *S. Maria dell'Anima. Die deutsche Nationalkirche in Rom* (Rome, 1909); J. Lenzenweger, *Sancta Maria de Anima* (Vienna and Rome, 1959).

countrymen in Rome, situated—like their more famous English, French, and German counterparts—in the pilgrims' quarter between the Tiber, the (old) Palazzo Farnese and the Piazza Navona, the area around the Via Giulia and the Via del Pellegrino. Even the Irish tried to follow this example, with the assistance of the then rector of the German foundation at Santa Maria dell'Anima, Dietrich von Niem.[46] Perhaps there is some irony in the fact that the prime mover and financier of this project was one who should be located in the *natio* of the English in Ireland. John Swayne, a cleric from the Kildare diocese, with good connections within the Pale, slightly more turbulent ones with the first Lancastrian ruler, Henry IV, a record of active performance at the papal court and the Council of Constance, finished his career with twenty years as Archbishop of Armagh and *primas totius Hibernie* (1418–39).[47] Swayne had clearly learned from experience and personal observation that it was desirable to have a place of residence for poor Irish clerics and pilgrims, and the implication is obvious: these were not welcome in the English hospice. In none of the published lists of visitors to the Hospice of St Thomas do we find Gaelic, or even Anglo-Irish names. However, for reasons beyond Swayne's control, his plans failed to materialize, and the Irish in Rome had to find alternative accommodation. That they did so, and that they continued to come in substantial numbers, is confirmed by the evidence of the papal registers, and also by tantalizing scraps of isolated information, such as the entry in the *Annals of Ulster* for 1466, in which we learn of feuding between the men of Ulster and of Connacht on the streets of Rome.[48]

It is therefore scarcely an accident that the man who saw the need to provide for the Irish *natio* in Rome was a far-sighted realist, who knew the value of money. He also knew that the ownership of house-property and vineyards in a sought-after area of papal Rome was an even better alternative to money.[49] He had a wider, more cosmopolitan experience—

---

[46] The best monograph is still H. Heimpel, *Dietrich von Niem (c.1340–1418)*, (Münster, 1932).

[47] Cf. K. Walsh, 'The Roman career of John Swayne, Archbishop of Armagh 1418–1439: Plans for an Irish Hospice in Rome', *Seanchas Ardmhacha*, 11 (1983–84), pp. 1–21.

[48] Cited in K. Nicholls, *Gaelic and Gaelicised Ireland in the Middle Ages — The Gill History of Ireland*, 4 (Dublin and London, 1972), p. 100.

[49] His vineyards were located on the Gianicolo, close to those of the papal household, cf. Walsh (as n. 47 above), pp. 9–10; A. Esch, *Bonifaz IX und der Kirchenstaat — Bibliothek des Deutschen Historischen Instituts in Rom*, 29 (Tübingen 1969); *idem*, 'Das Papsttum unter der Herrschaft der Neapolitaner. Die führende Gruppe Neapolitaner Familien an der Kurie während des Schismas 1378–1415, *Festschrift für Hermann Heimpel zum 70. Geburtstag*, 3 vols (Göttingen, 1972), 2, pp. 713–800.

at the Curia under Boniface IX, Gregory XII, and the Pisan popes, and at the councils of Pisa and Constance, where he appears to have acted in defence of his former master, Baldassare Cossa, the deposed John XXIII— than was customary among Irish candidates for a bishopric. It is further-more notable that Swayne—by contrast with a single-minded and stubborn prelate such as Richard FitzRalph—was flexible, and successful in maintaining the equilibrium between the two nations within his archdiocese and ecclesiastical province. He recognized no border or linguistic-ethnic divide; like Primate Colton he employed the services of bi-lingual canons and notaries in Armagh;[50] and he made a point of venturing in person to his episcopal city 'inter Hibernicos'.[51]

J. A. Watt originally decided to conclude his study of the Irish *nationes* with the Statutes of Kilkenny (1366).[52] These are a revealing document concerning the relationship of these nations and concerning the elements which were regarded by English authority as crucial for the maintenance of the lines of demarcation. Hence they are a justifiable *cesura* in the perception of English thinking about the Gaelic *natio* and its limited function in the Anglo-Irish polity. However, it is to be welcomed that Watt subsequently pursued the inquiry into the fifteenth century, enabling him to draw on one of the most important sources for the ecclesiastical history of later medieval Ireland, and that especially in the context of the Church and the nations.[53] The message of the surviving registers for a period of some hundred and sixty years between 1361 and the Reformation crisis in the archdiocese of Armagh is a curious blend of hostility and co-operation.[54] It reflects something more than a *laissez-faire*, and shows that there were phases when the archbishops, who were invariably drawn from the ranks of the Anglo-Irish or English clergy, displayed genuine pastoral concern for the welfare of their flock *inter*

---

[50] Watt, 'John Colton' (as n. 14 above).
[51] A rather eccentrically organized, but informative, calender of the unpublished registers of Archbishop Swayne appeared as *The Register of John Swayne, Archbishop of Armagh and Primate of Ireland 1418–1439, with Some Entries of Earlier and Later Archbishops*, ed. D. A. Chart (Belfast, 1935). It contains numerous references to the Archbishop's dealings with his flock *inter Hibernicos*.
[52] Cf. also Watt, in *A New History of Ireland* (as n. 6 above), pp. 386ff. on the implications of the Statutes.
[53] *Idem*, 'Ecclesia inter Anglicos et inter Hibernicos', and 'The Church and the two nations', (as n. 7 above).
[54] For an important study of the later registers cf. A. Gwynn, *The Medieval Province of Armagh, 1470–1545* (Dundalk, 1946). The only register to have appeared so far in a satisfactory modern edition is *Registrum Johannis Mey. The Register of John Mey, Archbishop of Armagh 1443–1456*, ed. W. G. H. Quigley and E. F. D. Roberts (Belfast, 1972).

Hibernicos. They pursued with some consistency a policy that had been inaugurated under FitzRalph's immediate successor, Primate Milo Sweteman, in the 1360s.[55] These prelates may not have engaged in the sort of theoretical reflection about the nature of coexistence which distinguished a lecture given in 1960 by the then Austrian Foreign Minister, Bruno Kreisky, to the Polish Institute for International Affairs in Warsaw.[56] But they practised (and presumably preached) a form of coexistence. Like Kreisky, they would have argued that whereas coexistence is undeniably a lesser good than peace, it is infinitely preferable to war.

The registers suggest that a state of harmony and goodwill between the archbishops of Armagh and the citizens of their cathedral city, which lay in the lands *inter Hibernicos*, may have been the rule rather than the exception. Even allowing for the one-sided nature of the evidence, the numerous occasions on which the archbishops protected both the rural and urban population in areas 'inter Hibernicos' from marauding and pillaging forces of the Gaelic chiefs, especially O'Hanlon, O'Neill, and McGuiness, have their own significance. This population was clearly not all on the fringe of destitution, exploited and oppressed by an alien regime. One example may suffice: in December 1406 Archbishop Nicholas Fleming gave the citizens of Armagh the use of three-quarters of the vault under the cathedral, so that their valuables might be safe from Gaelic robbers. The remaining quarter of the vault was deemed sufficient for the plate and other valuables of his cathedral.[57] Fleming's regular intervention to protect his flock 'inter Hibernicos' against aggression from local Gaelic leaders documents a vital point: the high level of physical violence, robbery, and murder, against which Archbishop FitzRalph fulminated from the pulpit on numerous occasions, is not always—nor apparently even in the majority of cases—to be explained as warfare across the racial-cultural divide. Even if we allow for the added tension provoked by differences between an urban and a rural population, and accept that the former in Armagh town was already perceived as part of a different social milieu from that of the O'Neill and O'Hanlon, the

---

[55] Cf. 'A Calender of the Register of Archbishop Sweteman', ed. H. J. Lawlor, *PRIA*, 29 C (1911), pp. 213–310.

[56] B. Kreisky, *Voraussetzungen der Koexistenz*. Vortrag des österreichischen Bundesministers für Auswärtige Angelegenheiten im Polnischen Institut für Internationale Angelegenheiten in Warschau am 2. März 1960 (Freiburg im Breisgau, 1960).

[57] 'A Calendar of the Register of Archbishop Fleming', ed. H. J. Lawlor, *PRIA*, 30 C (1912), no 36, p. 109 (19 December 1406).

examples of rural feuding among the Gaelic Irish and of urban rivalries among the Anglo-Irish are remarkable only for their intensity. It is difficult to escape the conclusion that these clashes had little to do with the *nationes* issue, and that they were caused by mundane matters such as economic rivalry and acquisitiveness—land and livestock, or the profits of manufacture and trade.

On the other hand, regular contact requires a medium of communication. If the archbishops of Armagh or their agents engaged in such contact with the Gaelic population, what language did they use? It seems that the linguistic boundary between the two *nationes* was fluid and by no means insurmountable. No more so than in the case of Germans and Bohemians, or of Silesians and Poles—even outside the Latin-speaking world of the university classroom—did the language barrier present impossible problems. It was not a barrier to communication, pastoral instruction, and the exchange of ideas for those who sought such contact, and some inhabitants of border areas appear to have had a little knowledge of both languages. This certainly applied to the long line of Gaelic deans of Armagh, who acted as a kind of permanent representative of the archbishop in his cathedral city, and it presumably applied to some notaries and administrators also.[58] Perhaps the provisions of the Statutes of Kilkenny should be taken more seriously than is often fashionable to do: when a prohibition was issued against the use of the Gaelic language by members of the English *natio*,[59] then it was issued precisely because they *were* using it. Once we allow ourselves to accept this fact, it comes as less of a surprise to find—as the first Reformation Archbishop of Dublin, George Browne, did—that attempts in the reign of Edward VI to introduce the vernacular Bible and the *Book of Common Prayer* were doomed to failure outside of Dublin and its immediate precincts because of the lack of Gaelic versions.[60]

There are numerous examples in later medieval Ireland, in which neither the high level of violence and tension nor the cross-cultural

[58] Watt, 'John Colton' (as n. 14 above).
[59] A royal decree of 1360 to the sheriff of Kilkenny also noted the abandonment of the English language in favour of Irish, and drew attention to the practice of English families in Ireland of sending their children to be educated among the Gaelic Irish, so that they would learn the Irish language, cited in *A New History of Ireland* (as n. 6 above), p. 713.
[60] Cf. B. Bradshaw, 'George Browne, First Reformation Archbishop of Dublin, 1536–1554', *JEH*, 21 (1970), pp. 301–26; K. Walsh, 'Luther-Rezeption auf den Britischen Inseln: George Browne, englischer Augustiner-Eremit und Erzbischof von Dublin († 1556); *Martin Luther: Leistung und Erbe*, ed. H. Bartel (†), G. Brendler, H. Hübner, and A. Laube (Berlin/DDR, 1986), pp. 299–308.

co-operation can be explained in either religious or ethnic terms. Unlike Hussite Bohemia, there was no compelling incentive here for the official church to identify with one *natio* against the other, on the grounds that heresy, chiliasm, or other forms of radical social teaching presented a threat to the divinely established order. Hence we must be careful not to exploit the *nationes* argument as a convenient scapegoat. It may be possible to learn from the analysis of this particular border situation between two *nationes* in Ireland, and from the Church's attempts to deal with the problems it presented. It should be considered, therefore, not as an isolated phenomenon, but in conjunction with strife in other medieval border areas: Czechs and Germans in Bohemia; Poles and Germans in Silesia, and in the conflicts in and around the lands of the German Knights. These indicate the need to reconsider the extent to which historians have been willing to over-interpret the medieval meaning of *natio* and read national conflict on modern lines into disputes of a totally different character. Socio-economic and structuralist determinism, attempts to minimize the extent to which religious and ethnic considerations could rouse instincts and govern actions, are unacceptable. But it is equally undesirable to sanctify as a kind of autonomous historical law the inevitability of religious and national strife.

University of Salzburg

THE SENSE OF NATIONAL IDENTITY
AMONG THE MARIAN EXILES (1553–1558)

by DAVID M. LOADES

Dr Cox and others with him came to Frankfort out of England, who began to break that order that was agreed upon; first in answering aloud after the minister, contrary to the church's determination; and being admonished thereof by the Seniors of the congregation, he, with the rest that came with him made answer, That they would do as they had done in England; and that they would have the face of an English church. . . .[1]

THANKS to the *Brieff Discours*, a partisan account published for polemical purposes almost twenty years later, the 'Troubles' which began with this gesture form one of the best-known aspects of the Marian exile.[2] However, because of the context within which the compilers of that work were operating, it is usually seen simply as a liturgical conflict between the protagonists of the 1552 Prayer Book, and those of the Geneva rite, which had been printed in English as far back as 1550.[3] In fact, the issues which it raised were far wider, embracing the whole conduct of ecclesiastical affairs, and the nature of the English church. Replying to Calvin's strictures on 20 September 1555, David Whitehead wrote:

These, your friends, however, are altogether a disgrace to their country; for whatever has been bestowed from above upon our country in this respect, with exceeding arrogance, not to say impudence, they are treading under foot.[4]

Recent historians of the English Reformation, from Norskov Olsen to Richard Bauckham, have demonstrated that there was among English Protestants of the 1550s no concept of 'elect nationhood' in the sense

---

[1] *A Brieff Discours of the troubles begonne at Franckfort* (1575); reprinted and edited by Edward Arber (London, 1907) [hereafter *Discours*], p. 54.

[2] A. F. Scott Pearson, *Thomas Cartwright and Elizabethan Puritanism* (London, 1925), pp. 144–6; M. A. Simpson, *John Knox and the Troubles begun at Frankfurt* (West Linton, 1975). Patrick Collinson has identified the main editor of this work as Thomas Wood; 'The authorship of A brief discours of the troubles begonne at Franckfort' *JEH*, 9 (1958), pp. 188–208.

[3] *The forme of common praiers used in the churches of Geneva; made by J. Calvyne*, trans. W. Huycke (London, 1550).

[4] *Discours*, p. 88.

postulated by William Haller.[5] If that came at all, it did not come until the
1590s. There was, however, a strong awareness of 'special providence'—
that God had a particularly significant part for them to play in the
preparations for his second coming. The roots of that tradition went back
well before the Reformation, and probably originated in the similar
convictions displayed by the French during the Hundred Years War. Both
the kingdom of England and the kingly office enjoyed a special place in
Divine favour.

'Regnum Anglorum regnum Dei est'
As the Aungell to seynt Edward dede wytenesse

a Yorkist propagandist had written in 1460, as a part of his attempt to
demonstrate that the Lancastrian usurpation had been a particular affront
to the Deity.[6] The later tendency of English reformers to celebrate John
Wyclif as the 'morning star of the Reformation' and to praise the 'Godly
proceedings' of Henry VIII stemmed from the same root, and was
regarded with incomprehension by their Continental friends.

There was, consequently, something special about the way in which
the English church had been reformed, and particularly about the person
of King Edward VI—the young Josias who had been destined to restore
the worship of the true God to Israel, but who had been removed because
his people had shown themselves unworthy.[7] In so far as that special
ingredient had been the Royal Supremacy itself, it was, of course, no
longer available to the Godly after 1553, and all the churches of the
diaspora realized that they would have to find some other method, both of
governing themselves and of preserving their identity. There were,
however, other ingredients which could still be made use of. One of these
was the continuity of the clerical office and authority, traced back to the
pure days of the primitive Church; another was the Articles of Faith,
authorized by Parliament in 1553; and the third was the English liturgy,
similarly authorized in the previous year. It was to these distinctive

---

[5] W. Haller, *John Foxe's Book of Martyrs and the Elect Nation* (London, 1963); V. Norskov Olsen,
John Foxe and the Elizabethan Church (Berkeley, 1973); R. Bauckham *Tudor Apocalypse*
(Appleford, 1978).
[6] J. W. McKenna, 'How God became an Englishman' in *Tudor Rule and Revolution; Essays for G. R.
Elton from his American Friends*, ed. J. W. McKenna and D. J. Guth (Cambridge, 1982), pp. 25–
43; quoting T. Wright, ed., *A Collection of Political Poems and Songs*, RS, 14 (1861), 2, p. 130.
[7] 'Our king has been removed from us by reason of our sins, to the very great peril of our
church', J. Hooper to John à Lasco, 3 September 1553, *Original Letters Relative to the English
Reformation*, PS (1846), 1, p. 100.

ingredients of the *Ecclesia Anglicana* that Whitehead alluded in the letter already quoted when he wrote:

> You must know that we do not entertain any regard for our country which is not agreeable to God's holy word. Neither in the meanwhile are we so ungrateful to our country ... as rashly to despise the benefits which God has bestowed upon it.

The fact that the church in England was 'under the Cross' by 1555 added point and poignancy to this defence. If suffering was a mark of the true Church, then the persecuted remnant of the Edwardian hierarchy was more worthy of credence in adversity than it had been in power. If the doctrine and worship of the English church had been truly reformed in the latter days of King Edward, then whatever the failures of implementation, that worship and doctrine was worthy to be maintained in exile and adversity, and should be so maintained.

> Nor have we such a mean opinion of the judgements of our countrymen who resisted ungodliness even unto blood, as that by reason of the clamours of individuals, possessing no weight whatever, we should brand them with the foulest marks of papistical impiety....[8]

Such arguments did not impress Whitehead's opponents, and indeed they contain distinct echoes of Charles V's judgment against Luther, or the general Catholic position on the traditions of the Church. At the height of the struggle in Frankfurt, John Knox preached a sermon, declaring roundly that it was precisely because of the abuses contained in the Prayer Book that God had turned his back upon the English church and withdrawn his 'Godly Imp'.[9] Calvin, although using more cautious language, clearly believed that the Prayer Book party in Frankfurt was more concerned with the validity of the English reformed tradition than it was with the Word of God. Cox and Whitehead responded vigorously. What they were doing was perfectly consistent with the Word of God. The 'English ceremonies' were things indifferent, and some, such as kneeling to receive Communion and the use of the surplice, had been abandoned out of deference to the consciences of Calvin's friends '... which might at that time have been piously adopted'.[10] The remainder

---

[8] *Discours*, p. 88.
[9] On 19 March 1555: *Discours*, p. 55.
[10] *Discours*, p. 8.

were retained, not out of wilful obstinacy, but as a 'concession to the love of our country'. They were, they protested, not 'so entirely wedded to our country as not to be able to endure any customs differing from our own . . .', but since these customs did not contain the substance of their faith, but merely a part of its form, they felt entitled to retain them within the constraints imposed by the circumstances of their exile. The magistrates of Frankfurt had given them permission to use 'the rites of our native country' and had been fully satisfied with the Forty-Two Articles as a summary of their doctrine. To some extent these justifications were disingenuous. The Prayer Book party were the aggressors in the 'Troubles', disrupting the previous understanding which had been reached with the senate of the city, and overthrowing the Geneva Order and Discipline which had previously been in use. The senate accepted this *coup*, simply because it appeared to be a decision made by the congregation itself, and did not transgress the limits of what they were prepared to tolerate. The main concern of the magistrates was that the English should not make a nuisance of themselves.

This, it soon transpired, was a forlorn hope because the removal of the Genevan Discipline had left gaps and uncertainties in the structure of authority. The English tradition was that of an establishment, where no such uncertainties existed, and the role of the congregation itself was negligible. However, it was one thing to transpose a modified Prayer Book into the context of exile, and quite another to decide how to run a church which suddenly consisted of a number of isolated groups. There were bishops among the exiles, notably John Ponet, but episcopal oversight would not have been practicable, even if it could have been agreed upon, and was scarcely suggested. The remaining alternatives were either appointment by the civil authority of the place in which the church was situated, or election by the congregation. The latter was universally adopted, for obvious reasons. However, the fact of election did not in itself fully define the relationship between the congregation and its officers, and it was that issue which was tried out during the next round of the Frankfurt 'Troubles', which began early in 1557. The origin of this dispute lay in an attempt by Robert Horne, the pastor, and Richard Chambers, the deacon, to discipline one Thomas Ashley for critical remarks which he had made about their ministry.[11] Ashley understandably complained that Horne and Chambers were proposing to be judges in their own cause, and appealed to the congregation at large. Horne did

---

[11] *Ibid.*, pp. 99–100.

not deny that he was proposing to act in the manner alleged, and according to one of his opponents took the view

> ... that, by his judgement, there is no ordinary way to meddle against the Pastors and Seniors, except they call themselves to be hearers of their own cause, and their own judges themselves. For other 'ordinary way' ... neither he nor any other shall be able to show.[12]

In other words, the fact of election did not make the pastor, or any other officer, answerable to the congregation for the discharge of his duties. Also, since there was no provision for re-election or review, such officers held what was effectively a freehold of their posts until they should choose to lay them down. The majority of the congregation held this position to be intolerable, but tacitly admitted that Horne was right in his interpretation of the existing constitution.

They therefore set out to draw up a 'New Discipline' which should remedy that situation, providing for two ministers in place of the original pastor, and for the annual re-election of officers. Horne and his friends objected to the first, on the grounds that it was contrary to custom and would breed confusion, but raised only a minor quibble about the second, presumably because the ministers (whose authority was really in question) were to be exempted. The main battle was joined over article 44 of the new Order, which ran:

> Item, that the Ministers and Seniors, thus elected, have now authority as the principal members of the Congregation, to govern the said Congregation according to God's word and the Discipline of the church as is aforesaid: and also to call together and assemble the said Congregation for causes, and at times, as shall to them seem expedient.
>
> Provided always, That if any dissension shall happen between the Ministers and the Seniors, or the more part of them, and the Body of the Congregation, or the more part of them, and that the said Ministers and Seniors, in such controversy, being desired thereto, will not assemble the Congregation: that then the Congregation may, of itself, come together and consult and determine as concerning the said controversy or controversies: and the said Assembly to be a lawful Congregation. . . .[13]

[12] *Ibid.*, p. 115.
[13] *Ibid.*, pp. 187–8.

To this Horne objected that it 'wiped away' the authority of the ministers and seniors, making them answerable to any temporary majority which might happen to arise, and was contrary to the terms upon which the church held its franchise from the city,

> That if there arise any dissentions or contentions among the Strangers, concerning religion or their discipline, they be set at one with all diligence by the Ministers and Seniors. . . . And in case the matter cannot be appeased before the Ministers and Elders; let them know that the Senate of this City will take order therein. . . .[14]

To which the supporters of the New Discipline responded:

> Except the matter be used as we have provided . . . both the authority and liberty of the Congregation is wiped away, and a mere tyranny established.

Although Horne admitted that there was no sensible alternative to the election of a minister in the circumstances of exile, in every other respect he was prepared to regard the senate of the city as a Godly Magistracy, with authority over the worship and doctrine of the church analogous to that of the Supreme Head to which they were accustomed.

The city fathers were not anxious to become involved, but they were anxious to see peace restored, and by intervening twice for that purpose embraced, unwittingly perhaps, the role which Horne wished to assign to them. However, they had many other more important matters to attend to, and in spite of the failure of the arbitration which they set up in April 1557 were prepared to let the matter rest once it was clear that the majority view was going to prevail. They had no interest in defending Horne, either to establish the principle of their own authority or to safeguard a concept of the ministerial function more appropriate to an established incumbency than to a church in exile. Although the controversy rumbled on after Horne and Chambers had left Frankfurt, for all practical purposes the autonomy of the English congregation, and its ultimate authority over its own pastors, was accepted by all parties.

Whether similar controversies were fought out elsewhere is not clear. The congregation which was originally established at Wesel seems to have been rejected by the authorities there for refusing to subscribe to the Augsburg Confession, but settled finally at Aarau, where it apparently

[14] *Ibid.*, p. 188.

used the Genevan Order both of worship and discipline without inter-ference. The other two congregations established early in the exile, at Zurich and Strasbourg, used a modified version of the 1552 Order, as is clear from correspondence between them and Frankfurt in October and November 1554. The original group in the latter city, led by William Whittingham and well pleased with their reception, had taken the ill-advised step in August 1554 of writing to the other congregations inviting their adherence. Zurich and Strasburg—the 'Learned men', as Whitting-ham somewhat disparagingly referred to them—responded cautiously, insisting upon adherence to the Prayer Book as a condition of any possible move.[15] When it became clear that Frankfurt had adopted the Genevan Order, the others not only backed off, but probably began to plot that incursion into Frankfurt which resulted in the establishment of the English Order in 1555, as we have seen. Neither in Zurich nor in Strasburg did disputes arise which threatened to involve the civil magistrates in the affairs of the congregations, and if there were quarrels over the nature of the ministerial authority, they have escaped the record. Strasburg did refuse burgher rights to some Englishmen who were suspected of purely political conspiracy, just as the magistrates of Frankfurt expelled John Knox for his intemperate attacks upon Philip and the Emperor Charles V. The attitude of all the 'cities of refuge' seems to have been substantially the same. They were all within the Reformed (as opposed to the Evangelical) tradition; they were perfectly satisfied with the doctrine professed by their English visitors, whether explicitly through the Forty-two Articles or not; and they were happy to leave them to run their own affairs, provided that they behaved themselves.

Nevertheless, considering that Zurich and Geneva had been in full communion since 1549, the differences between Bullinger and Calvin over the English Order were significant. Calvin objected to it in the strongest terms, supported its opponents wherever they appeared, and welcomed them to Geneva with enthusiasm. There could have been no Prayer Book congregation in Geneva, whatever its professed doctrine, while Calvin's influence prevailed with the Council. Bullinger, on the other hand, while denying that he would wish to use it himself, was perfectly happy for his guests to insist upon it in their own congregation, as something appertaining to their own tradition, the faults of which were matters indifferent. This was entirely consistent with the advice which he gave during the two Vestiarian controversies in England, in 1551 and

---

[15] *Ibid.*, pp. 31–7.

1563,[16] and indicates that his view of the discretion allowed to the Godly Magistrate was a good deal wider than Calvin's—perhaps reflecting the different circumstances in Zurich and Geneva. Calvin's only concession to national tradition in his dealings with the English was in the use of the vernacular, and that was not a concession, because it was a principle which he held as strongly as they did. Consequently, wherever the Genevan rite and discipline were adopted by the exiles—at Aarau, Basle, and Geneva itself—the only thing which distinguished the English congregations from their French or Swiss neighbours was the use of the English language. This complete, if temporary, absorption into the Continental Reformed tradition made a profound and lasting impression upon those who experienced it, detaching them not only from the liturgical tradition established by Cranmer and Ridley, but also from that broad interpretation of the role of the Godly Magistrate which had been necessary in England before 1553, and was going to be equally necessary after 1558. That this detachment was not carried out without some qualms, even on the part of its most earnest advocates, is indicated by Whittingham's claim in the early stages of the Frankfurt dispute that Cranmer had been about to produce a further revised Order 'a hundred times more perfect' than that of 1552, had he not been prevented by the King's death.[17] As far as I am aware, no evidence of any such intention has ever come to light.

To what extent either side was motivated during the exile by intentions, or even plans, of returning to England is uncertain. Although the restoration of the Gospel to England was a consummation devoutly to be wished, in practical terms it was only likely to come about through the death of Mary and her replacement with the more amenable Elizabeth. Given their distaste for the Prayer Book (which still represented Protestantism to most of the persecuted brethren who had remained behind) and their extremely limited view of the role of the Godly Magistrate, it is not surprising that the Genevans regarded the prospect with mixed feelings. Less than a month after the new Queen's accession, Christopher Goodman and his congregation in Geneva wrote to Frankfurt, rejoicing in the advent of the 'virtuous and gracious Queen Elizabeth' and proposing a common front among the returning exiles,

> that we may together reach and practice the true knowledge of God's Word; which we have learned in this our banishment, and by God's

[16] For a full discussion of this advice, see J. H. Primus, *The Vestments Controversy* (Kampen, 1960), *passim*.
[17] *Discours*, p. 75.

merciful Providence seen in the best Reformed churches, that (considering our negligence in time past; and God's punishment of the same) we may with zeal and diligence, endeavour to recompense it. . . .[18]

Significantly, by the time this letter was received, most of the Prayer Book congregation in Frankfurt had already left for England, and those who remained were under no illusions about the drift of their correspondents' intentions.

> For ceremonies to contend [they replied], (where it shall lie neither in your hands nor ours to appoint what they shall be; but in such mens wisdoms as shall be appointed to the devising of the same, and which shall be received by common consent of the parliament), it shall be to small purpose. But we trust that both true Religion shall be restored; and that we shall not be burdened with unprofitable Ceremonies. And therefore, as we purpose to submit ourselves to such Orders as shall be established by Authority, being not of themselves wicked; so we would wish you willingly to do the same.[19]

Although personal relations between many of the Prayer Book exiles and their co-religionists in Geneva and Aarau remained good, so that Horne and Chambers were able to pay an amicable call on Calvin during the summer of 1558, their visions of the English church remained a long way apart.

It is now generally recognized that Miss Christina Garrett overstated the case when she argued (almost fifty years ago) that the whole Marian exile was a calculated 'withdrawal and return'. Few Englishmen imitated Edmund Grindal in making a serious attempt to learn the German language, but their hopes for the restoration of true religion in England were vague and apocalyptic, at least until the onset of Mary's last illness. That the servants of Antichrist would be punished, none doubted. But with the End of the World so imminent, it was uncertain whether such punishment would antedate the Second Coming, or be part of it. Not surprisingly, it was Prayer Book men, such as Becon and Bale, who inclined to take the view that the Gospel would be restored in England before the End.

[18] *Ibid.*, p. 225.
[19] *Ibid.*, pp. 225–6.

'If we return unto the Lord our God', the former wrote, 'let us not doubt but that he will shortly turn unto us, mercifully behold us, and once again bless us with the benefit of his blessed word. . . .'[20]

'We shall find mercie in time convenient', Bale had declared at the very outset of Mary's reign, and the popular scriptural parallel of the exile in Babylon pointed hopefully in the same direction. However, to draw comfort from that, it was necessary to accept England as a manifestation of Israel, which brings us back to the concept of the special providence. In the last analysis, the difference between the Prayer Book exiles and their opponents can be reduced to the strength or weakness of their sense of such providence. To those whose model of the Reformation was the Consistory of Geneva, the church in England had never been anything other than a second-best approximation—true Reformation 'seen through a glass darkly'. To those who desired 'the face of an English church' in their exile, on the other hand, the Edwardian church liturgy, Godly Prince and all, had been an authentic expression of the Will of God. They did not defend it as perfect, but they did accept that the Royal Supremacy represented the divine purpose, and, like Bullinger, were prepared to allow a fairly generous latitude in their definition of Godliness. To a young queen who was keenly aware of the importance of being English, the availability of skilled and experienced clergy with such convenient principles must have carried a lot of weight in making the critical decision of 1559.

University College of North Wales,
Bangor

---

[20] Thomas Becon, *Works*, ed. J. Ayre, *PS*, (1843–4), 3, p. 220.

'I WAS A STRANGER, AND YE TOOK ME IN': POLISH RELIGIOUS REFUGEES IN ENGLAND AND ENGLISH REFUGEES IN POLAND IN THE SIXTEENTH CENTURY

by CLAIRE CROSS

ROM the moment of Luther's defiance of both Pope and Emperor at the Diet of Worms the sixteenth century became a period *par excellence* of *cuius regio*, *eius religio*, and of nowhere was this more true than for the very different societies of England and Poland. In England, for that time a highly centralized country, the nation's religious fate oscillated wildly with the change of monarchs and their respective governments, mildly reformist under Henry VIII so long as Thomas Cromwell held power, indisputedly Protestant during the rule of the boy king, Edward VI, as indisputedly Roman Catholic in the equally short reign of Mary I, and then Protestant, as it turned out permanently, on the accession of Elizabeth. In Poland, where, because of its proximity to Wittenberg, Luther's teachings began taking root at least within the German communities considerably earlier than in England, the spread first of Lutheranism and then Calvinism depended far more on the attitude of the nobility than of the monarch, though the succession of the more tolerant Sigismund Augustus in 1548 certainly accelerated the process. Apart from the five years between 1547 and 1553 in England, in neither country was life easy for converts to the Swiss version of Protestantism before 1560, and at different times both Polish and English Protestants suffered quite severe episodes of persecution: this essay traces the fortunes of the Poles who found a refuge in England and of the English who sought a temporary haven in Poland on account of their religion in the mid-sixteenth century.

By far the best known of this very select band of religious refugees is the Pole, John Laski, normally Anglicized as John à Lasco, whose influence upon the emergent Protestant church in England was thought sufficient to warrant his appearance in the British *Dictionary of National Biography*. Born at the very end of the fifteenth century, in 1499, the second son of a Polish nobleman, à Lasco owed his advancement to his uncle, the Archbishop of Gniezno and Primate of Poland, who brought him up first in his humanist household in Cracow, and later sent him to Italy for four years to study at Bologna. Following this he allowed him a further five years to travel in Europe, one of which à Lasco spent as a boarder in Erasmus's house in Basle. Recalled to Gneizno in 1525 and subsequently promoted to the deanery of Warsaw he remained in Poland, though vehemently suspected of favouring heresy, until 1538, when pressure to conform forced him to leave for Germany. For a time he studied in Louvain, where he made his commitment to Protestantism clear by marrying a burgher's daughter, and then for a time moved on to Ghent, before fleeing on the arrival of the Emperor to Emden in East Friesland, where in 1543 he accepted the superintendency of the local Protestant church. By this date he had abandoned Luther's doctrines for the more radical theology of the Swiss reformers, whom he had first encountered a decade earlier during his stay in Basle, and embarked upon a correspondence which continued for the rest of his life with Zwingli's successor at Zurich, Heinrich Bullinger. At Emden his congregation included at least one Englishman, the noted botanist and radical Protestant, Dr William Turner.

In January 1547 the death of Henry VIII brought about a major transformation of the English religious scene, permitting the Archbishop of Canterbury, Cranmer, to progress much further in a Protestant direction than he had dared to go so long as the old King lived. In his campaign to reform the English church he looked particularly to Continental Protestant leaders for advice, inviting a whole host of eminent theologians to visit England. Because of the Interim and its consequent harassment of those who adhered to the Swiss tradition, many responded to Cranmer's appeal and came to England to take up important positions, especially in the two universities. Among these Continental reformers was à Lasco. He first ventured to England in 1548, and actually stayed in Cranmer's own household at Lambeth. Back in Germany in the following year he found Emden closed to him because of its proximity to the Empire, and so entered the service of the Protestant duke of Prussia. In 1550 the duke sent à Lasco back to England as his diplomatic agent. In May he became naturalized, settled in London with his wife and four children, and, most important of all, was chosen superintendent of the Strangers' church. Since the Privy Council had granted this church complete autonomy, which placed it outside the jurisdiction of the bishop of London, à Lasco had virtually total freedom to make the re-named Jesus Temple, with its elders and deacons and full church discipline, into a replica of the churches in Zurich and Geneva, a pattern which he hoped might be emulated by the English church as a whole. From this base in London he went on to intervene in crucial developments in the English church, stiffening his friend Hooper's arm in the Vestiarian Controversy of 1551, advising Cranmer in his revision of the Prayer Book, sitting on the commission for the reform of the canon law. As with the so-called 'black rubric' which Knox persuaded the Privy Council to insert in the new Prayer Book to explain the reason for kneeling at Communion, à Lasco invariably supported the radical Protestant side. On the death, therefore, of Edward VI in July 1553 and the accession of the Catholic Mary Tudor, there could be no question of his remaining in England. He took sail for Denmark in the early autumn of 1553 with a hundred and seventy-five other religious exiles, and after wandering round north Germany went back for a year to Emden. Then at last the time seemed propitious for his return to his native land. In December 1556 he arrived in Cracow, and from there early in 1557 visited Sigismund Augustus at Vilna, where he was conducting a military campaign against the Livonians. The King received him favourably and allowed him to take up the superintendency of the Calvinist churches in Little Poland, where he remained both preaching and organizing until his death in January 1560.[1]

At exactly the same time in 1538 as à Lasco had felt compelled to leave Poland on account of his religion and seek refuge in the West, certain forward English Protestants to avoid having to conform during a period of religious reaction began to move east. They in particular made for Strasbourg and Zurich, and in addition to mature men of the calibre of the former monk, John Hooper, this little group included a number of young students among whom was a certain John Burcher. Almost nothing is known of Burcher's career in England before 1538, apart from the fact that he had already acquired a good classical education, though he subsequently claimed in a letter to Cromwell that the persecuting English bishops had forced him to abandon 'excellent prospects' in his native land. After his flight to the Continent he stayed for a time in Strasburg before going on in 1541 to Basle, where he lodged with Myconius, and during his period there visited Zurich and became acquainted with Bullinger. After a further period in Strasbourg he made his home in Zurich, in 1543, and married a Swiss, obtaining citizenship rights which helped in his mercantile ventures when he began trading, first in the export of bow staves to England and later in the import of cloth.

In 1553 another English Protestant merchant, Richard Hilles, entered into partnership with Burcher who then moved back to Strasbourg. There

---

[1] *DNB*, 32, pp. 159–61; C. H. Smyth, *Cranmer and the Reformation under Edward VI* (Cambridge, 1926), pp. 180–226.

he played a vital part in forwarding news and personnel between Zurich and the England of Edward VI, acting throughout as the chief intermediary of Bullinger and the other Zurich clergy. Although he followed the advance of Protestantism in Edwardian England with the greatest avidity, and did all he could to further the Zurich interest, Burcher had to content himself with watching from afar, and only paid occasional fleeting visits to his homeland. Then on the sudden death of the young King his world fell apart. Now, in the autumn of 1553, instead of promoting the movement of Swiss and other Protestant reformers to England, he took upon himself the melancholy task of succouring English religious refugees flocking to the Continent.[2]

In total Christina Garrett has calculated that almost eight hundred English people went into exile for their religion in the reign of Mary Tudor, the majority being university teachers and students. The exiles also included a redoubtable aristocratic lady, the Dowager Duchess of Suffolk, who seems first to have become acquainted with Protestantism at the court of Henry VIII. An intimate of the circle of Katherine Parr, the King's sixth and last wife, in Edward's reign she had been able to indulge her religious inclinations to the full: when her two sons went up to the university, she accompanied them and even attended Bucer's lectures in Cambridge, befriending the great reformer in his last illness. After Mary's accession, disregarding her own safety, she set about relieving Latimer and other imprisoned Protestant churchmen until forced to flee for her life to the Continent in February 1555. After many tribulations she, her second husband, Richard Bertie, and two small children eventually found a temporary sanctuary at Weinheim, in the Rhenish Palatine, where they received an invitation to come to Poland from Sigismund Augustus, who had been told of their plight by à Lasco. Understandably hesitant to venture so far east without further assurances, the Duchess sent her chaplain, William Barlow, to prospect the ground, and at some stage in this exploratory mission Barlow joined forces with John Burcher.[3]

John Burcher reached Cracow in late October 1557, his ostensible purpose being to introduce western methods of brewing into Poland, though a subsidiary intention must have been to open lines of communication between Bullinger and à Lasco, as his ensuing correspondence makes clear. From Cracow, Burcher immediately went north-east to the

[2] Smyth, pp. 89–93; H. Robinson, ed., *Original Letters Relative to the English Reformation*, PS (1846) [hereafter *O.L.*], 1, pp. 246–9; 2, pp. 637–8.
[3] C. Garrett, *The Marian Exiles* (Cambridge, 1938), pp. 32, 80; *DNB*, 4, pp. 403, 407–8.

town of Pinczów, which à Lasco had made his base, and at once reported back to Bullinger on the state of the Protestant church in Poland.

> The truth here in Poland, by the blessing of the great and good God, is deeply taking root. Master à Lasco is boldly instructing the nobles. He has today discoursed for two hours at a nobleman's table upon the true and genuine interpretation of the words of Christ, 'This is my body'. He has converted many, and maintains the real, and not the Lutheran interpretation. We must pray the Lord to give him strength. He has just been with the prince of Cracow, who is seventy years old, whom he has brought truly to acknowledge that the pope is antichrist. Nor does any thing make him hesitate, except the misapplication of church property, and the right understanding of the Lord's supper. They will easily be brought to agree that the property of the church shall be converted to pious uses; and Master à Lasco hopes that he will gradually come to the true understanding of the words of Christ. Commend them both to the Lord in your prayers; for if he can gain him over, there is great hope of the whole of lesser Poland.[4]

In a letter of 16 February 1558 Burcher enlarged further on the importance of patronage from the nobles in the dissemination of Protestantism:

> Master John à Lasco is actively labouring in the Lord's vineyard, and enforces no subject with greater earnestness than the pure doctrine of the Lord's supper. They hold their meetings, and sacred assemblies, but in the houses of the nobles. I have not seen any church purified, except only in Pinczów, where the word of God had its first beginning. For that brave nobleman of Pinczów, Nicolas Oleśnicki, a man certainly deserving of great praise, began the opposition to antichrist and the papists. The duke Palatine of Vilna has sermons in his house, and baptism, and the Lord's supper, and many of the citizens of Vilna assemble there. He alone, among the nobles of Poland, bears the heat and burden of the Lord's vineyard.[5]

Burcher had obtained his knowledge of the strength of Protestantism in Poland from a journey he and Barlow had made between November 1557 and February 1558 from Cracow to Vilna to visit Sigismund Augustus and the Polish court. The different races he encountered had particularly fascinated Burcher. 'I have many things to write respecting

---

[4] *O.L.*, 2, p. 688.
[5] *O.L.*, 2, p. 690; N. Davies, *God's Playground: A History of Poland*, 1 (Oxford, 1981), pp. 182–4.

the people of Poland and Lithuania, their manners and customs, which I defer till I return to you,' he told Bullinger:

> Thus much, however, I think right to add concerning their modes of religion. In Poland there are Jews, papists, and gospellers. In addition to these, there are in Lithuania Armenians, Tartars, Russians, Turks, and Muscovites. The Tartars acknowledge a God, creator of heaven and earth, but they worship moreover the sun, moon, and stars. The faith and religion of the Turks is well known to you. The Armenians, Russians, and Muscovites are of the Greek church and faith. They acknowledge as their head the patriarch of Constantinople, and are more happy than the papists in allowing communion in both kinds, and retaining the marriage of the clergy. They perform their sacred worship too only in the old Ruthenian language. They allow pictures, but not images, in their churches; but they place candles before them, and reverence and adore them just as the papists do. Their churches are divided into three parts, the upper, middle, and lower. The upper division they call, as the Jews do, the Holy of Holies, and no one enters therein save the priest and deacon. The unmarried part of the congregation occupy the middle division, and those who are married occupy the lower, not being allowed to enter into the middle division, till they shall have been introduced by the priest. They pray standing, and bowing down their heads to the very ground, as the monks do: they sign themselves with the sign of the cross, repeating these words, *Gospodi Pomilui*, which means, 'Lord, have mercy upon us'; and thereupon they sign and bow themselves. If any one laughs at their ceremonies, they immediately turn him out of the church, and sweep and clean the place where he stood. They bury their dead with great noise and howling; they array them in new clothes and shoes, and pour on their heads two cups of wine or beer. The corpse, moreover, receives a letter from the priests, and half a groschen from his friends; and is to present the letter and money to St. Peter, that the porter may immediately open for him the gates of heaven. They allow of no sermon, no teaching, and adhere to their ceremonies as tenaciously as the papists.[6]

The outcome of the deputation to the Polish King proved more fortunate for Barlow than for Burcher. Sigismund Augustus renewed his offer of hospitality to the Duchess of Suffolk and her household, and on their

[6] O.L., 2, pp. 690–1; Davies, pp. 172–7, 182–4.

arrival in Lithuania placed them in a castle at Kroze, in Samogitia, in the extreme north-east of the country, where they lived in something like the style to which they had been accustomed until news reached them late in 1558 of Elizabeth's accession, when they at once returned to further the restoration of Protestantism in England, Burcher, also, obtained his patent for brewing beer, but subsequently discovered it extended only to Lithuania and not to Poland where he wanted to exercise it. He, nevertheless, stayed on in Cracow for some time, describing with relish to Bullinger the hostile reception of the papal emissary in the autumn of 1558:

> The pope's legate was received here with kindness by his own friends, and with ridicule by ours. For as he made his entry, the trumpeter, the city watchman, sounded on his trumpet the melody, 'Uphold me herein by thy word': some of the nobles made a noise with horns, like the bellowing of herdsmen, along the way by which he entered; while others shouted in an extraordinary manner, whereby he might easily understand how acceptable his arrival was to the people of Poland. The bishop of Cracow had cited a preacher of the gospel to appear before his tribunal. He arrived here two days since, and, accompanied by a large attendance of nobles, came unexpectedly upon the bishop as he was sitting at his cups with the pope's legate, and demanded of him the reason of his citation. The bishop, astounded at the number of the nobles, replied, that he knew nothing at all about it. The nobles then, after having warned him against molesting in any manner or summoning any of their preachers for the future, went their way.[7]

By the end of 1558 Burcher realized that he stood little chance of making any substantial profit in Poland from his brewing patent and eventually decided to go back to Strasbourg, though before he left Cracow he urged Bullinger, at the request of à Lasco and his fellow minister, Utenhovious, 'to send an united letter to the king's majesty to admonish him touching both his kingly duty and his religion', and another letter to certain princes, such as

> the lord palatine of Vilna and the lord of Cracow, to persevere with diligence in what they have begun. . . . Do you act as it becometh Christians. For the time is certainly arrived in which the kingdom and truth of Christ can be advanced . . . The king is of an easy and tractable disposition, and may without difficulty be brought over to

[7] O.L., 2, p. 700.

our opinions . . . I beg, entreat and implore you by Christ, and by the salvation of your souls not to neglect this opportunity.[8]

Burcher had devoted too much of his time and energy to Polish affairs, and on his return to Strasbourg discovered he had lost both his family and his fortune. His wife's relations had taken advantage of his long absence to squander his capital, while his wife herself was living in adultery with another man. In 1561 he divorced her, turned her relations out, and married again before, in the summer of 1562, after almost a quarter of a century abroad, resolving to go back to England, 'very wretched and miserable'. Former exiles like the new bishops Jewel and Parkhurst, whom Burcher had helped in their extremity, now rallied to his aid, and the last notice of him is a happier one. Throughout his time on the Continent he had displayed as much, if not more, concern for theology as for his merchantile ventures. It is fitting, therefore, that John Abel could inform Bullinger in 1563 that 'John Burcher is now become a clergyman in the country not far from London, where he preaches the word of God faithfully, and is much beloved, and does much good. His wife has been delivered of a little girl, and is also well and hearty'. Exiles from their religion, each for a time a sojourner in each other's country, à Lasco and Burcher, like the Duchess of Suffolk and her household, were both able to live out their last days under a Protestant government (or at least a regime tolerant of Protestantism), at peace in their native land.[9]

University of York

[8] O.L., 2, pp. 701–2.
[9] Smyth, pp. 89–93; H. Robinson, ed., *Zurich Letters*, 1, PS (1842), pp. 90, 98, 105; *ibid.*, 2 (1845), pp. 108–9.

THE POLONIZATION OF CHRISTIANITY IN THE SIXTEENTH AND SEVENTEENTH CENTURIES

by JANUSZ TAZBIR

THE process of adapting universal religions to local cultures, conditions, and milieux is as old as the religions themselves. As far as Christinity is concerned, it was also subject to the continuous blending of general doctrinal principles with the national form of their expression, especially with age-old traditions in folklore. Consequently, Frankish or Germanic Christianity differed considerably from the Slavic version, while the latter again differed from that prevailing in the Eastern Roman Empire. Although in missionary areas the Church sometimes approved of investing the cult with specific features, taking into account the nationality and mentality of its congregations, in Europe itself conflicts between local church authorities on the one hand and Rome on the other often broke out over these matters. They found expression and were finally ossified in successive divisions of Christianity; beginning with the Great Schism of 1054, through the attempt to organize a national church in Bohemia (the Hussite Movement), to the permanent split brought about by the Reformation.

The Reformation put Rome on its mettle by forcing the papacy to approve values created outside the Church, often in spite of it. Its leaders, more or less willingly, decided to combine the mature—thanks to humanistic trends—national consciousness with the revitalized (through Counter-Reformation) religious content. It was all the easier as the greatly expanded Catholic ritual and dogma were better suited to combine with national culture and folklore than Protestantism: the latter restricted the number of feast days, and did away with patron saints and the furnishing of churches, which impressed the imagination. It was the Counter-Reformation that drew large numbers of folk artists to the job of decorating interiors with sculptures or statues, and to erect wayside shrines and sacred images. All these works reflect the vernacular, everyday reality.

Of particular interest is the Polonization of Catholicism through its 'Sarmatization' in the seventeenth century. The term denotes the adaptation of religious beliefs and ritual forms to the political ideas of the

117

gentry.[1] Attached as it was to the political system of the Commonwealth, it saw its reflection also in the immediate or remote past and in the other world. The free election of kings, rebellions against rulers who broke their obligations to the gentry—all this, it was argued, had existed already in the early Middle Ages. Moreover, the political structure of the Polish Commonwealth was supposed to have existed in the history of the Jewish nation, and priests in their sermons gave coats of arms to Old Testament figures (for example, Noah was given an ark). Preachers talked about the division of the Jewish state into twelve voivodships; Moses was called the hetman of the general levy; the Slaughter of the Innocents was supposed to have been perpetrated by the dragoons of King Herod, and the Annunciation was to be a sort of *pacta conventa*, concluded by the Creator with the people.[2]

Here we come to the Polonization of ideas about the other world. Thus there was talk about the election of patriarchs and prophets, of the martyrs' army of the quarter, infantry of holy virgins, a heavenly chamber of deputies, where sat 'common' saints, and a senate, where seats were reserved for the Apostles only. Canonization was compared with ennoblement gained by personal merit.

In the same specific way, adapted to the political doctrine of the gentry, the Conception of Our Lady was developed. In the seventeenth century her image underwent a clear evolution, from the patron saint of Poland to the Queen of Poland. She supports her subjects in their fight for the preservation of their faith and the inviolability of their national frontiers. From a celestial person she has become almost a terrestrial monarch, who—contrary to the women foreigners in the Warsaw Castle—sympathizes fully with the political and social ideas of the gentry's elected rulers. Mary's approval of the institution of 'golden freedom' was often contrasted by preachers with the support given by the Habsburg Archduchess, Louise Marie, or the Frenchwoman Marie Casimire, to the foul intentions to introduce absolute power. This was the meeting platform of the gentry of Catholic and other denominations, which also often turned for support to the Queen of Heaven.

The Calvinist and Lutheran gentry did not much oppose the idea that (together with the whole gentry class) they had in Heaven a ruler, a queen,

[1] They considered themselves to be the only descendants of the brave Sarmatians who, in the first centuries AD, having left their original habitations between the Don and the lower Volga, settled in the territories of the present Republic.
[2] Cf. J. Tazbir, *La République nobiliaire et le monde. Étude sur l'histoire de la culture polonaise à l'époque du baroque*, (Wrocław, 1986), pp. 124ff. (La polonisation du catholicisme).

and a protector. Perhaps this would not have been acceptable if Our Lady was supposed to be the ally of a strong royal authority, but she won full approval once it was established that she was the guardian of gentry freedom. Thanks to her presence in the political and metaphysical structure of the Commonwealth, she was the decisive factor in its ossification; she secured its system in the same way as did free election, the *liberum veto* or the right to deny allegiance to a monarch who had acted to the detriment of the 'golden freedom'.

Anyone who dared question such a system put himself beyond the pale of the gentry nation. One should remember that in the seventeenth century Poland considered itself threatened by nearly all its neighbours; at the same time, the Catholic states of western Europe were blamed for not hurrying with rapid and effective aid for the Poles. In this situation the awareness that up there in Heaven Our Lady of Victory was spreading her protective mantle was really invigorating. Her cult began to spread under the influence of conflicts with Turkey. Many Protestants, not only among the gentry, but also among the middle classes, must have shared that faith in her.[3]

The cult of native patron saints also formed a basis for a closer *rapprochement* on the grounds of national self-identification. Although the Polish reformers could not, of course, acknowledge the bishops St Adalbert and St Stanisław Szczepanowski, yet they had to rebuff the accusations of their opponents that they professed 'a new and different Gospel from the one which was taught by St Adalbert'. So they tried to make the two Bishops (who had lived in the tenth and eleventh centuries) ideological precursors of the Reformation. Krzysztof Krainski says in his Calvinistic *Postilla* (1611): 'In brief, in the times of St Stanisław there was not even one-tenth of the superstitions now believed in by papists'. Szymon Teofil Turnowski, a member of the Unity of Czech Brethren, wrote that 'the Christian services brought to our forefathers from Bohemia by St Adalbert, were closer to our evangelical or even Greek (Orthodox) ones than today's Roman'. For, apparently, at the beginnings of Christianity in Poland, the Holy Communion was given in both kinds, and services were celebrated in a language known and natural to all Poles—that is, not in Latin.[4]

---

[3] M. Wajsblum, *Ex registro arianismi. Szkice z dziejówe upadku protestantyzmu w Małopolsce* (Sketches from the History of the Fall of Protestantism in Little Poland) (Cracow, 1937–48), p. 278.

[4] J. Tazbir, 'Słowiańskie źródła reformacji w oświetleniu polemiki wyznaniowej' (Slav sources for the Reformation in the light of confessional polemics) in: *Z polskich studiów słowistycznych*, ser. 3, *History. Papers for the Fourth International Congress of Slavists in Prague, 1968* (Warsaw, 1968), pp. 104–5.

In their zeal to show the native roots of the Polish Reformation its
defenders went so far as to write that in the time of St Stanisław
indulgences were not known, nor were prayers for the dead or the cult of
saints. They did not believe in the transubstantiation of bread and wine
into the flesh and blood of the Lord, that is, in the corporeal presence of
Christ in the Eucharist. Consequently, the elements did not receive the
worship due exclusively to God; the monstrance was not carried during
processions as is now the practice. For this reason two charges were
continuously brought by Catholic polemists—that Protestantism was
something foreign, and that it was new to Poland. The terms 'new'
believer, used to denote its followers, and 'news' for their ideology, found
a permanent place in polemics against the Protestants. At the Sejm in
1648, the Chancellor, Jerzy Ossoliński, not a priest but a State dignitary,
presented this in a concise abbreviation, saying to the dissidents who
demanded religious freedom: 'Your religion is a newcomer which *recently*
[my emphasis] came to us from foreign countries, while the Catholic faith
was and is mistress in her own house'.[5]

In reply, people were reminded of the fact that among the so-called
'Witnesses of Truth', who at various times had opposed the teachings of
the 'Roman Antichrist', there were also Slavs. It was from their hands, that
is, those of Cyril and Method, that the Poles, as far back as the ninth
century, accepted the Slav ritual, that is a hundred years before the
baptism of Mieszko I and his subjects. Such a possibility was not denied
even by some Catholic writers. Bishop Paweł Piasecki wrote in his
chronicle that Poles had always been wary of things German and that is
why 'Polonia et Slavoniae tota' (the whole of Poland and the Slav
countries) preferred to be christianized directly by those two Apostles.[6]

Real differences began to arise when it came to the determination of
the ritual and dogmatic side of this 'Slav' Christianity. Thus the Catholics
professed that it had not differed in any essential way from the doctrinal
and liturgical forms of the contemporary Church. On the other hand, the
Calvinists argued that it was stripped of many 'idolatrous' elements,
incompatible with the teachings of the first Apostles. Many but not all; if
one adopted the thesis that corruption contaminated the Church as early
as the eighth or ninth century, it was impossible to maintain that at the
time of Cyril and Method even the Slav rites could have remained free
from certain imperfections.

[5] Wajsblum, p. 93.
[6] Tazbir, pp. 103–4.

An important figure among the Slav precursors of the sixteenth-century Reformation was, of course, Jan Hus. Martin Luther was considered to be the direct continuer of his teachings, which were supposed to prove that the Divine Truth had been preached 'in the Slav language earlier than in German'.[7] Hus's ideas reached Poland as early as the beginning of the fifteenth century: 'Reformation of the service polluted by papist superstitions' was supposed to have spread not only to the manors of the squires, but also to the University of Cracow and even to the royal court. 'And this light of the Gospel survived in our ancestors unquenched by various persecutions' until kindled again by the outburst of the Reformation in Germany, thanks to which the German Evangelicals followed the earlier Bohemian and Polish. Worth noting is the fact that the followers of the Reformation called their precursors Evangelicals not Hussites, which emphasized even more strongly the continuation of a certain tradition. Thus a certain line of development began, leading from Hus and Jerome of Prague, through the Czech Brethren to Lutheranism. So it may be said that according to Polish Protestants the Slav spark ignited the German fire. Andrzej Wegierski, author of an extensive outline of the development of the Reformation among the Slavs (1652), explained that the place of its birth was not an accident. For at the beginning of the movement there was the Unity of Czech Brethren, active in Slav territories which were later part of the Holy Roman Empire of the German Nation. It is easy, says Wegierski, to trace historically how the Slavs are mixed with the Germans in those lands. Evidence of this can be seen in certain place-names which have survived to this day (Rostok/Rostock, Lubeka/Lübeck, Lipsk/Leipzig/Szczecin), and in the fact that the inhabitants of some of the Empire's provinces still speak a Slav language.[8]

In this way, the charge of foreign origin against Polish Protestants was refuted. Of course, it was difficult to deny that their doctrine was based on foreign authorities. But as a rule the part played by great leaders of the Reformation was minimalized by emphasizing that the essential source of the faith of the Evangelicals lay in Holy Writ, not in the teachings of Luther, Zwingli, or Calvin. Even the Arians, particularly in the seventeenth century, liked to remind people that Fausto Sozzini did not play any important role in the birth of their doctrine, because it had been

---

[7] *Ibid.*, p. 107.
[8] A. Wegierski, *Systema historico-ichronologicum ecclesiarum Slavonicarum per provincias varias* (Utrecht, 1652), pp. 39–40.

shaped even before the emergence of Italian Antitrinitarianism in Poland. Generally, these arguments did not evoke much response; Cardinal Stanislaus Hosius, who dubbed sixteenth-century Arianism the 'Polish little faith', was an exception. Even the Calvinist opponents of the Antitrinitarians blamed the split in the Polish church on the Italians (one might remember here the famous cry uttered by Theodor Beza: 'fatalis Italia Poloniae videtur'). This, by the way, caused a new wave of Italophobia among Calvinists and Lutherans. They were joined by Catholics, who looked for the origins of the doctrine of the Antitrinitarians not in the teachings of Paulus Gregory, Peter of Goniadz, or Martin Czechowicz, but in the fact that the gentry supporters of the Reformation attracted to Poland the 'Servetuses, Gentiles and their disciplines, just as venomous' including Sozzini himself.[9]

Despite all this, the leader of the Polish Antitrinitarians did not become a symbol of the Italians as Luther became that of the Germans. Compared with the numbers of the latter who were settled in many towns and villages of the Commonwealth, the Italians were very few indeed. Although because of their great economic mobility and ruthlessness in business they were not much liked, especially among the Polish merchants, yet it was remembered that most of them had been very active in the defence of the Catholic Church, while most of the Germans sided with the Reformation. In their attacks on the papacy, the followers of the Reformation always underlined that its goal was not the salvation of men's souls, but the interests of the Italian clergy, who practised fiscal exploitation upon the entire Catholic Europe. Thus the confrontation between Rome and the Reformation acquired in Poland, as it did in Germany or France, a sharp national connotation and added fuel to the flames of Italophobia. The word 'Catholic' was replaced by 'Roman' (pope, bishop, priest, faith, and so on), naturally in the derogatory meaning of the term. In this way the foreign character of both the church institution itself and of its teachings was emphasized.

But the reason why—among the leaders of the Reformation known in Poland—only Martin Luther came to symbolize a German,[10] while John Calvin did not become the stereotype of the French (or the Swiss), John Knox of a Scot, or Sozzini of an Italian, lay much deeper. It is generally known that the settlement of German colonists in the Middle Ages on Polish land contributed seriously to the development of national ethnic

---

[9] Tazbir, pp. 102–3.
[10] Cf. *idem*, 'Luthers Bild im alten Polen' [in press].

consciousness (in the same way as the knowledge of other continents, spread in the fifteenth to seventeenth centuries, influenced the birth of European consciousness). In turn, the expansion of Lutheranism in the territories of the Commonwealth caused a consolidation of convictions about the Polish character, which identified with the Catholic Faith as opposed to the 'German' (Lutheran, 'heretical') and Ruthenian (Ruska or Orthodox). This was expressed in numerous proverbs (such as 'Any German is a heretic') and naturally in all the polemical discussions in connection with Reformation disputes. As early as the sixteenth century, the Catholic poet and polemist Wit Korczewski wrote in his mixed Latin: 'Nostri Poloni papizant et Germani lutherizant',[11] which in free translation means that Poles follow the pope while the Germans the reformer of Wittenberg.

Linking nationality with religion was not new in Poland and was not introduced by the Reformation. Even before its emergence Poland was a multi-confessional state, which reflected its multi-national character. The Ukrainian population was Orthodox, the Jews professed Judaism, the Tartars, who had settled in the Grand Duchy of Lithuania, Islam, the Armenians engaged in commerce—Monophysitism. In many Lithuanian villages paganism still survived, albeit in secret. This rule had only two exceptions: the Lithuanians and Germans who became Polonized in the Crown territories, but not in Royal Prussia. This would explain why Calvinism became strongly rooted in the Grand Duchy of Lithuania, which was keen on preserving its autonomy. On the other hand, Lutheranism became the religion of the minority of the German inhabitants of Royal Prussia, or the borderlands of Silesia and Great Poland. It was in this confession that they found the confirmation of their ethnic separateness, which until then they had not been able to find in a faith common with Poles or Lithuanians. Naturally, it did not mean that there were no Lutherans among the nobility, but their numbers diminished considerably in the seventeenth century, as a consequence of superimposing confessional divisions on class divisions.

Preachers liked to describe Catholicism as the religion of 'masters' as opposed to that of peasants, which Eastern Orthodoxy was supposed to be, or even the Greek-Catholic rite; while they called Lutheranism the 'confession of merchants'. Its founder became the symbol of the German neighbour with whom one brushed shoulders daily, in the town hall and on the street, in the market or at the inn. The image of Doctor Martin was

---

[11] *Ibid.*

beginning to be equated with a collective portrait of the Germans. It was composed of a liking for beer and banquets at which fatty foods were served, of broken Polish often ridiculed by satirists, and plebeian origins. The dislike of the economic rival, the nearest neighbour Hans or Heinrich, caused the stereotype of a Lutheran to be furnished with features which, when occurring in a German, were thought particularly funny, irritating, or even offensive.

Thus the fundamental information about Luther became part of a broad context of Polish-German relations. And not because of any show of continuous tension or sharp conflicts. On the contrary, the Polish Commonwealth, attacked as it was from three sides, could consider only its western frontiers relatively safe. But internally an antagonism developed in which the motives of economic rivalry were juxtaposed with class conflicts (dislike of the gentry on the part of the Royal Prussian middle class) as well as political (anxiety about the privileges guaranteeing the autonomy of that province). These two conflicts were strengthened by the adoption of Lutheranism.

The new faith stimulated totally contrasting phenomena. Through publications issued in Polish both in Ducal (Königsberg) and Royal Prussia, Lutheranism contributed to the development of Polish culture and language. But due to the connections with the universities of Leipzig and Wittenberg, by means of sermons and leaflets circulating in the language of Martin Luther, the confession slowed down the assimilation processes. It is impossible to accept the argument that the Reformation revived German characteristics moribund in Royal Prussia in the sixteenth century.[12] As a matter of fact, it was far from dying, all the more so as the Polish middle class in its fight for the right to use the Polish language in public life could count only on its own forces. Neither the local authority nor the royal court were greatly interested in the progress of civilization in the territories of Cracow or Poznań. And the monarchs were totally indifferent to these questions in respect of Gdańsk, Elblag, or Toruń. Although for a long time the local general diet in Royal Prussia demanded the exclusive use of the German language during its debates, this was more to emphasize the political autonomy of Royal Prussia than to manifest ethnic separateness. Although in the seventeenth century the Polish language gradually dominated in the debates over local gentry self-government, this happened without any pressure from Warsaw. Simply,

---

[12] A. Brückner, *Kultura, Piśmiennictwo, Folkor* (Culture, Writings, Folklore) (Warsaw, 1974), p. 334.

the gentry settled in Prussia gradually became Polonized to such a degree that they began to feel that the use of another language made it difficult to express their thoughts freely.

Despite everything, it should be noted that in Royal Prussia there existed between ethnic and religious identities a relationship which was *sui generis*. The German-speaking Gdańsk or Toruń burghers supported Lutheranism, which was culturally and territorially nearer to them; in turn, Lutheranism strengthened their feeling of national separateness. In the seventeenth century the Polish element in Protestant churches within the territory of the Commonwealth diminished. This was caused by the conversion to Catholicism of noble families as well as by the inflow of successive waves of political refugees. Especially during the Thirty Years War, Poland gained the honourable name of 'refugium Germaniae'— asylum for Germany. And not only for Germany since beside the many thousands of Lutherans it also accepted the succeeding wave of Czech Brethren, exiled from their country after 1628 (they had come for the first time to Great Poland in 1548).

These people formed an element which could not be Polonized, and if attempts were made to do so, we do not know anything about it. If Polish-German (or Polish-German-Latin) dictionaries predominated among the dictionaries published in the Commonwealth, this was due not only to the commercial contacts between Prussian towns and the gentry, but also to the appearance of various groups of newcomers who had not the vaguest knowledge of the Polish language.

Of some significance also was the formation of the notion of a 'gentry nation' as the sole representative of the whole ethnic community. This subjective category, which recognized that the nobles were the only successors of the brave Sarmatians, put not only the peasants, but also the burghers outside the pale of the nation. In the religious sphere 'Sarmatian Catholicism' was the counterpart of that notion. If in the seventeenth century the possession of the same class privileges meant for many Ukrainian and Lithuanian families the beginning of a path leading to Catholicism and Polishness, in the next century the situation gradually changed. For the conversion to Catholicism was fairly often preceded by an option for Polishness.

It is impossible to force the role played by a different confession (or even a different religion) in slowing down or stimulating the Polonization processes into the rigid framework of any scheme. Thus, orthodox allegiance to Islam did not prevent the assimilation of the majority of Lithuanian Tartars, who acquired the privileges of a para-gentry, while

Socinianism, which flourished in Volhynia in the first quarter of the seventeenth century, became one of the bridges crossed by the Ukrainian Orthodox gentry on its way to Polishness. At the close of the previous century the Babiński, Czaplic, Iwanicki, or Niemirycz families still spoke the Ukrainian language and went to the Orthodox church for Sunday service. By the mid-seventeenth century, they all belonged to a group of powerful and Polonized protectors of Arianism. The assimilation of the Volhynian nobles certainly paved the way for the progress of Socinianism, which in turn contributed to their further Polonization. So it is hard to differentiate between cause and effect.

On the other hand, it was their faith which kept the Dutch Mennonites, who had settled in the Żuławy, near Gdańsk, as well as the Jews in their ethnic separateness. Here the conclusion seems to be that social status was of essential importance. Differences in confession could not stop the progress of Polonization among the gentry, but the same differences served to maintain the ethnic separateness of plebeian masses. In other words, the higher a man's social status, the easier assimilation would come to him. The use of class privileges turned out to be more important than faith. Thus the ennobling of many Armenian families (or the confirmation of an earlier ennoblement) speeded up their denational-ization. The same applies to Antitrinitarians of foreign extraction, who, after obtaining a coat of arms would change their name and language for Polish ones. In this way the former Crells became Szpanowski, Statorius Stoinski, Ronembergs Naborowski.

This was not always the case: the daughter of Martin Ruar, Margareta, prayed for the King and the Commonwealth in fine Polish, though her father spoke German to the end of his life and was never ennobled. Many Socinians in the trials undergone by the Commonwealth in the mid-seventeenth century put the interests of their church above those of their homeland. The sobering up came only later. It was expressed by Stanisław Lubieniecki (d. 1675), who in his will warned his sons 'to keep as far as possible from the enemy of their homeland, so that they need not have to ask for his protection, to bind themselves to him, to stay with him'. The outstanding Socinian historian and polemist dotted the 'i's' in an unprinted contemporary theological treatise when he wrote that the banishment of the Socinians from their homeland was a divine retribution meted out for their collaboration with the Swedes.[13]

[13] S. Lubieniecki, *Compendium veritatis primaevae, Leisg. von K. E. Jordt Jørgensen*, 2, (Copenhagen, 1982), p. 92.

The Polonization of Christianity

A similar attitude was adopted in the first months of the Swedish invasion by the majority of the Protestant nobles. Later, when they were being critically assessed, it was forgotten that a considerable part of the Catholic gentry acted in a similar way. For in the years 1655–60, the Lutheran population of Royal Prussia, Gdańsk leading, remained loyal to the monarchs in Warsaw. The Swedes and the Brandenburgers were as much hated by their co-religionists of Toruń and Gdańsk as by the Catholic population of Cracow, Poznań, or Vilna. The conflicts between the Prussian towns and Polish kings were resolved amicably, and even Gdańsk did not undergo any serious reprisals for its armed action against them. But at the same time, while Lutheran towns flourished in Catholic Poland, in France the rebellion of La Rochelle was bloodily put down, though its inhabitants spoke the same language as their assailants. It is worth remembering that the verbal attacks on the biggest port of the Commonwealth accused it of arrogance, economic exploitation of its material sources, or tax evasion. Nobody argued that Gdańsk was a bastion of heresy and German influence.

Thus, from among the Christian confessions opposed to Rome which existed in the Polish lands only the Orthodox faith served as a flag for an armed fight against the Polish-Lithuanian state. Throughout the sixteenth century this did not constitute a political problem. The situation changed after the foundation of the Moscow patriarchate (1589), which claimed authority over the entire Orthodox Church, including Poland, which was bound to result in the political influence of Muscovy. The Union of Brest Litovsk (1595 and 1596) was to counteract that, but it was generally disapproved of by the Orthodox, from peasants and burghers to a considerable part of the gentry and even the great nobles (for example, Prince Konstanty Ostrogski). Its initiators must have overestimated the degree of political and mental cohesion among the gentry.

Many things indicate that if the union had been concluded half a century later, it would not have met with as much serious opposition on the part of the Ukrainian gentry as it did at the close of the sixteenth century. For under the rule of the two successive Vasas (1587–1648) it underwent considerable Polonization. But the union imposed in 1595 caused an inflammation, which the Cossacks later turned to their advantage by rebelling constantly, not so much against the Commonwealth itself as against the magnates ruling the Ukraine in its name. Opinions differed as to their true attachment to Orthodoxy. Some, headed by the voivode, Adam Kysiel, himself Orthodox, argued that the

Zaporoże Cossacks were 'religionis nullius' (of no religion),[14] and were less the 'salvation of Orthodoxy' than a constant worry. As late as 1612–18 they robbed many revered monasteries, often murdering the resident monks.

After *c.*1620, Orthodox protagonists who called the Cossacks the pillars of the 'Ukrainian Church', gained increasingly strong arguments. Under Cossack protection the church organized its illegal synods, and patronized the activity of Orthodox brethren, schools, and printing presses. Władysław IV, who needed the Cossacks' military aid, granted the Orthodox the same religious freedom as the supporters of the Union (among other things, many churches were restored to the 'Ukrainian' Church). The Compact of Hadiach of 1658 (never put into practice), which created the autonomous Grandy Duchy of the Ukraine within the framework of the Commonwealth, provided for Orthodoxy as the state religion.[15]

Not only did the Union have an impact on the political life of the Polish-Lithuanian State. By bringing to a head the matter of the separateness of the Eastern Church, threatened by the decisions passed at the synods in Brest Litovsk, it turned the Orthodox orders, printing houses, and schools into 'bastions of true faith'. From then onwards they began to serve religious aims as well as the development of Ukrainian culture, threatened as it was by 'lay' and Latin influences. Each energetic attempt to put the Union into practice was felt to be a danger to the national identity of the Orthodox faithful.

The opponents of the Union liked to refer to the continuity of that religious tradition in the Ukraine which had always been loyal to Orthodoxy. It was proudly argued that no Kiev metropolitan had ever come under the rule of the pope. The Uniates were charged with wanting to 'take Ukraine out of Ukraine'; but in order to uproot Orthodoxy it would have been necessary to destroy the Ukrainian nation first. Although the followers of the Eastern Church considered themselves the chief representatives of that nation, they did not deny that the Uniates

[14] T. Chyńczewska-Hennel, *Świadomość narodowa szlachty ukraińskiej i Kozaczyzny od schyłku XVI do połowy XVII wieku*, (National Consciousness of Ukrainian Gentry and the Cossacks from the Close of the Sixteenth to the mid-seventeenth Century) (Warsaw, 1982), p. 88. Cf. also F. E. Sysyn, *Between Poland and the Ukraine. The Dilemma of Adam Kysiel, 1600–1653* (Harvard, 1985), *passim*.

[15] Cf. A. Kamiński, 'The Cossack experiment in Szlachta Democracy in the Polish-Lithuanian Commonwealth: The Hadzizlach (Hadziacz) Union', *Harvard Ukrainian Studies*, 1 (1977), pp. 178–97.

also belonged to it. If the calling of a joint synod of the Orthodox and the Greek Catholics was suggested, this was in order to 'find a way to unite the Ukraine with the Ukraine'.[16]

In any case, ethnic community was an argument often used in anti-Union polemics. Its supporters were accused of being traitors to their own nation. These, in turn, would say that whoever changes his faith, does not necessarily change his own nationality. Thus, if a Ukrainian adopts Roman Catholicism, he does not at once become a Spaniard or an Italian, but remains 'a noble Ukrainian'. 'For it is not faith that makes a Ukrainian a Ukrainian, a Pole a Pole, a Lithuanian a Lithuanian, but his birth and Ukrainian, Polish or Lithuanian blood'.[17] In fact, in the first generation, among the followers of Rome, Wittenberg, Geneva, or Raków (capital of the Socinians), descendants of Ukrainian noble families, there were many who did not lose their original ethnic consciousness. In the next generations they usually became Polonized. This happened much more rarely among the gentry who remained faithful to Orthodoxy. In the first half of the seventeenth century it became the 'synonym of everything Ukrainian which was manifested at every occasion'.[18] But it did not prevent Union polemics after 1605 being conducted almost exclusively in Polish. Both sides were keen on reaching people who did not speak Ukrainian.

In the nineteenth and twentieth centuries the Ukrainian national revival found the confirmation of its political aspirations in Greek Catholicism. Orthodoxy equalled subordination not only to the confessional, but also to the political influence of Moscow. The Roman Catholic rite meant recognition of the superior role of Rome and Warsaw (in secular matters). Only one's own rite safeguarded independence from pressures coming from the two great neighbours of the Ukrainian nation.[19]

On the other hand, in the seventeenth century the adoption of the new faith in the Greek Catholic rite opened the door to Ruthenization, to which Polish peasants who had settled in the eastern borderlands of the Commonwealth also fell victim. Its mechanism has been convincingly revealed by Brückner:

---

[16] Chynczewska-Hennel, p. 102.
[17] M. Korduba, 'Die Entstehung der ukrainischen Nation', *Contributions à l'histoire de l'Ukraine au VIIe Congrès International des Sciences Historiques* (Warsaw, 1933), p. 65.
[18] Chynczewska-Hennel, p. 15.
[19] Cf. J.-P. Hinka, 'The Greek Catholic Church and national building in Galicia, 1772–1918', *Harvard Ukrainian Studies*, 8 (1984), 3–4, pp. 426–52.

Polish parishes, few in number, were dispersed over vast areas. On the other hand the Polish peasant had a Ukrainian pope in his own village, so he went to him for christenings, marriages and funerals because he was also Catholic after all ... the Polish peasant became Ukrainianized in his new surroundings. The Ukrainian gentry became Polonized in a different way, for with class privileges granted in plenty, it adopted the Polish language and customs.[20]

The Mazurians who settled in Ducal Prussia did not adopt the German language together with the new faith, because the difference between German and Polish was too great, while religious propaganda was conducted in the language of Rej and Kochanowski (the great figures of the Polish Renaissance, the former a writer, the latter a poet). The same Mazurians, when colonizing the Ukraine, had a very tenuous language barrier to overcome.

It was only the representatives of our Englightenment who hit upon the idea of a compulsory Polonization of Ukrainian peasants. They were the first to blame our ancestors for not doing anything about the assimilation of the most numerous section of society. Among them Hugo Kollatej, one of the leaders of the Polish Enlightenment, accused the Orthodox clergy of propagating a dislike for the Polish government, in addition to having a different language and faith. Although he acknowledged the services rendered by the Latin clergy in teaching the Polish language to the entire gentry, he held it against them that they taught the principles of faith in the Samogitian and Lithuanian languages, which isolated the population of the Grand Duchy from the State authority.[21] Likewise, the leader of the 1794 insurrection, Tadeusz Kościuszko, demanded uniformity of the church calendars of the two confessions: Orthodoxy and Catholicism. He wrote that 'care should be taken that poets should celebrate Mass in Polish ... In time the Polish spirit will enter them (the Ukrainian peasants). They will consider their enemy whoever would not know the national language ...'.[22]

But let us return to the seventeenth century in which no one worried about the imposition from on high of the 'Polish spirit' on the gentry, even less on the peasants. But at the same time Orthodoxy within the

[20] Brückner, p. 200.
[21] H. Kollataj, *Stan oświecenia w Polsce* (State Enlightenment in Poland) (Wrocław, 1953), pp. 11–12.
[22] *Pisma Tadeusza Kościuszki* (Writings of Tadeusz Kościuszko), ed. H. Mościcki (Warsaw, 1947), pp. 45–6.

frontiers of the Commonwealth remained under the constant pressure of Polish culture. In the seventeenth century the knowledge of the language reached the élite of the Eastern Church, who became bilingual, sometimes even trilingual, for religious treatises and poetry were written in Ukrainian, Polish, and Latin. They were usually educated at the famous Kiev-Mohylan Academy founded by Peter Mohyla in Kiev, then part of Poland. Both the founder and the lecturers and students used the Polish language 'in everyday life and in writing, preferring it to the specifically liturgical and moribund Old Slav Church language or the as yet unsophisticated folk Ukrainian'.[23] The Academy's manuals and lectures were based on Polish patterns, while the nascent Ukrainian 'scholar drama' within the Academy circle was patterned after the Jesuit model.

The 'return to Europe', to quote the term used by Soviet scholars, began in Russia at the close of the sixteenth century. It was then that Moscow established close contacts with the centres of Ukrainian culture which existed in the eastern territories of the Commonwealth. After the Union of Brest Litovsk, the middle and lower Orthodox clergy, who were inimical to it, sought help and understanding from their eastern neighbour, who also received polemical works about Union problems, published in Poland. Further Europeanization of Russian culture came with the Polish intervention into the internal affairs of that state (1608–11). Although False Demetrius (who surrounded himself with Poles) did not succeed in keeping the throne, nor any of the Vasas reigning in Warsaw in wearing the Russian crown, it did not stop the cultural impact coming from the West. Lately, Soviet historians of literature have reminded their readers that among the Poles then resident in Moscow 'there were not only adventurers but also educated intellectuals'.[24]

No wonder then that when the Moscow patriarch, Filaret, returned from Polish captivity in 1619 he was shocked by the scale of that impact. So he launched a determined fight against 'Lithuanian books' (as they were called in Russia) by ordering (1627) their removal from Orthodox churches and monasteries and replacement with books published in Moscow. This mostly concerned books published by Orthodox printing

---

[23] R. Luźny, *Pisarze kręgu Akademii Kijowsko-Mohylańskiej a literatura polska. Z dziejów zwiadków kulturalnych polskowschodnio-słowiańskich XVII–XVIII w.* (Writers in the Circle of the Kiev-Mohylan Academy and Polish Literature. From the History of Polish-Eastern-Slav Cultural Relations in the Seventeenth and Eighteenth Centuries) (Cracow, 1966), p. 10; cf. also A. Jobert, *De Luther à Mohila. La Pologne dans la crise de la Chrétienté, 1517–1648* (Paris, 1974), pp. 345ff.

[24] *Istoria russkoj literatury*, 1: *Dreverusskaya Literatura. Literatura XVIII veka*, ed. B. S. Likhachov and H. P. Magonenko (Leningrad, 1980), p. 294.

houses which operated in Lithuania and the Ukraine. Noteworthy is the fact that in the sixteenth and seventeenth centuries more books in the Ukrainian and Old Slav Church languages were issued there than during the same period in the State of Muscovy (only 500 titles up to the year 1700). In the second half of the seventeenth century, when knowledge of the Polish language spread in Russia, those prohibitions covered books in all languages coming from the territories of the then Commonwealth. They included primers, grammars, profane works as well as religious treatises, lives of saints, prayer books. Works of a religious nature were among those most frequently confiscated in Moscow.

Multiplying prohibitions and confiscations does not testify to their efficacy. If both the Orthodox Church and State authorities issued them as often as they did, this was because they feared dangerous political theories threatening the meaning and principle of absolute power being transplanted into an absolutely ruled State. An even more important role was played by the fear of infiltration from dangerous heresies, as well as the conviction that in the Commonwealth Orthodoxy was undergoing Polonization, which menaced its national and doctrinal integrity. Such processes did take place, mostly through the Greek Catholic rite; let us remember that its followers printed their books in the same Cyrillic alphabet as did the followers of Orthodoxy.

More generally every inhabitant of the Commonwealth knew where he belonged: whether he was a noble, a peasant, or a burgher. Relatively few knew on which continent they lived; only the intellectual élite could boast European consciousness. Between those two extremes lay the awareness of belonging to some definite ethnic and confessional community. These were so closely bound up that if a seventeenth-century noble were asked whether he was first a Pole or a Catholic, he would consider thinking it over a waste of time. Confession determined, so to speak, nationality, and social status confession. In the baroque period two convergent processes were taking place: on the one hand, the number of Polish followers of Protestantism diminished, which attests the truth of the earlier statement about the foreign character of the religion of Lutherans, Czech Brethren, or Calvinists. On the other, in the latter half of the seventeenth century areas populated mostly by Ukrainians were lost, which automatically increased the percentage of Poles in the population of the entire state.

Moreover, Polonization occurred among the majority of the gentry, eighty per cent of whom used the Polish language. If one did not learn it at home, one acquired its knowledge in the public forum (local diets, Seyms,

Crown Tribunals), during military service, or even at school. Even in the Jesuit colleges, which became the most popular form of secondary education, the students talked Polish after classes. But we do not know whether and to what degree ethnic communities belonging to entirely different language groups (for example, the Germans in Royal Prussia, Ukrainians, or Armenians) used Polish in their contacts.

It was Roman Catholicism not Orthodoxy which became the religious bond of the system of gentry democracy, a confession which was seen as the best guarantee of the stability of the system, and the privileges of individuals possessing a coat of arms. It also guaranteed the suppression of visible enemies of the State and Faith (Poland being surrounded by non-Catholic neighbours these two notions blended into each other).

Contemporary Catholic historians complain that Sarmatian piety invested the political system of the Commonwealth with a supernatural character. But it would be hard to deny that filling the supernatural world with institutions and offices well known to the gentry attenuated its dread of eternity. In such circumstances death became simply a change of residence, even the political system remained the same, since God was supposed to be a benevolent ruler whose rule was restricted by his own kindness and man's free will, not an absolute monarch. Only a few preachers broke out of this pattern, painting the image of a dread Creator who in meting out punishment did not take charity into account.

The system of heavenly clientele reminded one partly of the actual dependence of the gentry on the magnates; on earth and in Heaven people looked for more generous and influential patrons. The prevalence of the cult of saints, including the family of Christ himself, which was so characteristic of Polish Catholicism, resulted partly from the decline of intellectual life which occurred in the latter half of the seventeenth century. But it is difficult not to feel that this shift of gravity from God to the saints in a way reflected the socio-political changes occurring in seventeenth-century Poland. It was then that the power of the great nobles was on the increase, and the local diets dominated the Seym.

To the blooming of native culture the Counter-Reformation replied with the Polonization of religious culture. The demands for a national church were countered with a further nationalization of Catholicism which, beginning with the acceptance by the Polish clergy of the resolutions of the Council of Trent (1577) became, in several generations, more native than during previous centuries. Polonization of Catholicism was not instrumental in its victory, because the true defeat of the Reformation had come earlier and as a result of various causes. But it

consolidated the ultimate victory of the Catholic Church and strengthened its influence down to the twentieth century. In the years of national
captivity after the fall of the Polish State, there was both national and
religious oppression. To this was due the deepened symbiosis between
Polishness and Catholicism, which particularly under the rule of
Orthodox Russia and Lutheran Prussia increased the attractiveness both
of the Church and of Catholicism. It seems indisputable that this process
started in the seventeenth century, when the Sarmatization of post-
Tridentine Catholicism took place.

Among all the Christian confessions existing in the territories of the
gentry Commonwealth the most easily influenced by the processes of
nationalization was Catholicism, in the Latin rites, naturally not the
Greek Catholic. It was also Catholicism that paid the highest price for the
consequences of this process. For the complete restoration of its
hegemony, which took place under the reign of the Vasa dynasty (1587–
1668), did not mean that the Polish Church and Catholicism joined the
mainstream of life. On the contrary: in the baroque period provincialization took place, and the provinces stood aside from the great trends which
shook west European Catholicism, quickening its life. Thus the Polish
Church escaped the disputes about Jansenism, Jesuit casuistry, and finally
quietism, to cite only the most important examples. If Polish theologians
took part in the great discussions about tolerance, relations between
Church and State, and the limits of rationalism in matters of faith, their
works came not from the studies of Catholics, but from those of
Socinians, for they were written by Samuel Przypkowski, Andrzej
Wiszowaty, or Jonas Szlichtyng.[25] In the sixteenth century polemical and
theological treatises by Polish Catholic writers were very popular in the
West. In the next century, Calvinist theologians from Poland lectured at
Dutch universities, and Socinians gained in France and England the
honourable name of 'sect of philosophers'. But, at the same time, the
Catholic Church active within the boundaries of the Commonwealth was
sinking deeper and deeper into inessential doctrinal disputes. The
restriction of interest to internal troubles combined with an intensive
Polonization of Catholicism. These two processes, nationalization and
escape into parochialism, went together, although it is impossible to
determine which of these two phenomena came first.

The intellectual life of the Polish clergy developed along with the rise

---

[25] Treatises by Przypkowski and Wiszowaty have appeared lately (in Latin and Polish) in
Poland.

and fall of Sarmatian culture; as the Church submitted to its development pattern. The decline of that culture, especially distinct under the rule of Saxons (1696–1764) must have had an impact on the intellectual level of Polish Catholicism. This is clearly visible in, for example, the Jesuit schools: they started with an unusual impetus but—after years of triumph and development—underwent, more or less from the mid-seventeenth century,[26] gradual stagnation.

One more thing. If the seventeenth-century Sarmatization of Catholicism clearly harmed the Church itself, this was not only the result of the level of our culture in the late baroque period.[27] For a similar phenomenon occurred twice more in the modern history of Poland. For taking over the functions of the State and its cultural and educational institutions during the Partitions and again after 1945, the Church paid with its own provincialization, and intellectually lagged behind the transformations in contemporary Catholicism. This did not always follow from the exclusive concentration of interest on internal matters, political conflicts taking place in the country, or the struggle to maintain Polishness. It was frequently the outcome of the triumph of siege-mentality among church leaders, with all its consequences, including the conviction that violent reforms may be used by the besiegers. Here it would be proper to remember that precisely these two characteristics of Poland as a besieged fortress and as the bulwark of Christianity spread in the seventeenth century.

Historical Institute,
Warsaw

---

[26] Cf. S. Bednarski, *Upadek i odrodzenie szkół jezuickich w Polsce Studium z dziejów kultury i szkolnictwa polskiego* (Decline and Renaissance of Jesuit Schools in Poland. A Study in the History of Polish Culture and Schools) (Cracow, 1933), pp. 31ff.

[27] Cf. J. Tazbir, 'Culture of the Baroque in Poland' in *East Central Europe in Transition from the Fourteenth to the Seventeenth Century*, ed. A. Maczk *et al.* (Cambridge, 1985), pp. 167–80.

[28] Cf. *idem, La République nobiliaire et le monde*, pp. 83ff. (Le rempart place de la Pologne en Europe).

THE PROBLEM OF THE NATION IN THE PREACHING OF ARCHBISHOP JAN PAWEŁ WORONICZ, 1757–1829

by MIECZYSŁAW BRZOZOWSKI

JAN Paweł Woronicz—Polish archbishop, preacher, and poet, who lived in the second half of the eighteenth century and in the first third of the nineteenth century—presented in his writings a very characteristic and conceptually uniform vision of the nation. Generally speaking, one can say that this vision was based on the principles of divine finality and providence. It perceived individual nations as realities planned and created by God, aimed at precisely determined goals and provided with continual divine providence. These views are not the fruits of the Enlightenment, but can be traced back to biblical sources and to the writings of St Augustine and Jacques Bénigne Bosuet (1627–1704). However, in Poland these ideas are deeply rooted in the concepts already expressed by Jan Długosz (1415–80), Stanisław Orzechowski (1513–66), Stanisław Sarnicki (1532–97), Piotr Skarga (1536–1612), Wespazjan Kochowski (1633–1700), and Szymon Starowolski (1588–1656).

The synthesis made by Woronicz not only distinguished itself by its fresh insights, but also by the creative development of earlier ideas. However, most importantly, it played a very significant role in the lives of Poles living at the turn of the nineteenth century and in the shaping of the viewpoints and attitudes of several successive generations.[1]

Thanks to the ideas expressed by Woronicz, Poles in the most dramatic periods of their existence were confirmed in their conviction that the nation differs significantly from the State. From this, it follows that depriving them of political independence does not mean the end of the nation. Prominent among these ideas were (a) that the fate of nations is decided by God and rests in his almighty and just hand; and (b) that a miracle is always possible, and, in spite of obvious external circumstances, it will destroy the oppressors, and the oppressed will be set free.

One should bear in mind that the activities of Woronicz took place at a time when Poland had lost its independence; for 123 years the country was partitioned among Prussia, Russia, and Austria.

---

[1] Cf. J. Trybusiewicz, 'Zagadnienia historyczne w twórczości Jana Pawła Wronicza', *Archiwum Historii Filozofii Myśli Społecznej* (Warsaw, 1959), 4, pp. 5–65.

In order to present in a complete way the views of Archbishop Woronicz concerning the nation, as contained in his sermons, the whole problem should be divided into three parts: the genesis of the nation, the conditions of the nation's existence, and the specific character of the Polish nation.

1. The Genesis of the Nation

In the opinion of Archbishop Woronicz the genesis of each nation should be sought in the thoughts of the eternal God. It is God in his infinite wisdom and love who calls individual nations into being and endows them with numerous gifts.

Though not the most important element, and not decisive for the nation's existence, God gives nations a so-called sacred place, that is, fields, woods, rivers, and so on: in short, the earth and everything on it.

Further on comes the most important problem: God endows each nation with its unique, specific national character. The national spirit is an individual but invariable and timeless principle of the nation's existence. It includes supernatural and natural talents and gifts, customs, and habits. The national spirit determines the nation's identity, shapes its history, and is expressed in its consciousness. Thanks to the value which the national spirit represents, the history of the nation constitutes an inseparable unity, and the nation faithful to its spirit is faithful to itself and likewise faithful to God. In addition to the national spirit and character, each nation, from the moment of its creation, receives from God a specific and unique historical mission. The character of this mission is closely connected with the values included in the national spirit. It is possible to say that the features of the national spirit determine and make the historical mission possible. They simply predispose to its fulfilment.

At the same time, this historical mission gives each nation a specific purpose to fulfil in mutual relations between people and nations. The final conception of history is thus manifested. Each nation, by God's will, performs (or at least should perform) the tasks that God assigned to it.

Woronicz attaches special importance to the problem of the mother tongue. The native language is also an invaluable gift from God, and together with the national spirit creates 'a higher spiritual entity'. This entity shapes the nation and transforms it into one all-embracing family.

Finally, God enters into a special covenant with some nations. The prototype of such a covenant is the covenant that God set up with Abraham, Moses, and the whole Israelite nation. On the strength of this covenant, God gives the nation some extraordinary gifts, reveals to it his law, promises his special protection, and entrusts the nation with an important mission. The nation is obliged to guard with great care the gifts of God and to fulfil his will. Breaking the covenant is one of the most serious mortal sins, and may affect the fate of the nation tragically.

In summary, one may conclude that God intends individual nations to exist, and that he directs them and equips them with their essential features. The basic differences between individual nations depend on the peculiar character of the gifts received, primarily on the national spirit and on the historical mission.

2. Conditions of the Nation's Existence

Woronicz defines, in an obvious manner, the fundamental conditions for the nation's continued existence on the basis of his conception of the nation's genesis. Thus, respect for religion and for the moral obligations derived from it is placed first. God's law should be the guiding principle of life, and the good of the Faith should be the measure of the good of the nation. 'God's law is the primary link in the society, the primary principle of any government ruling it, the primary stronghold leading to its stability, and the primary guarantee of faith and public safety'.[2] According to Woronicz, love for God and respect for his laws is mainly expressed in everyday activities, in the totality of manners and national customs, in the morality of personal, family, professional, social, and political life. He pays special attention to respect for the Church and its institutions, and he demands that the role of the clergy and its importance in social life be maintained at its proper value. These conclusions, which are derived naturally from his conviction that the nation is created by God and directed by him towards precisely determined goals, acquire special importance where there exists a special covenant between God and the nation.

The second condition for the nation's existence is love of the mother country, expressed, above all, in respect for the national spirit and its historical mission, in affection for historical events, the mother tongue, and native land.

Woronicz often stresses the fact that continuous efforts at improving one's knowledge of the mother country's history help greatly in preserving one's love for the mother country. The nation which wants to

---

[2] J. P. Woronicz, *Pisma*, 4 (Cracow, 1832), p. 5.

live must know its history, because knowing history means knowing its national spirit and character and leads to the proper understanding of the covenant and historical mission. In getting acquainted with its own history, the nation consolidates its consciousness and identity. According to Woronicz, the history of the nation—enlivened by its spirit—constitutes an integral unity. The future is conditioned by the past, and is a faithful continuation of that past. History forms one integral whole, thus knowledge of history provides the knowledge necessary for the nation's existence, that is, for the conscious shaping of its present and future fate.

The third condition for the nation's existence is the continuous effort of all its members—in proportion to their capabilities—to work for the well-being of the country. Woronicz takes a number of things into consideration. He mentions in the first place efforts to keep the nation's political independence, fighting against foreign armed intervention. He stresses the military effort of the whole nation and of gifted individuals. Woronicz attaches great importance to individual heroism. In his opinion, outstanding individuals express the national spirit and greatly affect the history of the nation.

Further on he stresses social solidarity. Thus he demands the principles of freedom and equality before the law for all people, as a pre-requisite of the nation's existence. According to him, freedom may only be limited for the general well-being. On the basis of these assumptions, Woronicz proposed the abolition of serfdom and giving legal protection to peasants. He called the serfdom of peasants a 'moral disease of the political body'. At the same time, for the sake of solidarity, he pointed to the need for common agreement, especially among people who were to decide on the present and future fate of the nation. He developed the concept of solidarity out of the idea of the divine genesis of the nation. That is why the possibility of the realization of the above properties was perceived only on the basis of respect for God's law and for religious principles.

In addition to the defence of the nation's existence in the face of external dangers and the postulate of solidarity in the formation of its internal life, care for the common welfare ought to be expressed by 'civilizing efforts' and by artistic production.

He termed 'civilizing efforts' everything that a landowner or a peasant did to make the soil more fertile in order to obtain higher yields. Handicraft, development of workshops, commerce, and the national economy with all its branches were included in these civilizing efforts. In his opinion raising the level of civilization is necessarily connected with the spread of education. Particularly in this field, Woronicz showed himself as a man of the Enlightenment, combining the idea of the nation's life with the idea of progress conditioned by the spread of education at all levels, and beginning with elementary education.

He ascribed a great role to artistic creativity in expressing the national spirit and handing down the memory of important historical events to future generations to prevent them from falling into oblivion. Himself a preacher and poet, he often referred back to biblical times, and recalled events from Poland's history. He thus worked out a concept of the philosophy of history, trying to explain the present and future of the nation with the help of history. According to Woronicz, knowledge of a nation's history is one of the fundamental conditions of the nation's life, and relating it forms the basis of artistic production. It was said of Woronicz himself that he made history the background of his poetry.[3] Like the most famous Polish preacher, Piotr Skarga (†1612), he knew how to place it in his sermons.[4]

All that has been said about the conditions of the nation's existence, Woronicz termed 'faithfulness to yourself and faithfulness to the national spirit, which in consequence is faithfulness to God'. Upon those nations which are faithful to themselves, God bestows the light of faith. God gives political independence, wise rule, far-seeing legislation, and people of great spirit and mind. In this way not only is their existence secured, but they also come into well-earned power and glory. When, however, a nation proves faithless to God's law, betrays its national spirit and historical mission, and breaks the covenant—then it brings down upon itself various tragic consequences. These can be identified as chaotic legislation, anarchy, and, above all, laxity of morals. This demoralization spreads throughout all circles of society and spheres of life. The final and most painful effect of this loss of 'faithfulness to oneself'—that is, faithfulness to God—is loss of political independence. Although this calamity may sometimes be a test of faithfulness brought about by God, basically it is a sign of supernatural punishment. Loss of political independence does not yet mean the end of the nation's existence, just the opposite. Although under constraint, the nation continues to exist. What is more, God—who is infinitely merciful—may after many years restore its independence. The condition for regaining independence is taking up

---

[3] Cf. L. Dębicki, 'Pięści w Puławach. Jan Paweł Woronicz', *Przewodnik naukcowy i literacki* (1899), p. 604.
[4] Cf. K. Koźmian, *Pamiętniki*, 2 (Poznań, 1858), p. 164. Trybusiewicz, p. 59.

the tradition of the forefathers in which the spirit and national character dwell. According to Woronicz 'the national past owes its grandeur to the greatness of the spirit of its forefathers'; thus, only restoration of the past, of its timeless values, may guarantee regaining the national identity. In this way the sin of the nation will be absolved.

Woronicz's vision of history provides for the nation a source of unshaken confidence in God's Providence. Woronicz says that, irrespective of reality and political conditions, God may bring back the nation's independence at any time when he sees its internal change and regeneration. So, a miracle is always possible. Therefore, there is never any situation so tragic as to lead to hopelessness and despair.

In summary, one should note that the conditions of the nation's existence are rooted in a theological conception of history. There is a close connection between socio-political elements and religion and the principles of moral law revealed by God. Only a nation which respects the principles of God's law may exist and develop.

3. Specificity of the Polish nation

All the above views about the genesis and conditions of a nation's existence are exemplified in Woronicz with reference to the Polish nation.

(a) He describes the genealogy of the Polish nation against the background of other Slavonic nations. He goes far back into the past, claiming Assarme, the great-grandson of the biblical Sem, to be the first father of the Slavs. Searching for biblical roots, Woronicz at the same time tries to build support for his three ideological conceptions. He expresses his conviction that the Polish nation is included in God's plan of creation, he lays the foundations of Panslavic ideas, and he classifies the Polish nation with those which, due to their ancient origin, are entitled not only to exist, but also to be powerful and famous.

(b) Woronicz pays a great deal of attention to the problem of the Polish national spirit. He used to repeat these words to his fellow countrymen tormented by the disaster of the partitions: 'The national spirit is a weapon, and cannot be defeated by the power of time, nor by the severity of violence and oppression'.[5] 'One spark of the national spirit can raise from the dead all the urns of ashes and fill them with inspiration'.[6]

[5] J. P. Woronicz, *Dzieła poetyczne*, 3 (Lipsk, 1853), p. 54.
[6] *Ibid.*, p. 46.

'The nation, even oppressed very severely, will not die as long as the national spirit lives in it'.[7] 'A nation dies permanently only when it cannot save its national spirit. Then it can neither tell others about its great past nor feel it itself'.[8]

He wants to describe the Polish national spirit in detail, and among its basic features lists the following: piety deeply rooted in the Polish mentality, the love of freedom, and the willingness to ensure heroic sacrifice in dedication to the homeland.

In addition, Woronicz enumerates sincerity, simplicity of manners, religious tolerance, magnanimity in dealing with defeated enemies, and a readiness to respect ethical rules in political life. However, he does not regard the following characteristic features of western European nations as typically Polish national characteristics: the love of philosophical speculation, research dealing with fine arts, interest in the development of commerce and industry, and so on.

(c) According to Woronicz all the features of the national spirit given to the Polish nation by God help it in a special way to fulfil its historical mission. He sees this mission in the role that Poland has played as a bulwark protecting European Christianity. While other nations can, through the ages, devote themselves to the growth of science, fine arts, industry, and commerce, the Polish nation, by God's will, plays the role of a living barrier, holding back the nations approaching from the East. Woronicz drew this conviction from fifteenth- and sixteenth-century sources. Callimadius (Filippo Buonaccorsi, 1437–96) stated that only Poland was able to fight effectively against the Turkish threat and save Christianity.[9] Niccolò Machiavelli (1469–1527) in his *Discourses* wrote about Poland as a bulwark defending Europe against invasions from Asia.[10] The same thought was then taken up by Erasmus of Rotterdam and Philip Melanchthon.[11] Moreover, in 1627 Pope Urban VIII conferred the title 'Bulwark of Christianity' on Poland, and in 1678 Pope Innocent XI stated publicly that Poland was 'praevalidum ac illustre christianitatis Republicae propugnaculum'. Based on these and similar statements, Woronicz says that in carrying out the function of bulwark the historical mission of the Polish nation was expressed. God created the Polish nation

---

[7] *Ibid.*, p. 131.

[8] *Ibid.*, p. 55.

[9] Cf. F. Bujak, *Kallimach i znajomość państwa tureckiego w Polsce ok. początku XVI wieku* (Cracow, 1900), p. 15.

[10] Cf. *Korespondencja Erazma z Rotterdam z Polakami* (Warsaw, 1965), p. 22.

[11] Cf. *Corpus Reformatorum*, 8 (Hallis Saxonum, 1841), pp. 869–70.

on the frontier of Europe to be the protective tower of Christianity. After 1815—when Poland on the basis of the Viennese Congress received limited sovereignty within the Russian Empire—Woronicz modified his view, stating that the mission of the Polish nation is expressed now in the spiritual inspiration of the Russians. Poland has the power of spirit and Russia has the material power. In the future years Russia imbued with the spirit radiating from Poland may not only become the defender of Christianity, but also the propagator of freedom and peace among the nations of Europe.

(d) In his reflections on the Polish national spirit and its historical mission, Woronicz goes a step further, and says that God has entered into a special covenant with the Polish nation. He refers here to the past also. A well-known Renaissance writer, Stanisław Orzechowski (1513–66) wrote in his dissertation entitled *Quincux* in 1564: 'St Peter directed his words only to Jews and Poles: "You are the chosen tribe" [I Peter 2.9]'. In the sixteenth and especially in the seventeenth century, it was very common in Poland to believe that God had entered into a covenant with the nation, and by virtue of this covenant he offered the nation the gifts of true belief, political freedom, and a political system which guaranteed this freedom. The nation, for its part, undertook an obligation to guard the purity of the Faith, to keep God's moral law, and to protect European Christianity against the dangers from the East.

Woronicz, in talking about the idea of covenant does not repeat the thesis that God supposedly entered into a covenant only with the Polish and Jewish nations, but accepts other ideas known in previous centuries, introducing some elements taken from St Augustine and Bossuet's philosophy of history. In the opinion of Woronicz, the covenant with God is the essence of all Polish history. 'Mieszko I nurtured the state in the cradle of this covenant'.[12] The effect was the greatness and fame of the Polish nation, and its administrative, military, and economic achievements.[13]

(e) Paradoxically—according to Woronicz—the covenant initiated the fall of Poland in 1795. Since God punishes any nation that breaks his eternal moral law, all the more will he never allow evil taking place in the history of a chosen nation to go unpunished. The reasons for the fall of Poland which he singles out are, first of all, the deterioration of faith and the laxity of morals. In a general way he talks about the betrayal of the

[12] *Woronicz, Pisma*, 4, p. 214.
[13] Cf. Trybusiewicz, p. 39.

Old Polish virtues in which the national spirit dwelt. Consequently, he reproaches the Poles with excessive pride, pursuit of private interests, greed, lack of national unity, and oppression of the peasantry. These phenomena had grown particularly strong in the eighteenth century. Poles in this way betrayed their own national spirit and started to lose their specific national characteristics. Consequently the bonds of generations were destroyed, and likewise Poland lost its capability to fulfil its historical mission, that is, to protect the European boundaries of Christianity. All this led in a dramatic way to the breaking of the covenant. Then the Almighty allowed foreign brute force to use violence and treason to deprive Poland of its political independence.

(f) Nevertheless, Woronicz is far from pessimistic, at any rate he does not want to lose heart. Just the opposite: he says that the time will come when the nation, performing acts of penance in a religious sense, and restoring its historical consciousness, will reintroduce the old customs and virtues of its forefathers. Then, not only will God restore independence, sovereignty, wise government, just legislation, and the Polish State system, but also will enter into a new covenant with the nation. The fruit of this covenant will be a new, extended mission, the purpose of which will be not only to defend Christianity, but also to propagate freedom and peace among the nations of Europe. This will be a kind of care for the authentic state of European Christianity. The approach of this moment does not depend upon the state of international relations or socio-political conditions, but on the moral level of the Polish nation. God, after all, attains his goals with the strength of his power, independently of, and even in spite of, what people plan to do.

In order to precipitate this process of penance and time of new splendour, Woronicz constantly encourages the study of biblical history and the history of the nation, and thus the regeneration of the national spirit.

4. General Conclusions

Built in a complex system of philosophy of history, bearing the stamp of finality, and providence, Woronicz's studies of the nation played a great role in Polish thinking of the nineteenth and twentieth centuries.

(a) Above all, he protected the nation against the threatening danger of Russification or Germanization, clarifying the essential difference between the reality of the nation and the function of the State.

(b) Thanks to the stress put on the idea of covenant, the ideas 'a Pole', and 'a Catholic', which had existed since the eighteenth century, were strengthened. If God gave the Catholic Faith to the nation as the sign of the covenant, so it was the fundamental duty to keep that Faith.

(c) It confirmed respect for God's moral law, and made it clear that breaking that law was the basic reason for national tragedies.

(d) It strengthened the conviction that God's moral law must also be the principle of political life.

(e) It fortified faith in the infinite power of God's Providence and strengthened the belief that justice would always prevail and that all crimes would be punished. That was, among other things, the root of Polish struggles for independence in the nineteenth and twentieth centuries.

(f) It stressed the integral bond of Poland with Christian, west European culture, saying to the nation that it must spiritually belong to this part of Europe, the defence of which had become its historical mission.

(g) By showing the common origin of Slavic nations, there arose a basis for Panslavic movements, and a suggestion as to the possibility of a common historical role for Poland and Russia.

(h) There was a chance to note the Polish mission, anxious for peace, freedom, and authentic Christianity in the west European nations.

(i) It increased the value of outstanding and heroic people who play a great role in the life of the nation, above all, those people who distinguish themselves in the fight for independence (T. Kościuszko, J. Poniatowski, R. Traugutt, J. Bem, J. Piłsudski).

(j) Maurycy Mochnacki (1803–34)—theoretician of Polish romanticism and historian—wrote that Woronicz's contribution to the cause of Polish national consciousness rested, above all, in the fact that in his sermons and poetry, he reached back to historical sources: 'He awoke the memory of the past, mentioned virtues, and praised the courage, faith, and piety of ancient Poles'.[14] He restored to the defeated nation a belief in its own abilities. He saved the nation's identity and awoke the national consciousness.

Catholic University of Lublin

[14] Cf. *ibid.*, p. 10.

POLISH REVOLUTIONARIES OF THE NINETEENTH CENTURY AND THE CATHOLIC CHURCH

by STEFAN KIENIEWICZ

THE subject of my paper lies in a field of studies seldom pursued in Church historiography. Catholic historians in Poland are concerned principally with the study of the Church itself: its spiritual life, organization, political role, and contribution to national life. Much less attention is given to adversaries of the Church; so that, generally speaking, the study of non-Catholic (and non-Christian) trends or sectors in society is currently left to Marxist or liberal scholars. This is a pity.

How did Polish revolutionaries deal with, or behave towards, the Catholic Church? Why did they behave in such a variety of ways, as I shall try to explain? These are relevant problems for ecclesiastical history, not only in my own country.

When speaking of the Church, I mean it, of course, in a broad and modern sense, including the hierarchy and the entire 'People of God'. Whereas by revolutionaries I mean all Polish patriots who engaged in an open fight for the recovery of Poland's independence. It is well known that such activities included acquiescence in some kind of social reform or social upheaval. I intend to deal not only with militant insurgents, but also with those who prepared themselves for such a fight: in conspiracy, in propaganda, and in theoretical reflection. The scope of my perusal ranges from the ultimate fall of the Old Polish Republic in 1795, to the rebirth of a Polish State in 1918. I shall pay more attention to the period between the two major Polish insurrections of 1830 and 1863.

The obvious starting-point of my argument is that the period in question was a time of misfortune for Poland, and of hardships for the Catholic Church. Most Poles resented their submission to foreign domination; but their liberation was not conceivable without a European war, or revolution. Revolutions, however, threatened the Christian Faith. The pope, as the head of a temporal state, depended on the support of conservative courts who assisted him, when endangered by the Risorgimento. And if successive popes often tried to intercede in favour of persecuted religion in Poland, by and large they accepted the legality of Poland's partitions. The Polish Church, on the other hand, was headed mainly by dignitaries subservient to foreign rule, whose actions were determined by caution, or discretion, or fundamental reluctance to do anything illegal. As to the Polish laity, it was dominated, as everywhere in Europe, by conservative landowners, intrinsically hostile to revolutionary tendencies. Any political organization proposing the overthrow of the established order, even from patriotic motives, would face the hostility of the 'right-thinking' classes, the distrust of the bishops, and the condemnation of Rome. The attitude of the patriots towards the Church could not, therefore, be anything but antagonistic.

Now it seems to me that the mutual relations between Church and patriots actually proved much more complex. Let me adduce two significant incidents. In January 1798 French revolutionary armies occupied the Eternal City. To outside observers, the fate of the Roman Church appeared sealed: it was to be eradicated by impious Jacobins. The French garrison in Rome, however, included also some Poles, namely Dabrowski's Legion, who had enrolled one year before under the tricolour flag, in order to fight their common enemy, the Austrians. On that memorable day, 3 May 1798, the Polish soldiers paraded through the city from Porta del Popolo to the Capitol, watched with suspicious eyes by the Catholic population. Soon enough it became evident that these Slav *condottieri* were also Christians, attached to their faith and manifesting it emphatically. One could see privates (and even officers) attending divine services, serving at Mass, approaching the Sacraments, and kneeling in the street before the priest, bearer of the viaticum. Some simple-minded peasants, clad in uniform, were seen lying prostrated, in adoration ... before the Egyptian obelisk in St Peter's Square![1] Entering the service of the atheist French Republic, these Poles did not renounce the faith of their ancestors.

The second instance I am alluding to dates from thirty years later. In 1828, some members of the underground Patriotic Society appeared before the High Court in Warsaw, accused of high treason, of conspiring for the re-establishment of Poland. The High Court consisted of members of the Kingdom's Senate, which numbered among others eight bishops. It came as a surprise to patriotic opinion, while arousing the anger of Tsar Nicholas, when these loyal church dignitaries, led by Primate Woronicz, the well-known poet and preacher, sided with the majority of the senators and voted not guilty. They seemed unable to condemn illegal activities, inspired as they were by the love of their country.[2] The two

[1] See J. Pachoński, *Legiony polskie* (The Polish Legions), 2 (Warsaw, 1971).
[2] H. Dylagowa, *Duchowieństwo katolicki wobec sprawy narodowej 1764–1864* (The Catholic Clergy and the National Problem) (Lublin, 1981), pp. 79ff.

occasions quoted demonstrate that no insurmountable barrier separated revolution from religion in Poland.

The so-called November Insurrection of 1830–1 ran accordingly under the joint invocation of God and Fatherland. Solemn worship was held in Warsaw for the success of Polish arms; chaplains were attached to every regular or partisan regiment. The national government dispatched a special envoy to the Court of Rome. Some radically minded friars joined revolutionary clubs. Laymen and clergy joined in a common effort against the schismatic Tsar.[3]

The insurrection ended in defeat, and, still worse, it was to be severely condemned, after the defeat, by Pope Gregory XVI. The regrettable *Cum primum* encyclical of 1832[4] affected most painfully all believers among the patriots. The poet Słowacki reacted violently in his drama *Kordian* (1834). He depicted sarcastically a sovereign pontiff insensible of Poland's martyrdom, 'The Poles should pray and worship the Tsar; anathema on them, if they are defeated'. 'O Poland, Rome is your doom!' added Słowacki in a later poem.

Faced with this lamentable verdict, various groups of Polish *emigrés* reacted inconsistently, according to their temperament and political creed. Some flatly rejected all allegiance to the Holy See. Ludwik Mierosławski, the best-known leader of the Polish Democratic Society, described Pope Pius IX (1858) as 'this sort-of-a-monk foundling of Jesuits who sings today alone to himself in the Sistine chapel, dressed in a Chaldean nightgown and embroidered slippers!' Such an irreverent image was anti-clerical to be sure, but it did not amount to atheism. In the same breath Mierosławski alluded to 'the true God, the relentless Creator, naked as truth and as primeval force, a tremendous God, his beard dishevelled from Zenith to Nadir, from wrath and love', a God who will one day cleave the globe with St Michael's sword, in order to re-establish universal justice.[5] Beyond a doubt, the bearded orator identified himself with the formidable judge on Michelangelo's fresco.

Szymon Konarski, the hero of Polish conspiracy, who suffered torture during his trial in Wilno, and died without having betrayed a single soul, settled accounts with God in a long, versified confession, on the eve of his

---

[3] *Duchowieństwo a powstanie listopadowe* (The Clergy and the November Insurrection), volume of essays in *Roczniki Humanistyczne* (Humanist Annals), 28/2 (1980).
[4] See M. Zywczyński, *Geneza i następstwa Encykliki Cum primum* (The Genesis and Consequences of the *Cum primum* Encyclical) (Warsaw, 1935).
[5] L. Mierosławski's speech, first published in *Przegląd Rzeczy Polskich* (Polish Affairs Review), 20, 1 (Paris, 1859).

execution (1839). He too verged on blasphemy in exclaiming: 'I do not want Heaven, I spit into Heaven, so long as my countrymen are enslaved!' However, he ended his poem with the verse: 'O Lord, save Poland, O Lord, redeem Poland!'[6] Konarski, by the way, was a Protestant.

While radical democrats rejected all kinds of religion, allowing at the most for an abstract deity, other revolutionary groups, still attached to the Catholic Faith, contemplated an improvement or modernization of the Church, rather than its overthrow. Such an attitude was typical, among others, of Adam Mickiewicz, and I do not have in mind his membership of the Towianski sect. This mystical coterie, actually, cannot be included among the revolutionary groups. In 1846–7, however, the poet disentangled himself from the influence of Towiański, while giving support to the Italian cause in close alliance with Mazzini. As founder of the Polish Legion in Rome (March 1848) he stated in his famous *Credo* his allegiance to the Holy, Catholic, and Roman Faith, and to the Gospel, while proclaiming full freedom to all religious denominations, including Jews. He placed his trust, at that time, in the liberal attitude of Pius IX. Admitted to an audience with the Holy Father, he sought his blessing for the Polish cause. He dared, however, to burst out, before the Head of the Church: 'Be aware, that God's Spirit rests nowadays under the blouses of the People of Paris!' Of course, Pius IX soon disillusioned his radical admirers and supporters. The following autumn the Pope was obliged to flee the Eternal City; a Republic was proclaimed in Rome, under Mazzini's leadership; and Mickiewicz's legionaries eventually enrolled to defend the Roman Republic against French intervention.[7]

Mickiewicz at that time edited in Paris a French radical paper *La Tribune des Peuples*, called into being in order to promote the solidarity of all nations fighting for freedom. In one of the first issues (16 March 1849), the Polish poet pronounced a severe judgement on 'Rome and official Catholicism'. Under that last appellation he described those Italian and French reactionaries who campaigned against the Roman Republic, in order to re-establish the secular power of the Pope.

> We unofficial catholics [wrote Mickiewicz] consider that the only sin of our Roman brothers, a sin most scandalizing in the eyes of the Pope, the Sacred College, all major beneficiaries, the *Univers religieux* [a Catholic paper in Paris] and its subscribers, is republicanism. An unpardonable sin! In Rome one can easily absolve laxity in religious

[6] A. Barszczewska, *Szymon Konarski* (Warsaw, 1957).
[7] S. Kieniewicz, *Legion Mickiewicza* (Warsaw, 1957).

duties, or the breaking of Church discipline; one can tolerate, sometimes even encourage, religious indifference; the Romans, perhaps, can be allowed to proclaim atheism from the height of the Capitol—but under one condition: not to utter the word Republican at the Quirinal.[8]

Mickiewicz's main postulate against the 'official Church' was to put an end to the Pope's temporal power, which may seem sensible and innocuous in our eyes. Some Polish democrats proposed more far-reaching, one should say sweeping, reforms of religious life. It would be impossible to enumerate them all, so let us mention just one most original covenant of the Universal Church, that adopted by the so-called Grudziaz Commune established in Portsmouth. This tiny group of a couple of hundred emigrants, mostly privates and NCOs of plebian descent, deliberately isolated themselves from the bulk of the Polish exiles, burdened as they were with aristocratic prejudices. These simple souls, led by a group of radical intellectuals, proclaimed themselves as the only true representatives of the Polish people. They not only rejected all privileges of birth and social status, but also abolished in their manifestos private property as well, as a source of injustice and inequality. Cultivators were to receive their plot of land, craftsmen their workshop, from the Commune, and in usufruct only. Children were to be educated, trained, and endowed by the Commune.

In the Portsmouth barracks such a brand of agrarian Utopian communism went hand-in-hand with traditional religious feelings. In 1837, the Polish community of London approached the Portsmouth group with a proposal to merge, which would have been profitable for the latter, among others, for material reasons. After prolonged discussion, the negotiations came to nothing. The plebians of Portsmouth suspected their London partners of being infected with aristocratic traditions; but they also condemned their indifference, or even hostility, to religion.[9] No wonder, therefore, that their own covenant, cited above, elaborated by Zenon Świętosławski, was dressed in religious phraseology. It attempted nothing less than an organization of mankind, along Saint-Simonian lines. Complete equality of rights, equipment, and assets was proposed; strict centralism; and a long gradation of elected offices, from communes to

---

[8] A. Mickiewicz, *Dzieła* (Works), 12, pp. 27–8.
[9] P. Brock, 'The Birth of Polish Socialism', *Journal of Central European Affairs*, 13/3 (1953), and 'Na marginesie historii Gromady Grudziaż (On the Margin of the Grudziaż Commune's History), *Przegląd* Historyczyn (Historical Review), 52 (1961).

district, to province, to nation, to Universal Church. Its capital would be a new city built on the Suez Isthmus, on the junction of two seas and two continents, and its elected head was to be named Vicar of Christ. All mankind would unite in the Christian Faith: 'God of the only Faith, one God Creator of everything, is the only God, and every child of the Church will worship him'.

This singular document, complete in 19 chapters and 348 paragraphs, was signed in the 'Polish barracks' at Portsmouth on 24 March 1844, by 49 members, many of whom bore peasant family surnames like Papucia, Cimoszek, Bartosik, Grzyb, Czuchryta, and Jendroch.[10] Needless to say, their design remained on paper only, almost unknown to contemporaries. If I have dwelled a moment on the peculiar case of the Portsmouth Commune, it is in order to stress that one political group, forming the extreme left of the Polish Emigration, conceived their country's future in religious terms, as a kind of church, dissimilar, of course, to the existing one.

Another sort of approach by Polish revolutionaries to the problem of the Catholic Church was neither to fight it, nor to reject it, nor try to reform it, but rather to make use of it for the purpose of revolution. The main preoccupation of democratic propagandists in Poland, in the middle of the nineteenth century, was how to approach the peasants with slogans of freedom and national independence. The Polish villager was all too suspicious of every suggestion deriving from the manor, or from the town. Many patriots, therefore, placed their hopes in the clergy. They assumed—too eagerly, I suppose—that the parish flock, attached to their creed, obedient to their priest, would also respond to his patriotic invocation if he would call them to arms, for the defence of their country and of the Holy Virgin. Hence the importance attached to religious phraseology even by democrats otherwise lukewarm in spiritual matters. It seemed essential, in any insurrectionary venture, to ensure the assistance of the local priest, who was to deliver a patriotic sermon on 'D-Day', and take the oaths, thereafter, of the newly enrolled scythemen.

As a typical example of such an amalgam of religious and patriotic sentiments, one can quote the *Words of God to the People of Poland*, a tract published in Paris in 1848, commissioned by the Polish Dramatic Society. Its authors, Heltman and Zieńkowicz, did not stand out, before or later, as particularly pious. They were anxious, none the less, to counterbalance,

---

[10] H. Temkinowa, *Lud Polski. Wybór dokumentów* (The Polish People. Selected Documents) (Warsaw, 1957), pp. 230–314.

by religious apostrophe, the nefarious ascendency of Austrian officials over the peasants in Galicia, after the terrible massacre of the gentry, the year before.

> People of Poland! Brothers! Why are you so derelict, worse than the meanest worm, the tiniest blade of grass? . . . Why are you slaves on this earth, which God gave in heritage to all Mankind, without distinction? . . . God wants all men to be equal, that no one should be slave or subject to another, that everybody should have God as the only Lord. . . . Why do other countries enjoy liberty, learning and abundance, while we suffer bondage, ignorance and misery? I'll tell you why! Because other countries govern themselves according to the will of God, with laws which God himself gave to the human kind, while you are subjected to the will of God's enemies, to violators of the Divine law.[11]

I set aside the question to what degree arguments of this kind actually reached and influenced the Polish peasantry. I only want to stress that such appeals to God's laws, God's will, and God's justice did not always testify to their authors' sincere devotion. Some members of the clergy engaged willingly in this kind of propaganda, as early as the 1840s; and the current spread dramatically after 1860. This subject of a patriotic engagement of the Catholic clergy in Poland lies outside my considerations; I cannot, however, pass over in silence the very special case of Father Piotr Sciegienny.

Sciegienny, born in 1801, was the son of a peasant from a government-owned village in central Poland. He got some learning, tried to earn his living as a teacher, then entered holy orders in the teaching Piarist Congregation. He was noted for his patriotic attitude during the insurrection of 1831. Later, he occupied the posts of curate (eventually of vicar) of different villages in the south of Congress Poland. He joined the democratic conspiracy in the late thirties. He distributed among the peasantry handwritten leaflets of his own composition; the most famous of which bore the title, 'Brief of the Holy Father Pope Gregory, sent from Rome to farmers and craftsmen'. 'Go and teach the nations the word of Christ', ran the preamble. 'I, Pope Gregory in the name of Jesus Christ, Son of the Living God, grant fifteen years indulgence to everybody who reads this letter or listens to it five times with attention'.[12]

[11] *Boże słowa do ludu polskiego* (Words of God to the People of Poland) (Paris, 1848), pp. 10–13.
[12] W. Djaków, *Piotr Sciegienny i jego spuścizna* (Peter Sciegienny and His Bequest) (Warsaw, 1972), pp. 238–9.

Gregory XVI, a saintly but conservative-minded pontiff, who consistently opposed any kind of subversive movement, could hardly have been considered capable of inciting social upheaval, except in the most out-of-the-way recess of eastern Europe. The supposed papal bull announced that every peasant ought to own a plot of land sufficient to sustain his family, in full property and free of charges; and that in order to attain full liberty and ownership of land, the peasants ought to rebel against their lords and their foreign oppressors. They also ought to form an alliance with Russian soldiers and Russian peasants, against Russian generals, and the Tsar!

The author of this tract (and other similar compositions) was arrested in 1844, on the eve of an insurrection which did not eventually take place. He was solemnly deprived of his orders, sentenced to death, then pardoned and sent to Siberia, where he spent twenty-six years. I concentrated on his story, as his was the most blatant case of the misuse of the Lord's name by revolutionaries—still more questionable because perpetrated by a priest.

Moderate patriots did not venture, of course, to address their fellow countrymen in the name of a sovereign pontiff whom they knew to be indifferent or hostile to their cause. They tried another way: that of enlightening, advising, the Holy See, that it lay in the interests of religion and of the Church to intercede publicly for Poland. This was the line of conduct espoused by Prince Adam Czartoryski. One should not be surprised that he is mentioned when speaking of revolutionaries. Czartoryski was a liberal aristocrat, who aimed at restoring a moderately progressive Poland by the means of diplomatic pressure on, or occasionally of major war with, the partitioning powers. *Ipso facto*, he laboured to instigate a European upheaval. He did not hesitate to contact the right wing of the Risorgimento movement; nor to persuade Vatican dignitaries to enter the way of liberal reforms. Objectively, as an active Polish patriot, he played the game of European revolution, and was denounced and pursued as such by the combined police forces of all the reactionary powers.

Agents of the Hotel Lambert, as the Czartoryski group was called, from the name of his Paris residence, were continuously active in Rome, after the mid thirties. They informed the Holy See about the situation of the Polish Church, and denounced the tribulations it suffered under Russian and Prussian rule. They advised the Pope on the most appropriate course to be taken in negotiations with Petersburg, Berlin, or Vienna; and also in personal matters, such as providing to episcopal posts, recommending persons of worth, and cautioning against dubious candidates. During the first two years of Pius IX's pontificate, Czartorysky's emissaries in Rome acquired some influence at the Papal Court; they did not succeed, however, in preventing the conclusion of a concordat between Rome and Tsar Nicholas, an agreement highly detrimental to Polish interests. In November 1848, Ludwik Orpiszewski begged the Hotel Lambert to be released from his post at the Vatican. 'Our dignity and credit will suffer in sustaining relations with a government which appears to come more and more under Muscovite influence'.[13]

To encounter yet another style of Polish revolutionary approach to the Church and religion, we should recall the January insurrection of 1863. This was the most sizeable Polish national upheaval of the nineteenth century. People of all sorts joined it, from noblemen to peasants, Whites and Reds, men of other denominations, together with Catholics. Religious emblems figured on the guerilla banners; images of Our Lady of Częstochowa replaced portraits of the Tsar in communes occupied by insurgents. Some priests were seen, crucifix in hand, leading scythemen to the attack. One could argue, of course, to what degree the use of religious symbols implied sincere faith in the immediate help of Divine Providence. Was it one more attempt at winning the common folk's sympathy to the national cause? Opinions prevailing among the intelligentsia can be summed up in a radical pamphlet, dated Cracow, January 1864:

> We are most grateful to the Holy Father for his prayers; we also appreciate the patriotic preaching of our clergy. We would be glad, nonetheless, if the Pope did not so obstinately hold to his monarchic power (the golden tiara does not match Christ's crown of thorns), and if the parson did not squeeze too much out of poor villagers, for nuptial and funeral rites. . . .[14]

In this context, however, one character should not be passed over in silence: Romuald Traugutt, the last dictator of the insurrection. Traugutt was a consequent revolutionary; he was also a religious man; some people in Poland today consider him a saint. His understanding of the connection between the Christian Faith and the fight for freedom is best expressed in

---

[13] M. Handelsman, *Rok 1848 we Włoszech i polityka ks. Adama Czartoryskiego* (1848 in Italy. The Politics of Prince Adam Czartoryski) (Cracow, 1936), pp. 21–2.

[14] The text of this pamphlet, as well as Traugutt's letter of 28 November 1863, is included in a volume of sources: *Dokumenty organizacji terenowych powstania styczniowego* (Documents of Local Branches of the January Insurrection) (Wrocław, 1986).

his letter to General Różycki, written shortly after his seizure of power in November 1863. This beautiful text was recently discovered in one of the Cracow libraries. I limit myself to some essential paragraphs.

> Poland is a Catholic State. Its Government is Catholic too, and as such, founded on the principles of fraternity and Christian charity, those main features of true Catholicism. It extends its guard and protection to all sons of Poland alike, who flock under its wings, without distinction of religious belief, of which everybody will give account not on this Earth, but before his Creator.
>
> No miracle will deliver us from this captivity of the flesh, and Divine Grace will not descend and give us force to deliver our spirit from evil bondage, if we do not set to work with full zeal. You will get your bread by the sweat of your brow, corporeal bread as well as spiritual should be hard-earned; and God will help only those who toil.

We have briefly reviewed different approaches to religion among the fighters for Poland's independence. Condemnation of the Church, as hostile to the Polish cause; appeal from the actual Church to another, more ideal one; attempts, more or less sincere, to use the clergy's influence on common minds, for propaganda purposes; lost labours in persuading church authorities to take sides with Polish *irredenta*; and, last, but not least, confident pursuit of a desperate fight, in the humble hope that God will eventually assist the good cause.

The examples quoted until now pertain to a period when Polish patriots taking to arms, or preparing a new insurrection, were obviously anxious to ensure the help of Providence, or of its representatives on earth. Let us concentrate now on a later period, when chances of an armed struggle, and the will to undertake it, abated dramatically, and the majority of patriotically conscious Poles preferred to practise legal, that is, non-revolutionary, means of defending their nationality. The problem under consideration, that of the mutual relations between the Church and revolutionaries, loses its earlier importance. Revolutionaries became less numerous, and much less interested in religion. The Labour movement in Russian and Austrian Poland was led by Socialists of Marxist persuasion; its followers, in new industrial centres, held aloof from the Church.

> Religion [declared the first Socialist programme in Galicia (1881)] is in some measure a means of exploitation, it enjoys therefore the protection of the state and governing classes. Reduced to its proper

sense, it will become a private affair. With the advance of literacy, dogmatic religion will be replaced everywhere by positive science and art.[15]

The claim to a secular priority figured accordingly in most of the basic programmes of Socialist parties. If we consider that the entire clergy campaigned most vehemently against Socialist ideas, we should conclude that those Socialist factions who opted for revolution were necessarily against the Church. The matter was not as simple as that. Numerous workmen of the first generation, freshly transplanted from villages to big cities, remained attached to religious rites and habits. Socialist propaganda took this into account; it often tried to adapt traditional ceremonies to the new ideology. Weddings, for example, were held in church, but with an emphatic display of red scarves and ribbons. Red banners appeared at Christian funerals of Labour partisans. Revolutionary songs were composed to well-known church melodies, especially Christmas carols; and Jesus Christ was presented, in some Socialist tracts, as a forerunner of Communism, a friend of the poor, a victim of the exploiting classes. We are dealing here with tactics already noticed in a previous period: that of using religious terminology to convey revolutionary ideas.[16]

In 1896, an anonymous tract appeared in Poland, under the attractive title: *Can a Socialist be a Catholic?* Its author, Leon Falski (later exiled to Siberia), belonged to the elders of the Polish Workmen's Union. He wrote:

We do not advertise religious, nor anti-religious propaganda. . . . We do not base ourselves on religion, we do not impose faith upon anybody. . . . We are not a religious, nor an anti-religious sect; and that's our advantage, that we leave freedom of faith to everybody. Religious wars belong to the past. We workmen united in a Socialist party are fighting for our social and political interests, not meddling in questions of faith.

The brochure was a big success: five editions in various Polish provinces, a Czech, and even a Bulgarian translation. The booklet's evident aim: to

---

[15] Quoted in, *Polskie programy socjalistyczne, 1878–1918* (Polish Socialist Programme), ed. F. Tych (Warsaw, 1975), pp. 103–4.
[16] A. Chwalba, 'Obrzędowość i symbolika religijna w działalności partii socjalistycznych obozu rosyjskiego' (Religious Ceremonies and Symbols in the Activity of Socialists in Russian Poland), *Przegląd Historyczny*, 74 (1983).

STEFAN KIENIEWICZ

reassure proletarians not utterly detached from the Faith that they could
espouse Socialism without incurring Divine punishment. No wonder that
Falski's argument was violently opposed by clerical polemicists ... and by
left-wing polemicists, too. ...

Attachment to traditional religion survived still more markedly among
peasants, even among those emancipated enough to associate in an
independent political movement. The Polish Populist Party in Galicia was
violently attacked by the bishops, who supported the Conservative
establishment. The Populists, accused from pulpits of radicalism, and
even of irreligion, would not, however, repudiate their links with
Christianity. A relevant passage of the Populist party's programme of 1903
ought to be cited at length:

> Faithful to the principles which loftily distinguished Poland in times
> of general intolerance ... we want freedom of conscience for
> confessors of every creed and rite. ... We are conscious, nevertheless,
> of the exceptional role of the Catholic religion in our national life. Its
> persecution, under Russian and Prussian rule, is not only an outrage
> to human conscience; it is also a methodical undermining of the dam
> which religion represents against the hostile elements submerging
> our country. Defence against religious oppression associates itself so
> intimately with national defence, that every drop of blood, shed in
> defence of faith, implies also a martyrdom for Mother Country. The
> same ties, however, harm us beyond measure, when the clergy
> remains indifferent to the national cause, or if, in our society, it takes
> sides with the oppressors, against the oppressed.[17]

All underground groups in Russian Poland whose aim was their
country's independence had to confront the clergy's distrust or disfavour.
The National League, founded in 1893, broke unequivocally with the
Divine commandments, while claiming that the national interest over-
rode all other precepts and considerations. This was the thesis of Zygmunt
Balicki's book: *National Egoism versus Ethics* (1902). Some time later, Polish
nationalists modified their policy, trying, among other things, to win the
favour of the Catholic clergy; but by that time the National Democratic
Party had also abandoned its revolutionary aspirations.

In 1906, the Revolutionary Faction of the Polish Socialist Party
emerged from a rift in the ranks of the PSP. This was the origin of the

---

[17] S. Lato and W. Stankiewicz, *Programy stronnictw ludowych* (Programmes of Populist Parties)
(Warsaw, 1969), p. 73.

'radical independence movement' which, led by Pilsudski, played an eminent role in the reconstruction of the Polish State during World War I. Piłsudki-ites at first seemed unreliable to church dignitaries: as tainted with Socialism, disreputable desperados. None the less, Piłsudki's followers took care to avoid in their propaganda all anti-clerical accents; they even managed to secure the support of one auxiliary bishop of L'vov, Mgr Bandurski, who patronized Piłsudski's paramilitary troops, and became later the spiritual patron of Piłsudski's legions.

The rebirth of independent Poland in 1918 marked a turning-point in the history of our Catholicism/Patriotism syndrome. The Polish Church, hierarchy, and clergy embraced the national cause with enthusiasm and full conviction. In the inter-war period they supported, as was to be expected, the interests of the propertied classes, that is, of the Right. Hence the more or less virulent anti-clericalism of Polish radical parties. But that is another story, which transcends my present subject.

Looking back at the nineteenth century, the time of partitioned Poland, we may conclude with one fundamental observation. Polish patriots who aimed at regaining their country's independence, with or without some social reforms or upheavals, were bound to meet the hostility of the Court of Rome, and of most bishops. Nevertheless, facing this lack of support, Polish revolutionaries did not adopt a frankly anti-clerical, still less an anti-religious, position. They appealed from one ecclesiastical mentality to another, and better informed, one. They tried to oppose a Utopian, renovated Church to the 'official' one. They endeavoured, sometimes, to cover with religious phraseology their very worldly objectives. Some of them—the most eminent, most sincere Christians, and most sincere patriots—followed their own way, placing their trust in Divine Justice, and taking no notice of ecclesiastical condemnations.

What inference is to be drawn from these different attitudes outlined here very briefly? One only, it seems to me. That in the feeling of all these patriots, even those remote from religion, Catholicism remained so important a feature of Poland's identity and struggle for survival that it was unthinkable to ignore it, still more to combat it.

University of Warsaw

A VARIETY OF RELIGIOUS ARCHITECTURE IN POLAND

by TADEUSZ CHRZANOWSKI
Translated by Piotr Pieńkowski

BEFORE I attempt a brief survey of the numerous and varied examples of religious architecture in Poland let me mention a few well-known facts. Poland, having grown out of a tribal community, and having early developed a national character, after the Union with Lithuania (first a personal union in 1386 and then a State union in 1569) began expanding rapidly. At the turn of the fifteenth century a new model of parliamentary monarchy was established, a model functioning in an already multinational, federal state, which ceased to be the 'Republic of Two Nations' and became instead the 'Republic of Many Nations'. I do not intend to analyse here all the achievements, changes, and mistakes of Poland, but I would like to stress that between the fifteenth century and the eighteenth century the Poles were in a minority. This minority, however, decided the country's fate, as it was Polish noblemen (*szlachta*) who set the political and cultural pace. It has never been accurately assessed what percentage of the whole society the noblemen were, but it must have been high, probably the highest in Europe. According to some sources, the Poles who felt themselves free and regarded Poland as their commonwealth formed ten per cent of the whole population. We should also note that at that time the process of Polonization took place mainly among the nobility, and that the Poles who were in a minority in the Polish-Lithuanian State were at the same time a majority among those who ruled that State. I am not saying that as a Polish nationalist, but as an historian who has a deep respect and friendly feeling for all the nations and denominations which once inhabited this large and unique country. The Union of Lublin put the final touches to this distinctive commonwealth, which appeared too early in the Europe of nationalism and absolutism to survive.

I do not know whether Poles are tolerant by nature, but the tolerance which flourished in Poland at this time was necessitated by its internal situation: a newly fledged federation composed of an almost equal number of Roman Catholics and Orthodox, not to mention other denominations, the largest of which was the Jews.

The Reformation further complicated the situation, and the image of

Poland as a predominantly Catholic country remaining under the direct sway of the Holy See is an anachronism. The Reformation was divided against itself, a fact which led to its weakening and final collapse in Poland. The way it was divided reflected the national and ethnic variety of numerous social groups. For instance, Lutheranism positively differentiated the German or German-speaking inhabitants from other social groups in large towns. Magnates and rich noblemen embraced Calvinism, whereas noblemen of moderate incomes professed extremely radical antitrinitarian Arianism. Further, there were numerous independent religious communities embracing those who had fled from persecution. In Leszno, the Leszczyński family gave protection and support to Bohemian Brethren, who continued the tradition of Hussitism, whereas the Mennonites from the Netherlands found their shelter in the delta of the Wisla river.

The Polish-Lithuanian State, in fact the Republic of Many Nations, must of necessity have been tolerant, because otherwise it could not have survived for three centuries. This tolerance I understand as a tendency (expressed in the Confederation of Warsaw in 1573) to regard religion as a strictly personal matter, an attitude reflected in a famous statement made by Sigismund Augustus, the last king of the Jagiellonian dynasty, who said that he was 'the ruler of the citizens but not the ruler over their consciences'. Moreover, this tolerance had political connotations as well, since for the noblemen living in Poland, whether they were of Polish, Lithuanian, Ruthenian, German, Italian, or Jewish descent, the notion of *res publica* was a sacred one. This is one of the reasons why Poland did not witness religious wars, although religion was often treated as a vehicle of propaganda. This happened during the Cossack uprising under Chmielnicki (1648–51) and during the defensive war waged against the Swedish troops under Charles X Gustavus. Foreign invasions were launched in the name of 'religious freedom', a slogan which served purely political ends.

However, as a result of the Counter-Reformation, undertaken in the sixteenth century and gaining momentum in the seventeenth century thanks to the vigorous efforts of the Jesuits and other religious orders, Poland became largely a Catholic country and has remained so to the present day, a fact which helped the nation to survive the dark and long days of the Partitions. That is why I would like to begin the present survey with some general remarks on the architecture of Catholic churches.

1 Strzelno. Romanesque rotunda from the thirteenth century—interior.

2 Lublin. Gothic interior of the Holy Trinity Chapel in the castle, with Byzantine frescoes. Beginning of the fifteenth century.

3 L'vov. The choir of the Armenian cathedral from the middle of the fourteenth
century.

4 L'vov. The Orthodox cathedral, 1591–1634, with the Korniakt-tower, 1572–8 and 1672.

5 The Jesuist pilgrimage church in Święta Lipka, 1687–92.

6 Wilno. The Catholic church of the Missionaries, 1751–4.

7 Berezwecz (Bielorussia). The former Greek-Catholic church of the Basilians,
1753–6 (non-existent).

8 Kodeń. The former Orthodox church from the beginning of the sixteenth century.

9 L'vov. The Greek–Catholic (now Orthodox) cathedral, 1744–63.

10 Grywałd. The Gothic wooden church from the fifteenth century.

11 Dębno Podhalańskie. Interior of a Gothic wooden church with painted decoration from the beginning of the sixteenth century.

12 Tomaszów Lubelski. The baroque wooden church, 1728.

13 Szalowa. Interior of the wooden church with rococo decoration, *c.* 1760.

14 Sława Śląska. The half-timbered Lutheran church from the seventeenth century.

15 Chlastawa. Interior of the wooden Lutheran church, 1637.

16 Hrebenne. The wooden Orthodox church, 1600.

17 Banica. The Greek-Catholic wooden church from the Carpathian Mountains, from the end of the eighteenth century.

18 Czarna. Interior of a Greek-Catholic wooden church in the Carpathian Mountains, from the eighteenth century.

19 Cracow-Kazimierz. The old Synagogue (c. 1500 and 1555–7).

20 Cracow-Kazimierz. Interior of the old Synagogue from *c.* 1500.

21 Troki (Lithuania). The Karaimian 'Kenessa' from the eighteenth century.

22 Cracow-Nowa Huta. The church called 'The Ark', 1960–70.

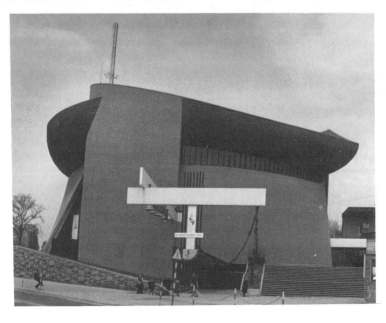

I

First let us consider the question of origins. Church building slowly spread in Poland and produced churches constructed both of stone and of wood. Romanesque forms reached the natural borderline of the Wisla river, beyond which they appeared only sporadically (Lublin, Halicz). At the same time Ruthenian architecture, steeped in the Byzantine tradition, was moving in from the East. During the reign of Kazimierz the Great, and especially after his conquest of the so-called Red Russia (the western parts of the present Ukraine, including the Duchies of Halicz, Wodzimierz, and others) in the years 1340–66, Gothic architecture spread eastward, reaching Kamieniec Podolski. In the north, the christening of Lithuania (1386–7) introduced Catholicism into Lithuania itself and into White Russia, where it mingled with local traditions to produce the so-called Orthodox Church architecture (Byzantine and Russian). In the fifteenth and sixteenth centuries the Catholic tradition and the Orthodox began to overlap: Gothic forms (and more precisely late-Gothic forms) made their way into Orthodox churches, whereas the Jagiellons introduced paintings of eastern origins into Roman Catholic Gothic churches (the so-called Russo-Byzantine frescos in Lublin, Sandomierz, Wiślica, Cracow, and earlier in many other places).

In the sixteenth century the Reformation impeded this process. The building of churches gave way to the building of palaces and sumptuous city houses. Yet already at the beginning of the seventeenth century church architecture was reviving. The 'Latin' architecture of mannerism and baroque spread into the East, reaching Kiev, Mohylew, Smolensk, and Polock.

After the Partitions and the ill-fated uprisings, the Poles put much effort into preserving their national identity, which made Neo-Gothic, the most popular style of architecture in the nineteenth century, a 'national style'. This was particularly pronounced in the second half of the century. Today the art historian realizes the extent of self-deception which accompanied these (not only Polish) aspirations, but they did create some sort of architectural individuality that deserves respect.

Generally speaking, all the changes of Roman Catholic church architecture in Poland reflected a steady desire to follow the fashions and styles flourishing in western Europe, and at an earlier stage in eastern Europe. Traditionalism in political institutions, custom and dress in the Republic of the Two Nations, and a certain cultural consensus, can be very misleading. Although the Poles tended to make themselves conspicuous and to stress their 'Polishness', at the same time they did not want to remain backward in comparison with other countries. Thus neither the Romanesque nor Gothic styles created their own tradition here, although they lasted longer than in the West and gave rise to multiple examples of churches that combined stone—relatively rare on the plains, and hence highly valued—with brick. It was in the first half of the seventeenth century that church architecture took a distinctive road. In addition to the traditional focus, embodying medieval patterns possibly interspersed with some ornamental innovations, there appeared a totally new style which, among others, promoted, almost overnight, patterns and motifs originating in Rome. For instance, well before the completion of il Gesu, a Jesuit church in Rome, its replicas were built in Nieśwież, Cracow, Vilna, and Kalisz. We should bear in mind that the Jesuits were ready to please those whose support they were seeking to secure. So in Poland, always sensitive to artistic novelties, baroque churches began mushrooming, whereas in the Rhineland, in France, and in Spain the Jesuits introduced a 'Neo-Gothic' style as early as 1600.

Although this swift process of assimilating western patterns first resulted in more or less faithful imitations, highly original, even unique forms were soon to follow. Particularly imaginative were the motifs utilized in churches built in late phases of architectural styles, magnificently exemplified by the brick 'fiery' Gothic of St Anne's Church in Vilna. The late phase of mannerism in the first half of the seventeenth century is equally interesting, especially the stucco decorations of its interiors. However, the style which produced the most idiosyncratic forms of high formal expressiveness was the late baroque, particularly that which expanded far to the east. This style absorbed local ornamental elements, rich and frequently fantastic, from the cultures of the Lithuanians, the White Russians, or the Ukrainians. White, highly graded architectural forms which emerged in the Grand Duchy of Luthuania matched in their originality such phenomena as Bavarian rococo or Spanish Churrigueresque.

A separate problem which I would like to discuss briefly is wooden architecture. It deserves special attention because it is always expressive of *genius loci*. The material used determined certain features which were subsequently repeated throughout the centuries without many alterations, and which retained, as it were, people's attitudes and ambitions. In Poland wood was plentiful and very cheap, which was taken advantage of by many carpenters. Thus, apart from 'great' architecture, commissioned by kings, magnates, or burghers, 'smaller' architecture, of a distinctively native character, found its enduring place. In spite of their vulnerability to destruction (by age or fire), we still have numerous examples of wooden buildings which date back to the Middle Ages.

A comparative study of this architecture in Poland and in other countries (from 'Stavikirker' in Norway to Russian Orthodox churches) yields an interesting conclusion. By comparison with Scandinavia, Romania, or other Slavonic countries, wooden architecture in Poland was much more affected by outside influences and tried to adapt 'official' styles, using a material which, after all, imposes certain technological limitations.

In the first place we should mention here wooden churches of the fifteenth and sixteenth centuries, which can be called Gothic, not because of any structural elements, such as vaults or buttresses, characteristic of the Gothic style, but because they were decorated with typical Gothic details, such as arched portals and windows or characteristically shaped beams which enhanced their Gothic proportions.

The seventeenth century witnessed attempts to adapt patterns first of mannerist and then of baroque provenance. What is really striking here is the skill of the (usually) anonymous artists, who for the most part hailed from town guilds which employed both carpenters and masons. Imaginative chapels, three-aisled foundations, apparent domes, two-towered façades, and above all a rich variety of vault forms make the architecture of this and the next century surprisingly original. Later, towards the end of the eighteenth century, classicism was skilfully utilized in wooden architecture. Finally there were some attempts to adopt Neo-Gothic and 'national' styles, the latter rooted in the tradition of folk architecture.

II

With 'Latin' architecture in the background it is interesting to trace the development of Ruthenian Orthodox church architecture and later of Greek-Catholic. In the Middle Ages there were two well-defined variants of this style. The Romanesque facilitated the process of adopting western patterns, especially in the border regions (for example, an entirely Romanesque portal in the otherwise Orthodox cathedral in Halicz).

This process gained some momentum after the inclusion of Red Russia in the Polish kingdom, and later after their union and the conversion of Lithuania new Latin elements entered the Byzantine tradition. Orthodox churches underwent a process of Gothicization in the fifteenth century and especially at the beginning of the sixteenth century, thanks to the development of brick architecture. Hence two types of churches developed in those times. Hall-like structures, like that in Synkowicze, closely resembled churches built everywhere on the northern European plains, and the Orthodox church belonging to the Basilian Monastery in Suprasl which fused (in the past tense, as it was destroyed during the last war), various traditions: Byzantine, Gothic, and Renaissance. Such unorthodox, unusual, and idiosyncratic architectural forms, which combined various heterogeneous elements, sprang up in the Ukraine (for example, a fortified Orthodox church in Sutkowice in Volyn), in White Russia, and in Lithuania.

However, when the majority of Orthodox clergy and believers entered the union with Rome in 1595, a new, and totally different, process began. The Latinization of Greek-Catholic Orthodox churches was undertaken in the seventeenth century, whereas the eighteenth century witnessed an 'explosion' of late baroque architecture, very unusual in its character, which served both Catholics and those following Orthodox rites. Interestingly enough, both types of churches were built by the same architects, for example, the Greek-Catholic Cathedral in L'vov, built by Bernard Meretyn in the years 1744–63 [see plate 9], and the huge monastery church in Lawra Poczjowska, in Volyn, built by Gotfryd Hoffmann and Piotr Polejowski in the years 1771–85.

We should differentiate between the occidental trend which influenced Russian architecture, especially in the eighteenth century, and the later trend. The former buildings showed traditional spacial arrangements, but were adorned after the western fashion, while the latter transformed the spacial and functional structure of Greek-Catholic Orthodox churches, making them resemble Catholic churches.

Just as in the case of Catholic architecture, wooden Orthodox churches fall into a different category. In their oldest forms, these churches were of a tripartite character, and consisted of three approximately square rooms, the middle of which was larger than the others. Either this middle part or all three were topped with domes having interesting structures which, in turn, were roofed with shingles. Architectural forms created in that way were most extraordinary: mansards, onion domes, and concave-convex roofs, resembling Chinese or Japanese pagodas. However, the most interesting structures were built in the Carpathian region, and it was there that a synthesis of the Orthodox and Latin traditions in church architecture was made by artisans who belonged to a local ethnic community, the Lemks. The Latin tradition yielded a characteristic tower topped with a small room (an echo of medieval fortified structures). A new and original form of the Greek-Catholic church was developed which retained three ornamental domes, yet it was the tower dome, and not the middle one, which was the structural focus.

On the other hand, the architecture which developed in the Volyn and Polesie regions had even more in common with the architecture of Catholic churches, and in a similar manner tried to accommodate baroque or classicist patterns to wooden material.

When the Russians annexed the regions which had belonged to the Polish-Lithuanian State they realized the extent to which the Greek-Catholic Church was Latinized. Although it retained its Old-Slavonic and Greek rites, which originated in the times of Saints Cyril and Method, mentally it felt a close affinity with western theology and, what is more, with a western way of thinking. The process of Russification of the Greek-Catholic inhabitants of western regions such as Podlasie or Chelm was much harsher and more rapid than Russification of the Poles. Brutal suppression of the Uniates and persecution of those who refused to embrace the Orthodox Faith, were accompanied by the propagation of new and alien architectural forms, such as those in the famous Ivan the Blessed Orthodox Church in the Kremlin. Smaller and simplified replicas of that model mushroomed in these regions towards the end of the nineteenth century.

III

Another Christian denomination which in the course of time entered the union with Rome (1667) was the Armenian. These people had come to Russia as early as the twelfth century, and when the territories they inhabited were included in the Polish kingdom, they acquired an autonomous status and some privileges, which resulted in a proliferation of their communities not only in L'vov, but also in other towns, both royal (Stanisławów, Kamieniec Podolski) and private (for example, Zamość). Originally they professed Monophysitism, and after their 1595 union with the Catholic Church they retained their rite and language. Their religious separateness helped them to keep a national identity; in other respects they underwent a swift process of Polonization, adopting Polish language, customs, and dress.

Only a few Armenian monuments now survive, but these include the oldest and most interesting; the Armenian Cathedral in L'vov, which was built in the second half of the fourteenth century [see plate 3]. This cathedral reflects more or less faithfully native architectural patterns which originated in a Genoese colony in Kaffa, where Armenian communities flourished. It is a three-aisled structure, whose middle part is accentuated by a high, many-sided domed tower. Iconographic sources suggest that the architecture of Armenian churches in Poland in the fifteenth and sixteenth centuries was closely connected with their native tradition. It was only after 1667 that the union hastened the process of Latinization and produced heterogenic forms. Some of these forms reflect the tradition (for example, three apses) whereas others, especially those of interior decoration, are westernized and often very rich (for example, the church in Stanisławów).

Although in the sixteenth century the Reformation, as we noticed above, gained momentum, there is relatively little to be said about the architecture of its early phases. Protestants built hardly any churches, as they were satisfied with converting Catholic ones or with adapting rooms in private houses. Moreover, some of the Protestant churches built at that time were subsequently rebuilt or destroyed, the fate which befell one such church in Cracow, which was destroyed during anti-Protestant riots at the turn of the sixteenth century. Similar riots took place in Poznań, Vilna, and Lublin. Judging from scarce evidence we can say that initially Protestant architecture differed from Catholic in the absence of a separate presbytery. Otherwise Protestant churches were spacious buildings, often with corner turrets which functioned at the same time as buttresses; for example, the church in Keijdany, in Lithuania. Many of them were fortified like the Protestant church in Kojdanów by Minsk Białoruski (unfortunately destroyed during the First World War) or that in Ostaszyn. In both cases the room-like structures were flanked by towers, obviously under the influence of Latin architecture. According to tradition, churches should be built with towers, the 'privilege' that was refused to synagogues.

Small rural Protestant churches were often built of wood, which was the cheapest material. Under the influence of western patterns, particularly those which had originated in the Netherlands and in Germany, they utilized framework constructions, combining a wooden frame with a clay or brick filler.

We must stress once again that the reformed churches, with the exception of the Socinian, most extreme in its antitrinitarian attitude, were not persecuted in Poland, although the Catholic kings of the Swedish Vasa dynasty turned a blind eye to anti-Protestant brawls initiated by students and townsfolk. Lutherans, Calvinists, Bohemian Brethren, and even the Mennonites enjoyed relative peace and welfare, although in the course of time it became increasingly difficult for them to be promoted to high State offices. It was the Enlightenment which brought positive changes. Protestants were allowed to build new churches as sumptuous as the Catholic ones, such as the imposing rotunda of the Lutheran church in Warsaw (1777–81), a dogmatically classicist design by the king's architect, Szymon Bogumił Zug. More or less at the same time a new Calvinist church was built in Vilna, and the Catholic cathedral was rebuilt (Wawrzyniec Gucewicz); in both cases the churches resembled ancient Greek temples, thanks to their monumental porticos. Later they ceased to resemble anything as the Soviet authorities turned the cathedral into an exhibition hall and the Calvinist church into a cinema.

After the partitions the territories annexed by Prussia changed into a Lutheran testing-ground. The authorities helped the German population to settle in previously Polish towns, established numerous garrisons, and at the same time began building. These identical Lutheran churches were ostentatiously placed in the middle of the market squares, often destroying the local town halls. No wonder that, whenever the chance arose, the Poles, openly inimical to these 'gifts' in the shape of boring bureaucratic architecture, tried to remove them. Any historian of art must deplore such a response, but I think that the same would happen in many countries. Suppose, for example, Nelson's Column were removed to make way for a mosque or an Orthodox church! At any rate the most sumptuous Orthodox-Lutheran church built in the Saski Square in Warsaw was destroyed the moment Poland regained her independence in 1918. Numerous Lutheran churches were also demolished after 1945. So when, in the years 1952–5, the so-called Palace of Culture and Science, a gift from the Soviet Union, was built in the centre of Warsaw, the townsfolk produced a puzzle: what is the Palace of Culture and Science? It is revenge for the demolition of the Orthodox church in the Saski Square!

IV

The problem of Jewish architecture in Poland is so extensive that I have to limit my discussion to a few representative samples. Although the Jews came to Poland in the thirteenth century, or even earlier, there are no traces of medieval synagogues. The Cracow synagogue, situated in the so-called Jewish town of Kazimierz, is widely considered to be the oldest in Poland. It is a Gothic building utilizing western patterns, and having two slender pillars placed in the centre of a rectangular room supporting a cross-ribbed vault [see plate 20]. As such it must have been built in the late

TADEUSZ CHRZANOWSKI

fifteenth century. In the sixteenth century it was rebuilt on the outside, after a contemporary fashion, and provided with a roof hidden behind a Renaissance attic [see plate 19]. The temple was destroyed by the Nazis. After the war it was rebuilt and now houses a Jewish museum.

It seems that a tendency to build synagogues as dissimilar from churches as possible was fully intentional; that is why they were modelled on palaces, manor houses, and town halls. The Polish manor houses of the sixteenth and seventeenth centuries were characterized by the frequent appearance of so-called alcoves, that is square corner annexes, whose origin can be traced back to fortified medieval structures. During the Renaissance the attic became the most popular method of coping an exterior masonry wall, which mainly played the functional role of shelter-ing the roof from fire, but was also regarded as a decorative element. Although the attic was known in Bohemia, Austria, Hungary, and later in Russia, its Polish variety was most decorative and fanciful. In the archi-tecture of manor houses and synagogues it served to make them less austere and more imaginative.

Perhaps the richest and most ingenious forms of Jewish architecture found their expression in wood. However, wooden structures, plentiful before the Second World War, did not survive the onset of *furor teutonicus*. What we have now are only the documents. We do not know who built those wooden synagogues, but we are almost certain that they were not built by the Jews themselves, as they had no tradition of carpentry. The builders must have been Poles or Ukrainians, who carried out the designs drafted by their employers. Wooden synagogues synthesize elements pertaining to residential architecture (alcoves), to manor house and town hall (multi-storeyed), to orthodox churches (mansard roofs), and to inns and town architecture (arcading in the shape of a loggia). The interiors were equally interesting, and abounded in false vaults, paintings, and wood-carvings. To sum up, one could say that wooden synagogues, along with mannerist and baroque synagogues, testify to the fact that the architecture of all the numerous denominations of Poland conformed to local traditions, customs, and experiences.

Apart from the denominations which we have discussed, there were a few small highly exotic religious communities. One such community was formed by the Karaites, who came from the Crimea and followed the dogmas of the Old Testament, rejecting both the cabala and other later sources. They used the Tartar language and their origin is still debatable. Their largest community was established in Troki, in Lithuania, in the fifteenth century, where their temple has survived until the present day. It is a wooden structure having a mansard roof and devoid of any ornaments—something between a synagogue and a mosque [see plate 21].

Mosques were quite numerous in Poland, since the Tartars and the Turks were not only our enemies but sometimes our allies. A number of the Tartars settled in Lithuania and Podlasie and built a dozen mosques which still existed in the nineteenth century. Now there are only two small countryside mosques within the borders of Poland. Although they were built as late as in the middle of the nineteenth century, they retained a characteristic architectural pattern—with the mihrab and the minbar.

Today Poland is predominantly Catholic. Such was the final choice made by the Poles who, as a rule, do not accept anything that is imposed on them from abroad. However, sometimes I feel intensely sad that the earlier variety has disappeared, the variety that was most obvious in L'vov, the city of my youth, where four cathedrals—Latin, Greek-Catholic [see plate 9], Orthodox [see plate 4], and Armenian [see plate 3]—coexisted in peace, and did not mind the prayers said by the believers in the nearby Lutheran and Calvinist churches, or in the nearby synagogues. Even if we concede that homogeneity is power, we have to remember that variety is wealth.

Catholic University of Lublin and University of Cracow

ABBREVIATIONS

AAWG.PH	*Abhandlungen der Akademie der Wissenschaften in Göttingen: Philologisch-historische Klasse*, ser. 3 (Göttingen, 1942ff.)
ABMA	*Auctores Britannici Medii Aevi*, British Academy (London, 1969ff.)
ACi	*Analecta Cisterciensia* (Rome, 1965ff.)
ADAW.PH	*Abhandlungen der deutschen Akademie der Wissenschaften: Philosophisch-historische Klasse* (Berlin, 1945ff.)
AFH	*Archivum Franciscanum historicum* (Quaracchi, 1908ff.)
ASC	*Anglo-Saxon Chronicle*
ASV	*Archivio Segreto Vaticano*
DA	*Deutsches Archiv für Erforschung des Mittelalters* (Cologne/Graz, 1905ff.)
DNB	*Dictionary of National Biography* (London, 1885ff.)
FS	*Franziskanische Studien* (Münster-Werl/Westfalen, 1914ff.)
GCS	*Die griechischen christlichen Schriftsteller der ersten drei Jahrhunderte* (Berlin, 1897ff.)
Hist. ecc.	*Historia ecclesiastica*
JEH	*Journal of Ecclesiastical History* (Cambridge, 1950ff.)
LThK	*Lexikon für Theologie und Kirche*, ed. J. Höfner and K. Rahner, 2nd edn (Freiburg im Briesgau, 1957ff.)
MHTB	*Materials for the History of Thomas Becket*, ed. J. C. Robertson and J. B. Sheppard, 7 vols, *RS* (London, 1875–85)
MIÖG	*Mitteilungen des Instituts für österreichische Geschichtsforschung* (Innsbruck, 1880ff, Cologne, Graz, and Vienna, 1945ff)
MRSt	*Medieval and Renaissance Studies* (Chapel Hill, 1965ff.)
NMT	*Nelsons Medieval Texts*, (London, Edinburgh, etc., 1949–71) [superseded by *OMT*]
ns	new series
OMT	*Oxford Medieval Texts* (Oxford, 1971ff.) [supersedes *NMT*]
PaP	*Past and Present. A Journal of Scientific History* (London, 1952ff.)
PL	*Patrologia Latina*, ed. J. P. Migne, 217 + 4 index vols (Paris, 1841–61)
PRIA	*Proceedings of the Royal Irish Academy* (Dublin, 1840ff.)
PS	*Parker Society* (Cambridge, 1841–55)
QFIAB	*Quellen und Forschungen aus italienischen Archiven und Bibliotheken* (Rome/Tübingen, 1897ff.)
RS	*Rerum Brittanicarum medii aevi scriptores*, 99 vols (London, 1858–1911) = *Rolls Series*
SBAW.PPH	*Sitzungsberichte der bayerischen Akademie der Wissenschaften in München: Philosophisch-philologisch und historische Klasse*, ns (München, 1898ff.)
SCH.S	*Studies in Church History. Subsidia* (Oxford, 1978ff.)